Spirit Guide Contact
Through Hypnosis

By

Dr. Bruce Goldberg

New Page Books
A division of The Career Press, Inc.
Franklin Lakes, NJ

SPIRIT GUIDE CONTACT THROUGH HYPNOSIS
EDITED BY KATE HENCHES
TYPESET BY EILEEN DOW MUNSON
Cover design by Lu Rossman/Digi Dog Design
Cover photo: Leslie Frank Hampton
Printed in the U.S.A. by Book-mart Press

To order this title, please call toll-free 1-800-CAREER-1 (NJ and Canada: 201-848-0310) to order using VISA or MasterCard, or for further information on books from Career Press.

The Career Press, Inc., 3 Tice Road, PO Box 687,
Franklin Lakes, NJ 07417
www.careerpress.com
www.newpagebooks.com

Library of Congress Cataloging-in-Publication Data

Goldberg, Bruce, 1948-
    Spirit guide contact through hypnosis / by Bruce Goldberg.
        p. cm.
    Includes bibliographical references and index.
    ISBN 1-56414-797-5 (pbk.)
    1. Guides (Spiritualism) 2. Autogenic training. I. Title.

BF1275.G85G65 2005
133.9'32--dc22

2005041504

This book is dedicated to the thousands of my patients who have been kind enough to share their spirit guide experiences using the techniques presented in this book.

Without their demonstrations of the benefits of these metaphysical, yet natural, techniques, this book would not have been possible.

I would like to thank Michael Lewis, Acquisitions Editor of New Page Books, for his interest and assistance in bringing this book to the public.

This book's final form would not be what it is without the assistance of my editor, Kate Henches. Thank you, Kate for your kindness, professionalism, and helpful suggestions.

Finally, I cannot express enough appreciation to my typist, Marianne Colasanti, for her tireless efforts and spiritual support.

Table of Contents

Introduction

Contacting spirit guides is as old as civilization itself. Shamans dating back to at least 50,000 B.C. had rituals of placing themselves in communication with nonphysical entities. The Mystery Schools of ancient Egypt, Greece, Persia, Rome, and India also dealt with contacting spirits.

This approach appeared to reach a zenith in the 19th century with the Spiritualism Movement. Today a reincarnation of interest has been manifested through the resurgence of attention brought to angels, the Higher Self and channeling in general.

Every major religion acknowledges the reality of discarnate entities or spirits. These may be called saints, angels, the Holy Spirit, and so on. One of the purposes of this book is to demystify this process. Hollywood films, television, and novels have incorrectly presented the view that some magical (if not evil) process is necessary to contact one of these spirits.

The media's conception of spirit contact has led to the false assumption that the individual who establishes this contact must be in great danger. In reality, this communication is natural, relatively simple, and is a wonderful growth experience. Spirit communication removes the fear of death and bereavement, and results in a form of spiritual empowerment. We now can have evidence of our immortality, in addition to receiving enlightenment from beings far more spiritually evolved than we are.

Other advantages of this communication are:

◎ Developing your intuition and other psychic abilities.

◎ Increasing your ability to love ourselves and others.

- ◎ Becoming more aware of the workings of the universe.

- ◎ Increasing your creativity and problem solving abilities.

- ◎ Establishing better contact with your own Masters and Guides and Higher Self to facilitate your own spiritual evolution.

- ◎ Spiritual protection from negative entities and/or other forces in the universe.

- ◎ Accessing the wisdom of the ancients.

- ◎ Establishing and maintaining your own physical, mental, emotional, and spiritual health.

This book presents many easy and perfectly safe methods to contact spirit guides. Absolutely anyone can master these simple exercises. The only obstacles in your path to apply these techniques successfully rests inside you. We refer to these obstacles as defense mechanisms or the ego. They try to prevent you from changing in any way.

Frequently, these defense mechanisms are easily overpowered by the use of simple meditative and self-hypnosis techniques. It is only the ignorance and prejudice that society has fostered upon the West that has misprogrammed you to feel that you cannot do this.

We are not the highest and only form of intelligent life. Being human is not the apex of evolution. There are nonphysical beings and dimensions that are far more evolved than any of us have ever imagined our species to be.

The ignorance that a soul illustrates during its life reflects and directs its actions after it crosses into spirit (dies). By establishing spirit contact now, you can better yourself and your destiny for this eventual transition.

I present several protection exercises in this book, so there is no need to fear being harmed while practicing the methods included. You will be helped tremendously by the spirits you contact. They may assist you in establishing abundance, provide insight on a variety of issues, protect you, and function as a nonphysical companion. Spirit guides can only help us if we request their assistance. The greater our awareness and more open we are to this communication, the stronger their help and guidance will be. It is always to our advantage to raise our souls' energies to facilitate this assistance and to grow spiritually.

Contacting spirit guides is a learned skill. You do not have to be born with a special "gift." With the methods presented in this book, you will learn how to expand your own consciousness and contact a high-level guide and your own Higher Self. All you require is a strong desire, perseverance, and patience to obtain positive results.

Using these techniques will increase the frequency of events in your life that just "seem to happen." You will receive insights and simply "know" about things and what to do to better your life and the lives of those you contact. This will result in your life taking on more meaning, and you developing a greater sense of karmic purpose.

Use the information and experiences that you obtain as a result of this book to be both enlightened and empowered. Make this a starting point in opening yourself up for guidance and spiritual growth. Be prepared for the adventure of your life as you bring higher levels of wisdom into your very own soul. Go forth into the light and share your new wisdom with others.

How to Use This Book

This book contains dozens of exercises specifically designed to train you to experience self-hypnosis. It doesn't matter what your background is.

You can accept or reject any of the principles and concepts presented here. Empowerment is vital and I stress that in my Los Angeles hypnotherapy practice and in my personal life as well. If you become rigid and stuck in your views, you become trapped by your beliefs. You are no longer empowered because you are no longer free.

Always use your judgment and free will in trying these exercises. Use the ones with which you feel comfortable and ignore the others. These exercises are all perfectly safe and have been tested for more than 25 years. You may create your own exercises from these models.

Read each exercise thoroughly to become familiar with it. Use the relaxation techniques that are given or use your own. You may practice alone or with others. I strongly suggest that you make tapes of these exercises. Read the scripts slowly and leave enough space on your tape to experience each part of the procedure.

Practice once or twice a day, in 15- to 20-minute sessions. In general, it is considered most effective to practice in the morning, as it may provide a relaxing start for the entire day. The more specific and realistic your schedule, the better the chances that you will succeed.

You should choose a part of your day when you are at your best. If you wait to practice until long after you get home from a hard day at work, you might only practice going to sleep, self-hypnosis is most effective if practiced when you are reasonably alert. Begin by picking a good time to practice.

If you wake up alert and rested first thing in the morning, practice then, before getting out of bed. Take into account whether or not you will be disturbed by spouse, lover, kids, pets, and so forth. Choose a time when you are not likely to be interrupted. Other popular times are before lunch or dinner.

Four components of successful self-hypnosis are:

1. A quiet environment.

2. A mental device.

3. A passive attitude.

4. A comfortable position.

When you enter into a self-hypnotic trance, you will observe the following:

- ◎ A positive mood (tranquility, peace of mind).

- ◎ An experience of unity or oneness with the environment.

- ◎ An inability to describe the experience in words.

- ◎ An alteration in time/space relationships.

- ◎ An enhanced sense of reality and meaning.

If you experience difficulty with an exercise, do not become frustrated. Some techniques are quite advanced, and you may not be ready for all of them. Return to the ones you could not successfully work with at another time.

Practice these trance states when you have time and are relaxed. Be patient. It takes time to master trance states and to become accustomed to this new and wonderful world. No one way is the right way to experience a trance. Your body may feel light, or it may feel heavy; you may feel as if you are dreaming; your eyelids may flutter, or your body can become cooler or warmer. All these possible responses are perfectly safe.

Because you will, at first, be unfamiliar with these techniques, your initial practice session should run as long as you need. As you become more proficient, you will be able to shorten these sessions. Some days nothing may seem to work. Try not to become discouraged. Remember that other days will be more fruitful. Always work at your own pace and with an open mind.

Note to the Reader

This book is the result of the professional experiences accumulated by the author since 1974, working individually with more than 14,000 patients. The material included herein is intended to complement, not replace the advice of your own physician, psychotherapist, or other healthcare professional, whom you should always consult about your circumstances before starting or stopping any medication or any other course of treatment, exercise regimen, or diet.

At times, the masculine pronoun has been used as a convenience. It is intended to indicate both male and female genders where this is applicable. All names and identifying references, except those of celebrities, have been altered to protect the privacy of my patients. All other facts are accurate and have not been altered.

—Dr. Bruce Goldberg
Woodland Hills, California

◎◎◎◎◎◎◎◎◎◎◎

CHAPTER 1

Who Are Spirit Guides?

A Historical Overview of the Soul

We have evidence of Neanderthal cavemen burying their dead equipped with food and tools—reflecting a belief that the afterlife was similar to the Earthly life. Kings and pharaohs in the ancient world were buried with elaborate preparations in order to assure a spirit life equal to the luxury experienced in the physical body.

Royal death pits in Ur (part of Iraq) were unearthed in the 1920s. Queen Shubad was found surrounded by 68 other people. These royal attendants voluntarily went to their deaths so that they could continue service to their queen in the afterlife.

Mummification procedures were common among the ancient Egyptians and Incas. According to Egyptian theology, in order for the spirit, or *ka*, to survive, the body must also survive. That is why the corpse was so carefully mummified and offerings of food were left at intervals in the pharaoh's tomb.

The Egyptian god Osiris and 42 judges sat in judgment over the transitee soul following the death of the physical body. The dead person's heart would be weighed on the scales of justice. The soul had to be able to say that in life the person had not been guilty of any one of a long list of sins.

According to the ancient Greeks, the soul of the deceased journeyed to an underworld called Hades, ruled over by the god Hades. This was a gloomy place where the spirits existed as vague shadows, somewhat similar to the Sheol, or "place of departed spirits," of the Jewish faith. The Greeks also had their hell, called Tartaros, and heaven, known as the Elysian fields.

Christians believe in a resurrected body and the best example of this principle is represented by Jesus. Following his death, Christians believe that Jesus appeared to them in his actual earthly body. Some interpret the story symbolically, saying that Christ was present among his followers in spirit. Still others believe that he appeared in his spiritual body, which resembled his Earthly body but was subtly different from it.

We find St. Paul discussing a spiritual body in the New Testament. "All flesh is not the same flesh: but there is one kind of flesh of men, another flesh of beasts, another of fishes, and another of birds...So also is the resurrection of the dead. It is sown in corruption: it is raised in incorruption: it is sown in dishonor; it is raised in glory: it is sown in weakness; it is raised in power: it is sown a natural body; it is raised a spiritual body. There is a natural body, and there is a spiritual body."[1]

No precise description of a spiritual body is given by Christian scripture. This theology does, however, recognize spiritual contact for a very significant reason. In these cases saints have appeared before a select few. A classic example of this is the communication received by Joan of Arc. She reported hearing the voices of St. Catherine and St. Margaret. Their divine message was for Joan to expel the English from France during the Hundred Years War and enable Charles VII to be crowned.

Joan of Arc persuaded Charles to allow her to lead an army to free the besieged city of Orléans. Her success resulted in Charles' coronation at Rheims in 1429, but Joan was later captured and burned at the stake by the English for heresy. She was canonized in 1920.

Spirit guides are entities from the "other side" who represent a mediator between the worlds of being and nonbeing, of reality and unreality. These teachers accompany us on our journeys to places in between waking consciousness and the realm of nonconsciousness. They come in many forms.

We have certain spiritual advisors with us from birth until death. A guardian angel is reportedly watching over us at all times. Other guides can come and go, changing according to our needs and levels of spiritual growth. There are specific spirit guides who are assigned to assist us for specific lessons only. These entities may be with us for a day, a year, or a lifetime.

It is not uncommon for spirit guides to present themselves as other than a human persona. They can take the form of animals, lights, or any other representation. You can more easily identify and recognize them when you are in an altered state of consciousness (ASC) such as hypnosis. That is why hypnosis will be the focus of this book.

The teachings that we receive from spirit guides may not be remembered after the particular altered state of consciousness in which we experience them is gone. This process can be recalled when we apply specific self-hypnosis techniques that will be presented throughout this book. Spirit guides have access to our *Akashic Records*, a type of "chart" of all our past, present, and future lifetimes, as well as a compilation of our spiritual growth and karmic lessons that still need to be mastered. These records are what psychics and channelers access when they initiate a reading. We have the capacity to access these records ourselves. I will present an entire chapter instructing you to do just that in Chapter 5.

Higher-level spirit guides are pure energy, having completed their karmic cycles long ago. They are referred to as "beings of light" because of their appearance and the manner in which they communicate with us telepathically. These beings travel throughout the fifth dimension into other dimensions, as well as the Physical plane, as we will discuss in Chapter 2.

These highly evolved beings of light are quite skilled at transmitting their thoughts from their dimension into ours. Their motive is one of love and devotion to the fostering of higher ideals. Their energy vibrations are so high and pure that we must adjust our receptive processes in our brain to accommodate these signals. We must be able to work with energy and our electromagnetic fields (aura) at very subtle and refined levels in order to accomplish this.

Hypnosis is, by far, the most efficient and easy mechanism to do this. We can access our Higher Self (the perfect component of our soul's energy) to facilitate the connection with these spirit guides. The purpose of our Higher Self and spirit guides are the same, to provide guidance, wisdom, compassion, and love and to assist us in manifesting our true karmic purpose, the main reason we are on the Earth in this lifetime.

Guides may appear to us in a variety of forms. They often assume a particular nationality, gender, and time period that is compatible with our mind sets. In other words, if you are male and expect a beautiful blond Greek goddess to be your spirit guide, that is the form the spirit would assume.

Guides may appear in a form they once had in a previous lifetime they shared with you. It is not unusual for a past-life acquaintance who has perfected his or her soul's energy, or is in between lives, to function as your spirit guide. The person may appear as a monk in robes, a religious figure such as Christ, Moses, Buddha, Mohammed, Native American or Chinese sage, St. Germain, an angel, animal spirit, or other manifestations.

Sometimes spirit guides come to us as sounds, colored lights, or simply a sensation of pure love. They may be male or female, or any representation that will best accomplish what they are here to do, or one to which you can most relate. We must remember that the soul has no gender, so these spirit guides are not really male or female, simply pure energy. There are as many identities for guides as there are for people, so be open to whatever form or appearance in which your guide presents him- or herself.

Guides can be specialists in their function as our counsel. Some impart only ideas of science, logic, math, art, or new systems of thought. We can always learn about the true nature of reality from a spirit guide. You may very well be disappointed if your goal in communicating with such an entity is to determine best where to live, whom to marry or what business direction to take.

This is not to say that your guide will not be of invaluable help to you; he or she simply won't run your life or foster a codependent relationship. You will experience far more inspiration and unfolding of spiritual truths than specific "Dear Abby" advice from a spirit guide.

There is a referral network paradigm in the spirit world, so that if you are working with a guide specializing in the fine arts and require business or scientific insights, an appropriate spirit guide will be brought in to fulfill this request. Occasionally, a spirit guide will refer you to a book or an individual on the Physical plane to assist your needs.

A particular spirit guide selects you to work with because you are most attuned to what the guide wants to bring to humanity and your own spiritual evolution. The only concern of these energy advisors is your higher good. They are there to help you with such things as remembering who you are, letting go of fear, and learning to love yourself and others. They come to add to your joy and to assist you with your personal growth and your work here on the Material plane. In other words, they are training you in the art of ascension.[2]

It is important to understand the limits and *modus operandi* of spirit guides. These beings assist you in making your own choices in life. Their approach is always accompanied with feelings of empowerment, confidence, and strength. They are the first to acknowledge that their truth is *not* the only or ultimate truth.

Higher-level spirit guides support your growth, but will not flatter you, patronize you, or blindly build up your ego. A sense of greater inner vision and expanded awareness is created by them. You will never be advised to "do something or else," or that you "must" do this or that. They support and encourage you to develop and use your inner strengths and deeper wisdom. I refer to this as psychic empowerment.

A truly developed spirit guide will *never* encourage you to blindly give your power to them. They rarely predict future events, or communicate anything to you that will encourage either codependency or self-destructive behavior.

There are spirit guides around that represent less than ideal levels of growth. The techniques presented in this book will protect you from them and steer these entities away from contacting you in the first place. You can easily detect whether a spirit guide is a high-level or low-level entity. If, for example, your response to a guide contact leaves you with a sense of fear, depression, or other negative emotion, then you have not been with a high-level guide. It's that simple.

High-level guides say much with few words. They teach love, forgiveness, and tolerance. This type of being offers practical advice that is never self-serving, always modest, and can easily be identified as good common sense. They speak only highly about people and things. Their universe is filled with love and goodness and they never use foul language or express cynicism.

If you persist in ignoring their counsel and wind up doing something that will impede your spiritual growth, a spirit guide will not stop you. They simply attempt to instruct you as to the probable negative consequences of your actions.

We must also remember that high-level spirit guides will never communicate with you without your permission and desire for this contact. These advanced entities will never lie to you or misrepresent themselves in any way. They will always respond to your requests for more or less information or contact.

Even if you do communicate with a low-level guide, you can simply dismiss the guide by assertively stating "go away" or "I demand that you leave and not return." You will always experience feelings of love, uplifting emotions and a sense of well-being when you are in the presence of a high-level guide. The reverse is true when a low-level being is in your sphere of influence. You can even ask a certain high-level guide to leave and request a more evolved or specific specialist in regard to an issue.

Much information has been written concerning personal spirit guides. My patients have confirmed that we do have certain guides that assist us throughout our lives. One thing I do know about these personal guides is that they are less evolved than a typical high-level guide, but far more evolved than we are.

Although your personal guide may have been someone you knew in a past life or a departed friend or relative from your current incarnation, the purpose of that being is to help you accomplish what you came here to do (karmic purpose). These guides are not less than high-level guides, but their span of dimensions and consciousness is not as broad or as all-encompassing as those of high-level master guides.

Your personal guide may function as an ethereal agent or go-between with these high-level spirit guides. A high-level guide may very well work with your personal guide to help you with detailed and specific information about your personal life and spiritual growth. Sometimes when you establish a regular link with a high-level guide, most of your contact with the spirit world will be with this entity. You may not directly communicate with your personal guide again, although he or she will be looking out for you as time progresses.

A Classification of Spirit Guides

With the information that I have provided as a foundation, let us now discuss the various types of spirit guides you may encounter. These are all high-level guides and certainly other categories do exist. This list is merely the most common ones that my patients report.

1. **Animal Spirits**. Shamans have been around for at least 50,000 years, having their origins in Siberia and Central Asia. This medicine man and *psychopomp* (guider of souls) prays mostly to guides in the form of animals.

They can appear as bears, wolves, stags, hares, and many kinds of birds (most notably the goose, eagle, owl, crow, and so on). When spirit guides assume the form of strong animals, they are referred to as protectors.

We see modern-day examples of shamanism among the Native Americans and certain Aborigine tribes, as well as many others.

The main Shamanic technique is called a "technique of ecstasy" and entails passage from one cosmic region to another—for example, from Earth to sky or from Earth to the Underworld. The technique of ecstasy is characterized by the Shaman's soul leaving his body and descending to the underworld or rising to the sky in search of lost souls. It is the Shaman's "guardian spirits" that protect the souls he has recovered on these journeys.

The Shaman is "protected" by a "spirit of the herd" during his ecstatic journeys. A spirit in the shape of a bear accompanies him on his descent to the Underworld, while a gray horse is with him in spirit as he ascends to the sky. The universe, in general, is conceived of as having three levels—sky, Earth, Underworld—connected by a central axis. This axis passes through an "opening," a "hole." This hole serves as a multipurpose vestibule: spirit guides pass through it to descend to Earth, the dead use it to reach the subterranean regions, and the soul of the shaman journeys through it in either direction while in ecstasy.

2. **Angels**. Angels theologically represent a separate being from humankind. These messengers of God were never human, and not a single human being has ever become or will become an angel. Although we possess a physical (corporeal) body, an angel does not. They are pure spirit, with their own activities, society, and hierarchy.

   The following characteristics describe these spirit guides:

   ◎ Angels are always messengers, protectors, and guardians.

   ◎ They are universal, being a component of all religions.

   ◎ Angels may appear in a human form or an event, such as a saving of a life or other miracle.

   ◎ Angels communicate by telepathy.

◎ Angels do not disturb our free will. We can ignore them if we want to. They will not learn our karmic lessons for us.

◎ They have consciousness, will, and purpose.

◎ They can be anywhere they want in an instant.

◎ An angel is going to appear to us in whatever way it believes is best suited for drawing our attention; such appearances are calculated to maximize our responses to their messages, spurring us to action.

◎ The only creed an angel has is love.

◎ Angels exist in a universe different from that of humans.

◎ They enter our world through a type of doorway from the fifth dimension to make themselves known to us.

◎ We always have access to angels and there are an unlimited number from which to choose.

◎ These spirit guides can inspire us through insights by entering our consciousness.

◎ Angels can be playful, and have a sense of humor as well as a serious nature.

◎ We will begin to experience angelic assistance in all areas of our lives once we initiate contact with them.

◎ Angels do not want to be worshipped, merely appreciated.

◎ They function through creating serendipity and synchronicities in our lives.

We find many references to angels in all holy scriptures. The angel Gabriel informs Mary that she will give birth to Jesus in the New Testament. The Old Testament sometimes refers to these spirit guides as *holy watchers*. For example, we read, "the king saw a holy watcher coming down from heaven." [3] The term ministering spirit is also used in the Old Testament: "Are they not all ministering spirits, sent forth to minister for them who shall be heirs of salvation?"[4]

Dionysius documented an angelic hierarchy in the fifth century in his book *Celestial Hierarchies*. He detailed nine orders of angels divided into three triads, each of which contains three classes of angels called *choirs*. The first triad is closest to the God energy complex, with the last triad being the most distant. We can list these groupings as follows:

First Triad

1. Seraphim

2. Cherubim

3. Ophanim

Second Triad

4. Dominions

5. Virtues

6. Powers

Third Triad

7. Principalities

8. Archangels

9. Angels

The Seraphim are described as pure light and thought, often referred to as *flaming angels*. We find pure knowledge associated with the Cherubim, who guard the Tree of Life, located east of Eden. God's transportation is provided by the Ophanim. Enoch reported their appearance as that of "fiery coals" in the Old Testament.

Within the second triad the Dominions regulate the duties of the various angels, while the Virtues are responsible for the miracles on Earth. The Powers guard heaven from demons and guide those souls who get lost after leaving the body.

In the third triad the Principalities protect religions, nations, and cities. The Archangels function as emissaries between God and man. Whereas Judaism and Christianity acknowledge seven Archangels, Islamic theology recognizes four. Angels include our guardian angels and are the closest to us.

The Old Testament only mentions Michael and Gabriel, whereas the seven angels who stand before God in *Revelations* in the New

Testament are assumed to be Archangels by theologians. We need only to recognize their presence and request their assistance to attract an angel.

Angels communicate with us in two distinct ways. In the active phase we invoke their help by praying. When we relax and allow them to work through us, we are engaging in a passive approach. Rarely do angels appear in human form. Most of their work is manifested by bringing people and synchronistic events into your life to protect you and promote spiritual growth.

3. **Chemist Guides.** These spiritual advisors train us in the art of altering our body chemistry to be able to more effectively adjust to communication from the spiritual dimension.

4. **The Doctor.** A spirit helper who assists in your mental, physical, or emotional healing is called a Doctor. This guide had lives on Earth as a healer or physician.

5. **Gate Keepers.** These spirits assist you in your spiritual protection from negative entities and evil forces. They function as guards to allow only positive beings to communicate with you. These guides are always present during hypnotic and meditative states.

6. **Message Guides.** These highly evolved beings aid us in the development of our psychic gifts, such as intuition, clairaudience (hearing spirit guides), clairvoyance (seeing spirit guides) and so on. These entities help you receive messages and other forms of information from the "other side."

7. **Poltergeists (Ghosts).** When an individual crosses into spirit (clinically dies), the soul enters another dimension known as the Astral plane. At this time that soul has not yet entered the white light (Higher Self) to eventually travel to the Soul plane where that soul will choose a future life.

    These recently departed souls remain on the Astral plane and visit the Earth plane. Other terms used to describe these spirits are apparitions and discarnates.

    You will be contacted by these entities during your dreams while sleeping. Family members and friends of yours who have passed away are examples of this category. Some of these souls are spiritually evolved, while others are trying to deal with their new dimension and comprehend precisely what is going on and why Earth souls can't see or hear them.

8. **Masters.** Masters are spirit guides who assisted other humans when they lived on Earth. They have perfected their souls and now counsel large numbers of people from a dimension called the Mental plane, which we will discuss in the next chapter. One difference between a Master and an individual guide is that Masters work with great numbers of people, whereas your own spirit guide will work with you and a small number of other souls.

When these Masters lived on the Physical plane, they spent much of their time in deep trance and out-of-the-body. The purity of their lifestyles, along with daily practice of deep meditation, allowed them to occupy the same physical bodies for more years than the average human occupies his or her body.

Masters communicate telepathically with anyone they feel needs this spiritual wisdom. Part of their highly developed powers allows them to enter the inner consciousness of an individual by focusing their perfect consciousness on any specific person. One result of this contact is the inspiration I alluded to earlier that is seen in artists and scientists. We can more readily attain this inspiration by daily accessing our Higher Self through hypnosis.

Another skill Masters possess is the ability to receive advice from beings who reside on the seven higher planes, which we will discuss in the next chapter. These dimensions are beyond the karmic cycle and the entities who function there ultimately receive their source from God. We can make better decisions and speed up the completion of our karmic cycle by listening to these Masters. Buddha, Jesus, Moses, Krishna and the Mahatmas of Tibet are examples of Masters.

The most important factor in determining which particular spirit guide you attract into your life is your level of spiritual growth, which is reflected by the *frequency vibrational rate* (fvr) of your soul's electromagnetic energy. These spiritual advisors may appear to you by way of voices, symbols, fragrances, animals, colors, or in the form of a human being. They will tell you their names and relationship to you, if any, in previous lifetimes.

It is quite common to have a certain spirit guide act as a representative of several other guides who advise you. You have both an inner band of a select number of guides who work with you on a regular basis and an outer band of these spirit guides to assist you when you are ready for a particular spiritual lesson in growth. It is an infrequent communication compared to that of the inner band.

We can summarize the workings of these various spirit guides as follows:

◎ A spirit guide will assist you in any way you request, as long as it does not result in harm to others or interfere with your own spiritual growth. What I mean by this is that no spirit guide is going to learn your karmic lessons for you. You must do that yourself.

◎ The compatibility of your purposes and goals is the main factor that determines the choice of a particular guide or group of guides to work with you.

◎ The control and direction of all communication with your spirit guides always rests with you. If you are not ready or willing to be contacted, you can simply dismiss this guide. This usually is not a problem, as your spirit guides can telepathically read your mind and are well aware of when you are most and least receptive to them.

◎ You are in no danger at any time from establishing communication with a spirit guide. Do not be concerned with being "possessed," or harmed in any way.

◎ There are no shortcuts to spiritual growth. Your spirit guides will assist you by their communications, but you always have the free will to reject their advice. Some lessons are harder than others. The contact with these beings will efficiently speed up your spiritual growth, but do not expect instant revelations each time contact is made.

◎ Spirit guides communicate with you only with your permission.

◎ The higher-level guides serve as sources for clarity, direction, and guidance. Their main concern is your higher purpose.

◎ Do not follow a spirit guide's advice blindly. You are encouraged to test them. Refer to my description on angels to see what to expect and what not to expect from a true spirit guide.

◎ It is not necessary for you to be in a trance, meditative, or dream state in order to communicate with your spirit guides. Angels, for example, make most of their contacts with humans while we are in our waking, conscious state. The trance state will facilitate this contact.

❀ As a result of contacting spiritual guides, you can expect the following to occur:

◎ You will be enlightened spiritually.

◎ Your compassion toward others will grow.

◎ Your goals that may not have been attained in the past will now be achieved.

◎ You may experience physical, mental, emotional or spiritual healing.

◎ An increase in your psychic abilities will be noted.

The Mechanism of Spirit Guide Contact

The hypnotic state allows us to focus and create a clear channel to receive communication from our spirit guides. These beings make direct contact with our souls by way of telepathy and any manner that will permit transmission of this necessary counsel.

An alignment of the electromagnetic fields of both the guide and our soul (subconscious mind) takes place to make this contact possible. Once these frequency vibrational rates match, we can receive their communications. Spirit guides will remain both invisible and silent to your senses until you alter or expand your consciousness so that you can receive their thought-impulses.

From the spirit guides' vantage point in their dimension, they can see and hear us only when they adjust their frequencies in such a way as to make our universe visible to them. They do not see us as we see each other. We are perceived as moving energy patterns, colors, and harmonies. They perceive our world as moving harmonics of energy and life-force.

Our physical brain contains a left and right hemisphere, each specialized to perform certain functions. The right sides of our brains deal with intuition, feelings, nonverbal communication, creativity, and inspiration. The left side concerns itself with memory, logic, words, and language. It functions to coordinate, categorize, and synthesize data received from our five senses in a completely rational fashion.

We receive spirit guide communication from our right brains, but a synchronization of both brain hemispheres is necessary to allow a greater reception of these signals from higher-level dimensions. This is where hypnosis comes in. This natural daydream state functions to synchronize our brain hemispheres quickly and efficiently.

We can see this brain synchronization mechanism at work when we receive the higher flow of information (a right-brain function) and, at the same time, speak or write (left-brain functions involving action, organization, and vocabulary). This now results in a particular communication from a guide to be transmitted with precision and accuracy.

In actuality, our brain creates additional nerve cells (dendrites) as a result of this spirit guide contact. One obvious effect of this process is a change from our usual mode of thinking, so that we now think in higher and more spiritually focused ways. Our level of psychic development also is increased, so we at times "know" the message (*clairsentient*), "see" the information (*clairvoyant*), or "hear" the information (*clairaudient*).

The spirit guides transmit information to us in several ways, as I described above. They can send thoughts, light images and other forms of energy to our soul and eventually our right brain to present us with data that we can understand and hopefully act upon.

We sometimes have to interpret their transmissions, as some of their images need to be translated into our conceptual framework. A guide may speak to us in the form of a parable, use metaphors, or present shapes, color, or sound to illustrate their spiritual wisdom. Some spirit guides are quite serious and philosophical, while others use humor, poetry, or art to make their point.

These spiritual beings tend to specialize as I have previously discussed. If you are involved as an artist, an artistic guide will communicate with you. Scientific guides select scientists to counsel and so on. We still have a representative guide that oversees all of these communications, although your spiritual guide may not be involved in direct communication with you for quite some time.

The main point I am trying to make is that guides will use whatever method is most suited to you and the information at that moment. They will choose the easiest way to get their messages through. This data will be received by you in whatever way it feels the most natural to you. The method of transmission may change as you continue to grow spiritually.

Spirit guides give you the counsel and recommendations that you can apply, as well as understand, in the present moment. They may very well use ideas that you have read about and present them in a new way. For example, it is not unusual for a spirit guide to say "this principle is similar to what you read in So-and-So's book."

At other times spirit guides may utilize a certain "trigger" word to get their message across. This term by itself will have no special meaning to others, but it brings to our awareness an association of certain thoughts, ideas, or concepts that illustrate the guide's communication. In other words, a spirit guide relays information to us so that we may understand it from *our* vantage point and look upon our own life in a more spiritual way.

These high-level beings often convey their spiritual wisdom by using comparisons, metaphors, and examples from our own lives. It is important to keep a journal and record their insights, so that you can reread these messages and perhaps see a greater wisdom in this enlightened information, more so than you originally suspected. Very often a guide's communication appears even more profound and significant to our spiritual evolution when seen from a future date.

You must always be aware of any moment when you have your connection to your guide interrupted. This can be easily discerned if you experience boredom at any time information is relayed to you. Only data from your ego will come across as boring. You may choose to ignore the advice of your spiritual guide, but it is never boring. The hypnotic exercises presented in this book will train you to differentiate input received from your Higher Self and spirit guides from that of your own ego (defense mechanisms).

Creation and Origin of Spirit Guides

The reports from spirit guides concerning the origin of our universe may surprise you. God created perfect souls many eons ago. Although these primordial souls felt nothing but love for the God energy complex, they expressed a great desire to create their own worlds and bring forth a new energy that never before existed.

These original souls lived in the higher planes that I will detail in the next chapter. For now just accept these perfect dimensions as the "eternal now." We may look upon this desire to create, not as an expression of boredom or rebellion (contrary to the Old Testament), but one of a sense of love and desire to propagate the joy and magnificence of the God energy into new forms of creation.

In this manner a vast number of souls contributed to a huge force that represented an intense desire to create new realities of love for which they would be responsible, and of which they would be masters. Within this new coalesced force, each individual soul's ideas became a type of individual energy pattern that functioned as the primary causative forces of the physical universes we know of today. This may be looked upon as what theologians describe as the First Cause.

God acted as their teacher, always loving and nurturing these souls and their united force, while encouraging them to create freely and independently of His energy. No restrictions were placed on these souls.

God had nothing *directly* to do with the creation of our universe. We may look upon creation as these energy patterns functioning as creative forces by way of nonphysical energies that eventually evolved into physical atoms and molecules forming gases, liquids and, subsequently, minerals, plants, and animal life.

This does not discount evolution, but all of these processes can be traced back to these original God-created souls, whose forces of creation may be viewed as sounds, light, and various forms of vibrational energies all composed of love.

To effect this plan of creation these souls required a new dimension for their independent reality. This dimension would exist within the eternal now in which these souls resided. This new wavelength, or frequency vibrational rate (fvr), had never before existed. We may call this dimension a type of physical space, although there is no concept of space in the eternal now of the higher planes.

These higher planes consist of overlapping experiences of beauty, love, and magnificence that take place in completely nonphysical realities, all of which are interconnected with one another. You must understand that the creation of this new space did not previously exist within the eternal realities. The external realities have no beginning and no end.

Soon these original souls, whom I shall refer to as *Oversouls*, became able to inhabit the dimensions they created. It must be remembered that there existed other divine souls who took no part in this creation. These souls never inhabited these new dimensions and viewed this new creation from a distance.

Only the Oversouls could directly experience this new space by inhabiting it. Although these Oversouls became temporarily separate from their divine colleagues by creating and inhabiting these new dimensions, in all other ways these Oversouls retained their connection with God and the eternal now.

These new energy forces began a process of solidification, resulting in the creation of the first physical matter in the universes. This physical matter took the form of vapors and gases. Later these elements coalesced into liquids, with water being the most abundant representative. Soon chemicals were created and eventually solid matter was formed. Throughout this process there was a depth of love, beauty, and magnificence of soul forces woven into these creations.

Our current galaxies, stars, suns, and planets are an expression of the infinite variety of the Oversouls' choices reproduced endlessly to reflect the divine nature of their true eternal existence and origin from the God energy complex. There is a beginning and end to our physical universe from our perspective, but it is contained within the endless eternal now. This means that the forces within our universe are external.

These Oversouls created and directed the evolutionary mechanisms, which caused all of the permutations and all of the changes that led from the single-cell organisms to all of the many present forms of the minerals, the plants, the animals, and eventually our species. In reference to our evolution, the Oversouls gave our predecessors a certain cleverness and rapidly growing cerebral cortex of our brain that was implanted with creativity, imagination, and resourcefulness.

Feelings came next, mostly in the form of love, beauty, kindness, compassion, togetherness, and oneness with God. This was done in order to have us reflect the perfection of God and the Oversouls community of existing together in harmony and understanding of one another.

These early humans were perfect and had no karmic cycle, no negativity and consisted of societies in which love, kindness, and harmony manifested. They were given the full human capacities of creativity, inventiveness, intelligence, and feeling, but not yet that sense of each person being one unique individual. Early human beings did not have that unique awareness of self, but considered themselves as the entire wholeness of the group in which they lived.

The love, beauty, and perfection exhibited by these early humans were devoid of any form of negativity. There was no inhabiting of these early humans by the Oversouls at this time. Not until this experiment was refined enough so that these spirits could enter into and subjectively experience the new dimension they created, did they become a part of us.

We must also recognize that these early humans were not purely physical. Their components were of eternal nonphysical force origin, in order for the Oversouls to be able to place a portion of their own self-awareness (the Higher Self we possess) into these nonphysical bodies. These bodies that existed alongside the physical animal-human forms would appear to physical eyes as being etheric or vaporous in form.

Subsequently, these Oversouls began to make changes in the nonphysical forms that eventually, over vast periods of time, resulted in these etheric human forms becoming more physical. These nonphysical humans contained within their structure a divine projection of the Oversoul known as the Higher Self or superconscious mind. We refer to these as "the sons of God," who were a contrast to other humans lacking this Higher Self and who were known as "the sons of man." Indeed, the Old Testament makes reference to both.

Eventually the sons of man were given this Higher Self by their Oversoul creators. Now these sons of man shared a portion of the God energy complex and soul awareness that characterized the sons of God, to a degree. This ancient time took place long before recorded history and is represented today only in myth and legend. The lost continent of Lemuria (Mu) is one such place. Mu was located in the Pacific Ocean and it covered most of the area between California and the Pacific Rim countries. This vast continent sunk at approximately 11,000 B.C., long with Atlantis in the Atlantic Ocean.

We can now see a type of separation occurring in the sons of man. They understood that their physical bodies followed the cycles of life and death, but were also aware of their Higher Self and their own eternal nature. Those early humans deduced that they were only borrowing the physical forms that were ruled by life and death. Thus, they understood the ultimate truth of the universe while still possessing the ability to manipulate matter at will, with the mind and the powers of their Oversoul creators.

Later on, the Oversouls initiated an experiment that backfired. They brought certain changes upon the sons of man through expanded psychic abilities, feelings, and other human capacities, which resulted in our ability to focus clearly upon ourselves as physical beings; to experience ourselves as one unique ego; and to temporarily lose sight of eternal realities from whence we came. At this time there was still no negativity exhibited by our species.

Just as God instilled free will to the Oversouls, the latter gave us free will and allowed us complete freedom to do as we pleased and create whatever our hearts and minds desired. The Oversouls only knew of good in the universe and didn't concern themselves with the possibility of our creating negativity and evil acts. That was their biggest mistake.

This represented a turning point and over several generations the sons of man (us) began to think of themselves as being unique and freely expressing this feeling in their creative efforts and aligning it with their own unique desires. Throughout this process a further separation and diminishing awareness of the eternal portions of reality persisted.

A new cycle of creation began and these sons of man began to emphasize their own personal desires more and more. The first aspect of negativity that arose centered around possessions. These early humans were now more concerned with physical objects than they were with the love and well-being of their fellow humans. This led to the development of fear, a fear of losing these possessions. Stealing and violence resulted from this unfortunate sequence.

We should never blame the universe, God, nature, or evolution for the negativity we see all around us. Negativity and evil action is a human creation. It does not exist in the eternal now. All of this came about because of the development of a single ego and a loss of feelings of love for our fellow human beings.

The Oversouls tried to correct this situation through the use of the sons of God, who retained their clear and distinct awareness of their eternal origin. Primitive man referred to these as *enlightened beings*, whose appearance physically was identical to that of the sons of man, but who were able to expand their conscious awareness to directly perceive their own soul and the union with all other souls. These sons of God maintained direct communication with the divine Oversouls.

We can see how these enlightened beings translated their inner intuitive knowledge into human words and deeds that they believed were the most understandable to the ordinary human beings of the day. They became the Ascended Masters and channelers of all of the various holy scriptures present throughout the world. Differences in these teachings arose due to the variations in time and locations in which these translations were made available to the sons of man.

These differences in spiritual teachings came about because the enlightened beings of each period needed to communicate as human beings of their day in order to be understood. Our predecessors were being guided both by their ego, subconscious, occasional Higher Self contact and enlightened beings (sons of God).

The sons of man on the whole ignored the guidance from these sons of God. A form of rigidity and narrow-mindedness ensued and these sons of man would no longer listen to their inner voices of truth or the sons of God.

To resolve this difficulty the Oversouls tried another innovation. They called upon other highly evolved souls to function as spirit guides in order to augment the force of love and wisdom flowing into each one of the sons of man. We rejected this new form of guidance and our negativity and evil acts expanded.

Early man formed tribal groups and then nations to protect their possessions and commit various nefarious acts against one another. Wars resulted and the struggle and competition we see today all originated not so much from free will but from an unwillingness to care for other human beings more than we cared for material possessions.

With complete freedom we all possess the capacity to create our own reality and understand the origins of our species, our consciousness and the universe. Our human form is an excellent vehicle for what the Oversoul attempted to accomplish by projecting human personality into physical bodies.

We are all quite capable of witnessing a subjective experience free from excessive pain, fear, or extraordinarily difficult Earth challenges. A life characterized by happiness, joy, and balance, even though there may be difficult challenges in the life, is well within our range of attainment.

It is when we allow, by our own free will creation, our subjective experience of our lives to become saturated with fear and pain, that our healthy human consciousness is distorted and fear results. Fear is the only obstacle we need to overcome, because it leads to all other forms of negativity. We intentionally created this fear out of our own free will and it is the purpose of spirit guides to assist us in removing this fear.

Let us learn from geese. Scientists have discovered that the reason geese fly along in V formations is due to the aerodynamic fact that as each bird flaps its wings, it creates an uplift for the bird immediately following. By flying in a V formation, the whole flock adds at least 71 percent greater flying range than if each bird flew on its own.

When a goose falls out of formation, it suddenly feels the drag and resistance of trying to go it alone and quickly gets back into the formation to take advantage of the lifting power of the bird in the front. When the head goose gets tired, it rotates back in the formation and another goose flies as leader. And when a goose gets sick or is wounded by gunshots and falls out of formation, two other geese fall out with that goose and follow it down to lend help and protection. They stay with the fallen goose until it is able to fly, or until it dies; only then do they launch out on their own, or with another formation to catch up with their group.

Let us adopt the sense of a goose and stand by each other unconditionally. Human nature finds this idea foreign, but with the assistance of spirit guides we can become sons of God.

I quite realize that the paradigm I just presented will likely offend many religious beliefs. We must understand that there is a great difference between religion (which is based on dogma) and spirituality (which is based on universal truth).

These are commonalities among the various religions, such as a belief in a power higher than humans. Another thread is to love and honor this higher power. Even though the terminology of the teachings is different, the message is similar.

Universal Laws

Although there are dozens of universal laws, I will summarize what I feel are the most important ones. Because these universal laws (truths) represent the main difference between religion and spirituality, let us discuss them:

1. **The Law of Free Will.** Because the soul always has free will, it is our decision to be born at certain times and places. It is our decisions to choose our parents, friends, lovers, and enemies. We cannot blame other people or a bad childhood or marriage for our present problems. We are directly responsible for our lives because we have chosen the environment. The basic framework of your new life will be preplanned

by you, but you can't plan every situation. Not only does *your* soul have free will, but so do *all* the souls with which you will come into contact in this new life. The main point there is that you choose the tests.

Although many of the major events in your life are laid out by you on the soul plane prior to your birth, you have free will to sidestep your destiny. Also, you always have free will in how you respond to any situation. If you respond with love, compassion, and integrity, you have probably learned your karmic lesson and will not have to repeat the experience in the future.

We alone have the power to choose good over evil and growth over stagnation or degeneration. Only you can facilitate your spiritual growth and perfect your soul. Never blame any person, place, or thing for your lot in life. It is free will that caused our fall from grace originally.

2. **The Law of Grace.** Karma can be experienced to the letter of the law or in mercy and grace. Wisdom erases karma. If you show mercy, grace, and love, you will receive the same in return. This is also known as the *principle of forgiveness*. If you eliminate a negative behavior or weakness now, you erase all previous karma debts and don't have to work out any past life carryovers with every individual you may have wronged in the past, or who may have hurt you in previous existences.

3. **The Law of Challenge.** The universe never presents us with opportunities we cannot handle. You may be emotionally or physically overwhelmed, but not spiritually. Each obstacle and reward is placed in our path to both challenge us and facilitate our growth as a soul.

4. **The Law of Karma.** This law focuses on cause and effect. For every action there is a reaction. Nothing happens by mere chance. We select the framework, including all obstacles and rewards, on the soul plane prior to our birth. Because we choose all of these lessons, there is nobody else to blame for our circumstances. "To thine own self be true."

All of our actions, particularly our motives, have consequences. If you follow universal laws you will perfect the soul and ascend, as wisdom erases karma. If you continue repeating mistakes and fail lessons (you choose those lessons on the Soul plane), you are asking for a long and frustrating karmic cycle of many dysfunctional lives.

5. **The Law of Attraction.** Like attracts like. Whatever you focus your energy on you will attract. If you are negative, you draw in and experience negativity. If you are loving, you draw in and experience love.

6. **The Law of Resistance.** You tend to attract those individuals and karmic lessons which you have resisted. This is a "mirror of karma" law.

7. **The Law of Divine Flow.** By accessing our Higher Self (superconscious mind), we are functioning as a channel for the God energy complex and can accelerate our spiritual growth at a rapid rate. This law also explains how miracles occur.

8. **The Law of Polarity.** Everything has an opposite on the physical plane. These opposites (left, right, up, down, love, fear, good, evil, hot, cold, and so on.) are identical in composition but only differ in direction or degree. This law is the foundation for the dual aspects of our world.

9. **The Law of Reciprocity.** The more you give, the more you will receive. The more you assist others, the more you assist yourself.

10. **The Law of Manifestation.** Our mind, not our brain, creates the material world we live. Quantum physics demonstrates how this mechanism works mathematically. Be careful for what you desire, it may very well come true.

11. **The Law of Consciousness.** Our consciousness (soul) is constantly expanding and thereby creating more opportunities for our spiritual growth. We can also lengthen our karmic cycle if we fail to follow universal laws.

12. **The Law of Abundance.** It is our mind (consciousness) that creates abundance. Through self-hypnosis and visualization techniques we can attract, money, relationships, fame, better communication, spirituality, and other goals into our reality.

13. **The Law of Correspondence.** This principle deals with what is known as the "mirror of karma." "As above so below" also applies here. The outer world (macrocosm) we live in is a reflection of the inner world (microcosm) of our consciousness. All objects created on the physical plane have a counterpart on the Astral plane. This law helps to establish an interconnectedness between all components of our universe.

14. **The Law of the Present Moment.** We live in a space-time continuum in which the past, present and future occurs simultaneously. It is only within our mind that we limit ourselves to the concepts of linear time. In reality, all that exists is in the present moment. In the higher planes, where all souls are perfect, this is referred to as the "Eternal Now."

15. **The Law of Cycles.** As we discussed with the Law of Polarity, our universe is characterized by cycles. Day becomes night, winter ends and spring begins, and whatever rises eventually falls and rises again. This principle helps explain how our universe began (Big Bang) and will eventually collapse and rise again in a 40-billion year cyclic pattern.

16. **The Law of Reincarnation.** This law is also known as the wheel of reincarnation or law of cyclic return. As long as we have lessons to learn (karma), our soul will be required to reincarnate into a body. It is only when perfection of the soul is achieved that this seemingly endless cycle is terminated and our soul merges with our Higher Self to ascend into the higher planes to reunite with God.

From this discussion I hope you can see that spirituality is about that evolutionary process of self-realization and God realization and has nothing to do with religion.

◎◎◎◎◎◎◎◎◎◎◎◎

CHAPTER 2

Where Do Spirit Guides Live?

Spirit guides originate from many other realms, or dimensions. I have briefly discussed the fact that Masters are often found on the Mental plane. We find spirit guides on many other dimensions and realities and will discuss these worlds in this chapter.

One principle you do need to be aware of is that spirit guides represent various stages of their own evolution and growth. Not all guides symbolize perfect energy, and it is important for you to be discriminating about with what guide you establish a link. Competent and helpful teachers exist in every plane of reality. You can always dismiss a guide who is not helping you at any time. However, the real key is to attract spiritual teachers that are both sufficiently skilled and committed to assisting you with your spiritual growth.

Spirit guides often (but not always) have lived on Earth and evolved spiritually to the extent that they perfected their souls. This state of grace allows this being the option of ascending into the higher planes to reunite with God, or remaining on the lower planes to function as teacher assisting others in perfecting their souls.[1]

Not all guides have perfected their souls. Some are trainees and are still working on their spiritual paths. Your Higher Self will assist you in making this distinction.

Spiritual teachers may originate from multidimensional realities, such as hyperspace, which we will discuss later in this chapter. There are extraterrestrials and angelic beings who have never lived on the Earth, but function as spirit guides nonetheless. Always bear in mind the fact that all guides are highly skilled at transmitting energy from their world to ours.

Here is a paradigm I have discovered over the years of training my patients to contact their spirit guides that explains how this mechanism of spirit communication works:

God energy from the higher planes

Thought

Dimensional matter (Astral, Causal, Mental, Etheric, or Soul plane)

Life force (prana, chi, and so on), which now occupies

Physical body on the Earth plane

Spirit guides live on dimensions where thought instantly creates a reality. They can change their physical appearances instantly and appear thinner, younger, and acquire any other characteristic they desire. There is no time concept as we know it. All time is simultaneous in the space-time continuum on these realms, so these guides can literally view our past, present, and future all at once.

There are many spiritual laws on these dimensions to which these beings must adhere. Although the "physical" laws that control their world are quite different from those that govern our Physical plane, these guides are bound by those spiritual laws and can never override our free will. We can accept or reject their advice, but regardless of how necessary and beneficial their counsel may be, they will never force their intentions upon us in any way.

The main point here is that we always possess free will choices. We can choose to follow a guide's advice, or adamantly refuse this option. The assistance presented to us by our guides can only go so far. It is up to us to consciously work at opening our hearts to them and raising the frequency vibrational rates of our own souls. Accessing the Higher Self through a technique I developed called the superconscious mind tap, which will be explained in chapter 4, is one method of attaining this spiritual unfoldment.

The Plane Concept

1. **Physical, Material, or Earth Plane.** The world in which we live comprises the Earth plane. As previously mentioned, the physical body is composed of the densest matter on this dimension and has the lowest fvr. We can add to or subtract the largest amount of karma when we exist on this realm.

   The realm of illusion or *maya* is the term the Easterners would apply to our plane. This dimension is one of energy, matter, space, and time and is characterized by the sound of thunder.

2. **Astral Plane.** The Astral plane is divided into an upper and lower component. We can ascribe a misty or foggy environment, the presence of bizarre and evil inhabitants and feelings of confusion and bewilderment to the lower Astral plane. No spirit guide is found in this part of the Astral plane, as there is no possibility of spiritual growth in the lower astral component.

   The upper Astral plane is characterized by Earthlike majestic scenery with human inhabitants, feelings of peace, and spiritual fulfillment. Our psychic abilities originate from the Astral plane.

   When we cross into spirit this is the dimension our soul first enters. Those who live dysfunctional, or are simply not prepared to handle changing dimensions, wind up in the lower Astral plane. The upper astral component is your destination if you evolve spiritually and learn how to handle the transition from the Physical plane. The sound associated with the Astral plane is the roar of the sea.

3. **The Causal Plane.** The main characteristic of the Causal plane is that it is the location of Akashic Records. These records represent a chart of our soul's growth and development encompassing the entire range

of past, present, and future lifetimes. Whenever we learn or fail a karmic test, it is noted in these files. It is possible to access these records from any of the lower five planes and I will present an exercise to do this in Chapter 6. Spirit guides have complete access to these records at all times. The tinkling of bells is heard continuously on this dimension.

4. **The Mental Plane.** I have previously cited the fact that many Masters reside on the Mental plane. When the ancients visited this realm during their out-of-body experiences (OBEs), they identified their gods with the inhabitants of this world. Ethics, moral teaching, philosophy, and thought dominate this dimension.

   Mental plane inhabitants wear white flowing gowns, live in homes that have the appearance of abstract geometric designs, and travel on blue highways, because the soil of this realm is deep blue in color and this soil is used in the construction of their roads. Running water represents the characteristic sound of this plane.

5. **The Etheric Plane.** The reported source of our primitive thoughts and subconscious is on the Etheric plane. Its vast size gives this world the appearance of being flat.

   With this dimension we associate truth and beauty, the sound of buzzing bees, and a sky filled with brilliant white lights 24 hours a day.

6. **The Soul Plane.** I refer to the Soul plane as a type of "demilitarized zone," because it neither represents the lower planes nor the higher dimensions. This is where we choose our future lifetimes, or ascend, if our souls are perfected. The very last plane in which we possess any type of body is the Soul plane. We associate a single note of a flute with this world.

   One nice thing about this realm is that it represents the closest working relationship between your Higher Self and spirit guides. As with all of the other planes except the Physical plane, telepathy is the mode of communication. All souls eventually end up here following the death of the body on any of the lower five planes.

All of us would just love to ascend following a particular incarnation, but as long as we have a karmic cycle we cannot enter the seven higher planes—our vibrational rate would be too low to permit it. It is the purpose of spirit guides to instruct us on how to perfect our souls so that we may ascend and terminate the cycle of birth and death that has come to be known as the karmic cycle.

The Seven Higher Planes

When you finally perfect your soul, you shed the last remnants of a body (Soul plane body) and now enter into the first of the higher planes—the seventh plane. Of course, you could always choose to remain on the lower planes as a spirit guide yourself.

The disadvantage in describing the higher planes is that the source is always secondhand. From the Soul plane we can eavesdrop and receive data from these more advanced realms. Spirit guides can relay information about these dimensions, but we cannot travel there until our souls are perfect.

The higher planes represent the eternal now. There is absolutely no form of negativity or stress there. Because there is no real relation to a finite mode of being, no cause and effect exists. A *newness, isness,* and *hereness* are all that one finds on the higher planes.

One dominant feature of the higher planes is the presence of the God energy. We refer to the presence of this energy as the *isness.* The specific reality of God's presence is what I mean by nowness, while hereness implies the continual presence of God in these higher realms. An indescribable orchestra-like music may be heard continually throughout each one of the higher planes.

The eternity concept we theorize about is actually the higher planes themselves. There is no time or space on these realms, just an eternal now. We cannot begin to comprehend the 13th plane or God (nameless) plane, because this is the location of ultimate truth and reality.

Our thoughts and actions determine our fvr, and to ascend from the seventh to the thirteenth plane requires a continual increase in this fvr. Logic, cause and effect, time, birth, death, and changes of seasons are unknown on the higher planes. There are no perpetrators or victims.

We cannot even describe one plane being on top of or farther away from another dimension—they simply exist, as do temperature and barometric pressure on our plane. Figure 1 on page 44 represents a comparison and summary of each of the 13 planes.

Name of Plane	Sound	Description
13. God or nameless plane 12. _____ 11. _____ 10. _____ 9. _____ 8. _____ 7. _____	Indescribable orchestralike music is heard continually, representing the sounds of the universe.	The true Heaven or Nirvana. The details of these planes can only be ascertained when you have perfected your soul's energy and have ascended. There is no time, space, or cause and effect here. Souls occupying eternity do not possess a body of any kind. They are all perfect energy.
6. Soul Plane	Single note of a flute	This is where souls go following death on the lower 5 planes to close their next life. Beyond this plane there is no body of any type. Self-realization and ascension occur here.
5. Etheric (Intuition)	Buzzing of bees	The source of the subconscious.
4. Mental (Mind)	Running water	The source of moral teaching, ethics and philosophy. The home of the God of most orthodox religions.
3. Causal Memory	Tinkle of bells	Akashic Records are kept here.
2. Astral (Emotion)	Roar of the sea	The source of emotions and all psychic phenomena. All ideas concerning Physical plane inventions of orginate here.
1. Physical (5 senses)	Thunder	Illusions of reality; the plane of space, time, matter, and energy.

Figure 1. The Sounds and Description of the 13 Planes

The one element of our psyche that prevents spiritual growth is fear, and this is the main lesson that spirit guides attempt to teach us. When you overcome all fears, ascension is just around the corner.

Hyperspace

We define the three dimensions of the Physical plane as length, width, and depth of an object. Time represents the fourth dimension. Einstein established the concept of space-time by demonstrating the curved nature of this aspect of the universe.

As hard as he tried, Einstein was unsuccessful during the last 30 years of his life in his attempt to unify all known physical phenomena into a *unified field theory*. Hyperspace can also be called the fifth dimension and beyond. There are mathematical models to show that a 26-dimensional universe exists.[2]

We can define hyperspace as anything beyond the fourth dimension, or the time component of the space-time continuum. All of the lower planes, including the Physical plane, lie in hyperspace. The hyperspace concept unifies all known physical phenomena into a simple paradigm and accomplishes what Einstein could not do.

Light and gravity, for example, are not similar and adhere to very different mathematical laws. Hyperspace theory simply demonstrates that light and gravity are merely vibrations in the fifth dimension. This theory looks upon matter as also vibrating from the fifth dimension.

Hyperspace has other odd qualities. Light was created from the warping of the geometry of hyperspace. This unusual dimension is located topologically in a circle, so that anyone walking in its direction would eventually wind up back at the point of origin.

The interesting thing about hyperspace theory is that it provides for a unification of the four forces of nature, which no other paradigm has been able to accomplish. The four natural forces to which I am referring are:

1. **Electromagnetic force.** Electricity, light, and magnetism compose this force.

2. **The strong nuclear force.** This energy fuels the stars. All life on Earth owes its very existence to the energy from our sun (a star).

3. **The weak nuclear force.** Radioactive decay is an example of this force.

4. **Gravitational force.** This force is responsible for keeping all planets in their orbits. All of us and our atmosphere would be flung into space without this force. The world itself would nova (explode) devoid of gravity.

Scientific Evidence of Other Dimensions

It is important to understand the universe in terms of spirit guides function. Descriptions of the "other side" have been presented by those people who have had near-death experiences, clairvoyants, mystics, and others sensitive enough to relate their out-of-body encounters.

There are three main schools of thought on exactly what these encounters are or represent. The first type is that of the scientist. Hard science attempts to rationally explain these observations by such principles as hypoxia (a lack of oxygen to the brain), in the case of near-death experience (NDE).

A careful reading of the literature on NDEs will illustrate the errors in rationale advanced by science. For example, hypoxia would result in complete unconsciousness, and the patient would have no memories of experiences he or she had. How could these patients possibly describe the core experience of a NDE in 40 percent of these cases throughout the world, long before they appeared in popular books, such as Dr. Raymond Moody's *Life After Life?*[3]

As I stated in my book *Peaceful Transition* when describing NDEs, "The typical encounter is described as being in a dream. Surprisingly, this experience seems more real than ordinary waking consciousness. The five senses are heightened; thought processes are rational and crystal clear.

The main difference noted is a disconnectedness from your physical body. A floating sensation ensues and the soul views the lifeless body from a corner of the ceiling. A sense of calm and serenity dominates now, and time has no meaning. The soul feels drawn to a dark tunnel with a brilliant white light at its end.

As you enter the white light, a loved one or a religious figure [spirit guide] greets you. At this time you become aware that you will return to your physical body. Prior to this, however, you have perceived in the form of flashbacks an instantaneous panoramic review of your former life.

Most people do not remember these events when they are resuscitated. Some people report becoming aware of discomfort or being propelled uncontrollably back into their body. Reports prevail of a greater appreciation of life, an increase in the importance of personal relationships, and a determination to maximize the opportunities afforded to them.

In summary, the core experience of an NDE includes (1) hearing loud noises very early in the death process; (2) moving through a long, dark tunnel; (3) seeing a white or gold light that is separate from oneself; (4) seeing religious figures like Jesus or Buddha or Moses; (5) a panoramic life review/judgment; and (6) indications that this is a learning process."[4]

A dismissive explanation as that of fraud, imagination, hallucination, or delusion is usually presented by the parapsychology debunkers. The fact remains that there is overwhelming scientific and clinical evidence to substantiate these reported contacts. The documentation of precognitions obtained from NDEs is but one example. Transformations in the individual's life that have positively affected others are additional evidence.

Metaphysical explanations represent the third category. There are theological and philosophical components to this group. The Easterners long ago postulated the existence of different spiritual dimensions or planes. These other planes of existence are occupied by life forms as energy beings. Many of these energy beings are spirit guides.

In reference to hyperspace, two important scientific verifications should be mentioned. The first refers to the mathematical models establishing the existence of hyperspace. The Indian mathematician Srinivasa Ramanujan worked out a rather complicated series of equations demonstrating the existence theoretically of a 10- and 26-dimensional universe.

A second factor relates to Thomas Banchoff's work at Brown University. He has developed computer programs that actually demonstrate the existence of fifth-dimensional objects and beyond. Our eyes are not able to see these higher dimensional objects but their shadows can be viewed on computer screens.[5]

In answering the question where do spirit guides live? We can say that they occupy any of the lower five planes, as well as the Soul plane. Hyperspace proper is also home to spirit guides and in chapter 6 I will present exercises to travel to these other dimensions both in and out of the body to visit these spiritual advisors.

◎◎◎◎◎◎◎◎◎◎◎◎

CHAPTER 3

Preparing Yourself for Spirit Guide Contact

You are probably wondering why it is so difficult for the average person to converse with a spirit guide. The answer is simple. In the West, fundamental religious teachings portray spirits as devils or saints, demons, or angels. Theology leaves us with the impression that only certain select people can communicate with spirits, and anyone else who claims to do so must be psychotic or evil. The rational Western mind makes fun of any paranormal or psychic ability. It is only recently that the media has taken a more serious attitude towards parapsychology.

Another factor rests in your preparedness. Most people are unprepared to communicate with a spirit guide. In addition, these guides are not always available. Your attempts at communication with these energy beings will be successful only if you are properly prepared and if this attempt coincides with this guide's availability.

Oftentimes a spirit guide will communicate with us without our acknowledgement of this interaction. For example, a dream, symbol, or shadow seen in the corner of our eye or unusual insight that solves a problem may be easily overlooked by us in our hurried lives.

Certain sounds such as whispers, pops, soft buzzings, and ringing noises are sometimes the beginnings of audible spirit communications. You might even have had the experience of waking up in the middle of the night thinking you heard a voice in your room.

Some other signs of spirit contact are a sensation of coolness, warmth, or a tingly feeling on certain parts of your body. Sudden urges to repeatedly scratch an area of our body also can reflect a spirit's attempt to catch our attention.

Before describing specific techniques to meet a spirit guide, I would like to discuss fragrances. Certain fragrances can actually assist you in your ability to communicate with your spirit guide. These are:

Gardenia: This fragrance stimulates telepathy and attracts only spirits.

Rose: This attracts guides of love and joy and assists the development of psychic abilities in general.

Wisteria: This odor brings in guides who stimulate creativity and acts to initiate and expand healing energy.

Frankincense: This fragrance functions by cleansing the aura.

Apple Blossom: Mythic images are facilitated by using this fragrance.

Lavender: This herb stimulates higher levels of psychic vision and facilitates altered states of consciousness.

Rosemary: This herb is very protective and useful in facilitating spirit contact when used as a bath oil. Its fragrance works best that way.

Chamomile: This fragrance helps to balance the aura and attunes you to nature spirits.

Carnation: This fragrance protects you from negative entities.

Lilac: This fragrance assists in developing your ability to actually see spirits.

Violet: This fragrance attracts all nature spirits and develops telepathic communication abilities.

Using Stones, Herbs, and Oils to Establish Spirit Guide Contact

A very simple technique to induce spirit guide contact during the dream state is to place an unset stone under your pillow at night and simply go to sleep. I recommend you only use only one stone at a time.

Amethyst: This violet stone has been used to treat anger, hallucinations, fear, hate, and grief. Its high vibrational rate makes it ideal for producing OBEs and attracting guides.

Aquamarine: It is supposed that this stone gives clarity to mental visions. A gem of this clear blue or blue-green color assists our spiritual judgment and clears our minds.

Azurite: This stone is reported to aid our psychic development.

Crystal, Quartz: The rock crystal also assists in facilitating our ESP powers.

Lapis Lazuli: The ancient Egyptians referred to this as the "Stone of Heaven." It is said to promote sound sleep and aid in spiritual vision.

Malachite: This dark green stone creates a feeling of positivity and general well-being.

Moonstone: Your ability to unmask enemies and facilitate dreams will be experienced by using this stone.

Peridot: This light green stone promotes a good night's rest.

Tourmaline, Blue: In addition to being available in red, green, yellow-green, pink, honey-yellow, violet, and black, this stone gives us confidence, inspiration, and tranquility.

Ancient cultures used the scent of certain oils to improve their psychic senses. You may smell crushed herbs or fresh flowers instead. Do not ingest either the herbs or the oils. Use only one at a time to keep both your physical and astral head clear.

Bay: This herb promotes psychic awareness.

Calendula: Marigold is another name for this flower. It reportedly induces psychic dreams.

Chamomile: This herb relieves tensions and produces restful sleep.

Cinnamon: You will improve your psychic awareness by smelling this fragrance.

Clary sage: The musty scent of his herb promotes calmness and dreams.

Deer's tongue: Smelling this vanilla-like herb will facilitate OBEs and guide contact.

Frankincense: This oil allows you to become more aware of other planes, your Higher Self, and spirit guides and reduces stress.

Honeysuckle: Your psychic awareness will be increased by smelling this sweet flower.

Hyacinth: This flower is used to eliminate nightmares and promote a restful sleep.

Iris: The odor of this flower root or oil is associated with a strengthening of the connection between the conscious mind and the psychic centers facilitating spirit guide communication.

Jasmine: You will have more psychic dreams and feel less nervous by using this oil.

Lilac: Use of this scent will aid in the recall of past lives.

Lotus or Water Lily: Inhaling the scent of this flower creates peace and tranquility.

Mace: The odor from this nutmeg enhances psychic awareness.

Mimosa: Dreams of the future will be facilitated by the sweet fragrance of this yellow flower.

Mugwort: This plant induces OBEs and guide contact.

Myrrh: The bitter scent of this herb will improve your awareness and other dimensions.

Sandalwood: Your frequency vibrational rate will be improved from its scent.

Yarrow: The rich scent of this garden flower promotes psychic communication.

Absolutely every one of us can learn how to contact the Higher Self and spirit guides. All it requires is patience and persistent practice. With just a little bit of effort representing an investment of about 30 minutes daily, you can establish this link to high-level entities.

We are all composed of energy that originated from the God energy complex. Our Higher Self and spirit guides are simply an expression of this perfect energy. All you need to do to begin this work of accessing your guides is to invite them in. This can be accomplished by sitting or lying down in a relaxed position and clearly stating your desire to establish a communication with your guide.

Keep in mind the basics of the spirit world *before* you initiate this contact. Your guides do not know how every future event in our lives will manifest. The reasons for this will be explained later. Suffice it for now to say that they can receive only probable paths.

This leads to a second principle relating to our free will. It is our free will and choices that we make that ultimately determine our destinies. Even if a spirit guide were capable of seeing into every aspect of your future accurately, the guide would not risk interfering with your free will. This is a basic law of the universe that is *never* violated by a spirit guide.

Keep your questions or goals simple to prevent confusion on both the guide's reception of your query and its response to you. Always bear in mind that data from guides does not represent the ultimate truth, but a step in our understanding so that we may discover this truth for ourselves.

The information from spirit guides has to be filtered and subsequently interpreted by our physical brains. This wisdom is presented to us in a way that permits our understanding and acceptance through our present belief system. Some of our interpretations may be biased by our beliefs to various degrees.

Guides may work with you on pure energy levels. They can assist you in balancing your psychic energy centers located within your astral body known as *chakras*. We will discuss these in greater detail later and I will present a simple self-hypnotic exercise in Chapter 5 to train you to do this yourself.

You may not be aware that these processes are taking place even during hypnosis. Do not assume you are being ignored if you are not aware of this energy mechanism. "When the student is ready, the teacher will be there" applies daily to spirit guide contact.

Guide contact will always be facilitated by establishing a level of trust with them once you determine that they are high-level advisors. It is also helpful to begin each communication by specifically requesting that they work with you in every way to stimulate your spiritual growth. Take the time to connect with your guide and Higher Self daily for your own spiritual unfoldment.

Begin this process slowly using the exercises presented in this chapter. Use only the techniques that you find comfortable. Your guides will customize their approach to meet your needs and not go any faster than you can comfortably handle. You are never given spiritual lessons to learn that are beyond your growth level (fvr).

Occasionally, a spirit guide will communicate with you while you are in your physical body. Here are some principles you should know exist concerning your communication with a guide. I have previously mentioned some of these, but they are worth repeating.

- ☉ You are in no danger at any time from establishing communication with a spirit guide. Do not be concerned with being "possessed," or harmed in any way.

- ☉ The compatibility of your purposes and goals is the main reason why a particular guide or group of guides chooses to work with you.

- ☉ The higher level guides serve as sources for clarity, direction, and guidance. Their main concern is your higher purpose.

- ☉ The control and direction of all communication with your spirit guides always rests with you. If you are not ready or willing to be contacted, you can simply dismiss this guide.

- ☉ A spirit guide will assist you in any way you request, as long as it does not result in harm to others or interfere with your own spiritual growth. No spirit guide is going to learn your karmic lessons for you. You must do that yourself.

- ☉ There are no shortcuts to spiritual growth. Your spirit guides will assist you by their communications, but you always have the free will to reject their advice. The contact with these beings will efficiently speed up your spiritual growth.

- ☉ Do not follow spirit guides' advice blindly. You are encouraged to test them.

- ☉ Spirit guides communicate with you only with your permission.

- ☉ As a result of contacting spiritual guides, you can expect the following to occur:

  - ◎ You will be enlightened spiritually.

  - ◎ Your compassion towards others will grow.

◎ Your goals that may not have been attained in the past will now be achieved.

◎ You may experience physical, mental, emotional, or spiritual healing.

◎ An increase in your psychic abilities will be noted.

◎ You are always left feeling confident and empowered.

◎ All messages and advice are designed to give you freedom to choose your actions.

◎ You are always left feeling changed for the better in some way.

◎ There is no difficulty in understanding the information provided. It agrees with and expands upon your own basic knowledge.

◎ You will find new information presented that always betters your life in some way as you apply it.

◎ Others will be attracted to you because of your new and higher energy.

◎ A sense of sincerity, simplicity, humility, and spirituality will always be demonstrated as a result of these contacts. These entities will never make demands or brag about their abilities or knowledge.

The Aura

As long as you maintain good health and control over your life, absolutely nothing in the other dimensions can harm you. Later in this chapter I will present several spiritual protection exercises. For our current purpose we will focus on strengthening your subtle energy and physical body.

Please bear in mind that contacting spirit guides affords us the opportunity to be inspired creatively, attract a significant other, attain abundance, be protected from psychic attack, become informed by their insights, experience their companionship, unconditional love and myriad other benefits. This spiritual contact should always be viewed as a way to supplement and enrich your life, not replace or control it.

Our subtle bodies are energy components to our being that allow us to both tap into and enter other dimensions. We use the term aura or auric field to describe this electromagnetic extension of our soul. This aura is weakened by drugs, stress, bad habits, poor diet and lack of fresh air, rest, or exercise.

The aura comprises three auric bodies, referred to as the *physical auric body*, the *etheric auric body* and the *vital auric body*. A light-blue or bright white band extending from one-eighth to one-half inches is the *physical auric body*. This is the densest of the auric bodies and bulges when injured.

The *etheric auric body* extends out from one to four inches from the physical auric body and is an exact replica of it. It is interesting to note that this etheric auric body is necessary to maintain life and is responsible for transporting the soul's energy to the nonphysical dimensions following the death of the physical body. This etheric auric body is hazy light-blue or gray in appearance usually, although it may be seen as violet, blue, green, orange, and yellow.

Extending from two to six inches from the etheric auric body is the *vital auric body*. This latter auric body is composed of fingerlets of lines of energy extending out in all directions. The functions attributed to the vital auric body connect the physical body to the astral body and project your personality and charisma to others.

The stronger and more vibrant our auric bodies are, the better our communication with spirit guides will be and the healthier our bodies will function. To assist our bodies in their functioning, a proper diet is also necessary. Fish, white meat, vegetables, pineapples, papaya, lemons, oranges, and so on, are high-vibrational foods, and result in raising the quality of the soul's energy.

Lower vibrational foods, such as red meat, slow our metabolism and interfere with our ability to communicate with spirit guides. It is advisable to drink more water and lower salt intake to facilitate spirit guide contact. Fasting also helps us bring these spiritual advisors into our awareness. You should avoid heavy meals following a contact with your guide.

Mindfulness

The ability to focus is critical in contacting spirit guides. Without this ability to focus, you may not be able to receive information from your spiritual advisor. The natural ability we possess to eliminate robotic behavior and maintain high levels of awareness of our actions and the world in which we live is called *mindfulness*.

To accomplish the state of mindfulness, you must end stereotyped perception. It is so natural to ignore differences in our world and assume everything is as it has always been. Mindfulness involves carefully observing each event in our life as though it were occurring for the first time. This is done by continually paying attention to each phase of an event when our mind is receptive, not reactive.

By simply registering everything you observe, a form of objectivity is exhibited. This is how scientists conduct experiments. There are three different types of mindfulness. The first type is *mindfulness of the body*. Each moment of your bodily activity is noted, regardless of what you do about it. The focus is on the body itself, not on the motives behind your actions.

Mindfulness of feeling is the second category. The focus now is on your internal sensations. The degree of pleasantness or unpleasantness is ignored. All you do at this juncture is note any internal feelings as they surface and become a part of your awareness. The specific feeling itself is registered, then disregarded.

The third grouping is called *mindfulness of mental states*. This type focuses on whatever mood, mode of thought, or psychological state presents itself. Each is simply noted as such. If, for instance, there is frustration at a disturbing noise, at that moment you simply note frustration.

Mindfulness trains us to use our awareness as distinct from the modalities contributing to it. The knowledge we now acquire is not easily expressed verbally, but more a realization obtained by direct experience.

Mindfulness gives us an understanding and enlightenment of the separate nature of awareness and its objects. We can now gain a clear understanding that these dual processes are devoid of self. Each moment of awareness goes according to its own nature, regardless of one's will. This allows us to see the big picture and the fact that awareness is in a state of perpetual flux.

Our world of reality is renewed every mind moment in an endless chain. We now come to know the truth of impermanence in the depths of our very being. Reality is understood to be devoid of self and ever changing. This assists our spiritual unfoldment by directing us to a state of detachment from our world of experience.

It is helpful to keep a log and note the date and your responses to the exercises presented in this section. You can jot down how long you were actually able to focus your concentration. It may have been only a minute or two the first time you tried this exercise. Additional trials will train you to hold your focus for at least six minutes.

Here is an exercise designed to assist you in focusing:

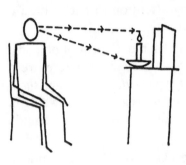

Figure 2

Place a lit candle at eye level and sit in a chair within four feet of it. Make sure there are no drafts in this room. Set a timer for ten minutes and end this exercise the moment the timer sounds.

Relax and breathe deeply. Ask your Higher Self to assist you in projecting colors onto this candle flame. Concentrate on the color blue and mentally project that color onto the flickering candle flame. When you see the blue color, look away from the candle and begin again.

Stare at the candle flame once more, only this time focus on the color green and repeat this procedure.

Your conscious mind might tempt you with outside thoughts. Ignore these mental distractions and continue gazing at the candle flame. You cannot succeed with this exercise if you focus on these thoughts. You must discipline yourself to deal only with the candle. This applies to any other type of potential type of distraction that may be around this room or your home.

In future sessions you might want to make the candle flame higher or lower with your mind as you develop your mindfulness and your ability to focus on one thing at a time.

Spiritual Protection Techniques

Contacting spirit guides by the methods presented in this book is perfectly safe. Spirit guide contacts help you to discover the psychic powers within you that can help empower your life. You will always be strengthened and enlightened with a greater sense of meaning of life as a result of these exposures. Your life will always be improved in some way when you access a true spirit guide.

Yes, there are negative entities on other dimensions, and we will discuss them shortly. It is always wise to apply protection techniques when contacting spirit guides, because some of these dysfunctional spirits attempt to communicate with inexperienced and unprotected receivers.

You can rest assured that you are in contact with a high-level spirit guide when the following factors are observed:

- ◎ A sense of sincerity, simplicity, humility, and spirituality will always be demonstrated as a result of these contacts.

- ◎ You are always left feeling changed for the better in some way.

- ◎ You will find new information presented that always betters your life in some way as you apply it.

- ◎ Your true spirit guide will be able to accurately perceive not only future trends in your life, but also how you will respond to them. They will limit these precognitions so as not to violate your free will choice rights.

- ◎ There is no difficulty in understanding the information provided. The information agrees with and expands upon your own knowledge acquired throughout your life.

- ◎ As a result of these contacts, you will be stimulated to be stronger, encourage others, and initiate healing powers within yourself.

- ◎ All messages and advice are designed to give you freedom to choose your actions.

- ◎ The psychic powers you have will increase so that you yourself receive additional data beneficial for your own growth. This is part of your psychic empowerment.

- ◎ You are always left feeling confident and empowered, never bored, frustrated, angry, or compromised in any way.

If you have the experience of running into a dysfunctional or downright negative entity, the following patterns will be noted by you:

- You will develop a sense of alienation to those people and things normally closest to you.

- The spirit expects you to accept its teachings blindly and discourages questions.

- You note an impatience with this entity and the use of foul language.

- You suddenly develop medical and emotional problems.

- The spirit flatters or patronizes you and appeals strongly to your emotions.

- You become obsessed with material or personal gains.

- A series of incidents of "bad luck" occurs in your life shortly following your communication with this spirit.

- The spirit communication leaves you with uncomfortable feelings and results in stress.

- You experience paralysis felt as a wave rising through your body with no known cause or past history of this symptom.

- Observing a glittery red light in your eyes, or the eyes of someone close to you.

- Inner voices urge you to do destructive things to yourself or others.

- Dark threadlike or tubelike connections are observed leading from you.

- Relentless nightmares destroy your ability to obtain a good night's rest.

- You see visualizations of the spirit perched on a throne combined with statements such as, "I am the God of the Mental plane."

- Negative statements are made in reference to God.

- Encouragement is given to the karmic cycle and reincarnation as the solution to your problems. All high-level spirit guides will assist us in *escaping* the reincarnation mechanism.

- Advice is given to ignore all other spirit guide contact except that of this entity.

- An attitude of vindictiveness, impatience, anger, and irritation is noted.

- Attempts are made at possession of your physical body.

- Statements are given to the extent that this is your only chance to communicate with God.

- You are treated as if you are specially chosen to receive this spirit's wisdom.

- Your past failures or current problems are mocked.

- Coercive attempts are made to force you to comprehend a concept.

- Any form of lying or misrepresentation.

- Attempts at name dropping. For example, "I was Moses' spirit guide."

- Allegiance to entities other than God.

- Pressure to perform certain functions.

- Any expectation of trust, such as statements like, "Why don't you trust me?"

Psychic attacks may be viewed as the nonphysical component of any form of an attack. This can range from a nasty look (evil eye) to casting a curse, as in black magic-thought-forms being created and evil entities conjured up in certain rituals of the dark arts.

The greatest likelihood of being contacted by a negative entity are with groups of people practicing malicious magic, or just experimenting with conjuring up spirits without spiritual protection techniques applied. Individuals who are emotionally and psychologically compromised attract these negative spirits like ants to a picnic. It is statistically more common to find such unhappy souls in large gatherings.

You know a group is dealing with negative beings when these traits are exhibited:

- The group leader does not represent the standards that he or she is professing.

- The material given by the spirit is simply a rehashing of popular metaphysical trends.

- You cannot verify any of the data given.

- The group leader purports himself or herself to be a superior being or possess some unique knowledge of the universe.

- The leaders demand absolute obedience to their authority.

- The group requires you to make drastic changes in your life and/or turn over all of your worldly possessions to them.

- You are given inadequate time to think about their doctrines or demands.

- The spirit delivers material in subsequent sessions that contradicts previous data.

In my book *Protected by the Light*[1] I present a thorough discussion of negative entities and how to recognize metaphysical traps. For our purposes let me state that for all psychic attacks to be effective, there must be some connection established with your aura, a telepathic suggestion and a reinforcement of this suggestion by way of invisible forces.

Many of us associate the term possession with psychic attacks. Possession has a most unusual history. The ancient Greeks of 1250 B.C. believed that the body of man could be "possessed" by a god so that this being could perform physical acts. Heroic deeds in war and sexual acts were the most common examples cited.

By 800 B.C. the Greek gods had acquired their own physical bodies and possession seemed to have disappeared. For example, in Homer's *Iliad* the goddess Aphrodite saves the injured Paris by carrying him in her arms, rather than possessing him bodily, as was characteristic of pre-Homeric Greek literature.

These possession paradigms were not looked upon as evil until Roman times. Now an exorcism was required to rid the poor unfortunate victim of this evil demon. This technique consisted of talking directly to the evil entity quoting holy scripture and dousing it with holy water.

It is relatively easy to protect yourself from a psychic attack, or contact with a negative spirit. Showing care for others brightens your auric bodies and this automatically attracts high-level spirit guides into your arena. These positive beings now easily see your radiant aura against a mostly gray background of this section of the universe. Dark entities avoid all forms of light and this further protects you.

Recalling positive episodes in your life that are accompanied by feelings of happiness also helps keep negative beings from singling you out. Think of a trip to the Grand Canyon or a time you did something kind for someone else. Sing your favorite song and reflect upon a tender moment of love in your life. These examples will assist you in spiritual protection.

Evil spirits are attracted to people who are greedy and focus on getting versus giving things. If you want sex, money, success, or psychic powers at the expense of or to control others, you are a candidate for psychic attack. You will attract benevolent spirits by adopting a philosophy of helping others and giving of yourself.

Love, peace, and self-discipline repels negative entities. Showing true concern and empathy for those less fortunate and challenged in some way goes a long way to attracting high-level guides. People who are possessive, pessimistic, cynical, and hateful attract dark spirits.

Avoid depressing and fanatical reading, especially if your health is compromised in any way. Concentrate on the positive side of life. If you should encounter a negative entity simply say "God bless you" or "God is with me" and send out light, warmth, and love to that entity. They will then leave you alone. A strong, active mind is your best defense against a dark spirit.

Other helpful hints to prevent psychic attacks and repel malevolent beings are:

- Act in an organized and purposeful manner. You are most vulnerable when you are confused and disorganized. Focus your attention on something productive.
- Keep a mental image of a bright, radiant white light around you at all times.
- Refrain from watching television news, listening to depressing stories on the radio and reading such items in newspapers. Keep your thoughts positive.
- Stay in well-lit areas and avoid synthetic clothing. Synthetics block the protective effect on spiritual energy.
- Keep up your own physical and emotional energy levels.
- If you have foolishly made a pact with a dark entity or the Devil, renounce it. God does not recognize these agreements anyway.

◎　Not all radiant spirits are positive. Some merely reflect or channel light instead of generating it themselves. Refer to my previous discussion on how to determine whether this is a good or bad spirit.

◎　Never argue or debate with a dark spirit. They are more knowledgeable than you and can read your mind. Just send them away and apply white light protection.

Here is an exercise to assist you in the arts and science of spiritual protection:

1. Take a deep breath and hold it for a count of six. Let it out slowly. Now repeat this and hold this breath for a count of eight. Again, let it out slowly.

2. Imagine a bright white light surrounding your entire body and merging with your aura. Feel the warmth of this light as it penetrates every cell in your body, energizing them and emanating a feeling of safety and security.

3. This white light enveloping your very being is both cleansing you from all negative thoughts and feelings and shielding you from those originating elsewhere.

4. You are totally protected by this white light.

5. Now perceive a pulsating silver cord connecting this white light to your Higher Self. Only positive thoughts, feelings and energy can enter your awareness.

6. Acknowledge this complete protection and connection to the perfect part of your essence, your Higher Self.

7. You are totally protected by this white light.

Now try this protection method:

1. Sit comfortably or lie down with your shoes off and dressed in loosely fitting clothes. Breathe deeply for two minutes.

2. Breathe in deeply and as you exhale, visualize a circle of energy in the form of a white light above your head. Sense this energy moving in a clockwise direction as it moves down your body.

3. This circle of white light now takes the shape of a funnel and appears as a corkscrew as it slowly descends down your body. See certain fragments of negative energy being ejected from your aura as it makes its descent.

4. Imagine this energy field finally moving into your feet. Now see a gold band of energy moving up from your feet to your head. As this gold band rises, it leaves a thin gold shield around your aura. This is a protective covering that only allows positive energy to enter your auric field.

5. Spend five minutes with this last visualization. Now take a few deep breaths and relax.

Another visualization in which you again call upon your Higher Self is as follows:

Light three white candles and lie down placing one candle two feet from your feet and one candle two feet from each side of your body. Say this: "In the name of the positive powers of the universe I call upon my own Higher Self and masters and guides to come and be with me at this time.

My masters, guides, and Higher Self are now with me and I am totally protected from any negativity, from the adverse thoughts of others through psychic attack, or from forces beyond the physical realms. To begin, I am going to release all negativity from my own body. I feel the negativity leaving my body and mind. All negativity has now left my body and mind and I am beginning to expand the white light that already surrounds me. This protective aura of magnetic white God light is now beginning to expand. I see it in my mind. My own guides, Masters and Higher Self are helping to create a protective magnetic bubble of pure white light. The God light is expanding which totally protects me from any negativity being projected at me. With the power of my own mind and the power of my own Higher Self and with the help of the unseen who love me, I have created a totally effective force field...a magnetic, protectory bubble through which only good can penetrate...through which only love can penetrate. Any outside negativity being directed at me will simply bounce off this protective aura of white light. Now I'm surrounded by a bubble which totally protects me and all negativity will now bounce off this protective bubble like a mirror. It will bounce off and I ask that it bounce out into outer space, where it will dissipate harmlessly. I now want to send love to all who send me negativity. Love is the most powerful force in the universe. It will mitigate and put an end to the misuse of power on the part of others. I feel love manifesting around my heart area and it is now flowing from me. I feel it happening. I see it happening. I am sending love and am totally protected by the light."

Exercises for Connecting With Your Spirit Energy

1. Sit quietly, relax, and breathe deeply. Apply protection and ask your Higher Self to assist you in connecting with your spirit energy.

2. Place both hands, with their backs toward you, on your forehead. Point both of your thumbs down and continue breathing deeply. Now lift your hands up and move them out in front of you at the level of your shoulders.

3. Turn your hands around so that the palms face you and make sure your hands are shoulder width apart. Slowly exhale and say, "Om." While you are doing this, bring your hands to rest in front of your throat, again with their backs facing you and the thumbs pointing downward.

4. Repeat numbers 2 and 3 four times.

5. Sit in this relaxed position for two minutes. Enjoy this state as you breathe deeply. You have successfully connected with your spirit energy. End this exercise by opening your eyes.

The next exercise is designed to balance your psychic energy with your physical body. Do not end the preceding exercise but continue with this one as follows:

1. Breathe slowly with your hands, palms down, on your lap. Focus your energy as a white light, and visualize it rising through your body from your toes to the top of your head.

   This is your soul's energy and as you continue breathing rhythmically this white light will be joined by other colors. During this time you are very relaxed and experiencing a feeling of harmony, peace, and balance.

2. Stay in this state for five to 10 minutes. End this exercise immediately by opening up your eyes.

3. This exercise is completed by asking your Higher Self to disconnect you from your psychic energy. Visualize the colors of the rainbow leaving the white light and the white light itself leaving your physical body from the top of your head. Open up your eyes and pick up a solid object. You may also want to drink some water.

You must be patient and conscientious in practicing these two exercises. Do not expect immediate results or try to rush them.

Receiving Rhema

The ancient Greeks spoke of *Rhema* as the spoken word of God that is heard by an individual. Only certain people in ancient times exhibited this ability. We read about Adam, Eve, Noah, Abraham, and other Old Testament personalities opening to Rhema. At other times in history certain inspired people, saints, and prophets received Rhema.

Religion has almost always tried to maintain its monopoly on Rhema by taking the position that we cannot receive God's words or have a two-way communication with the Creator without intermediaries such as priests or saints. The church has always discouraged attempts to receive Rhema by lay people and judged such communication as evil and dangerous.

According to theologians, only church authorities have the training and wisdom to evaluate true Rhema. You may pray to God, but don't expect an answer. It is unheard of for you and me to have an audience with God. Prayer is meant to be a one-way communication and God apparently ceased presenting inspired writings and revelations following the writing of the Old and New Testaments. This is what formal religions would have you believe. I respectfully disagree with this ecclesiastical dogma.

Receiving Rhema has a long history in Biblical times. For example, Mary received a message from the Angel Gabriel and an angel also told Joseph in a dream about the coming birth of Jesus; angels announced the birth of Jesus to the shepherds; the Magi were warned, through a dream, not to return to Herod contrary to his wish; and an angel advised Joseph to flee with his family to Egypt.

We can eliminate this aloofness to the concept of communicating with God and learn to receive Rhema through the Higher Self and spirit guides. God did not simply favor ancient peoples with His wisdom. The Creator, by way of Oversouls, is available today through your Higher Self and spirit guides and more than interested in communicating with us.

Today an increasing number of people are requesting and exhibiting an openness to receive Rhema. We can see this occurring in the Philippines, where several indigenous and evangelistic/charismatic religious groups have continued the practice. In the Tagalog language, the word *kaloob* (literally, meaning "that which is given within") means Rhema, and *patotoo* means the internal and external corroborations to *kaloob*.

The key to safe Rhema is to be able to discern between good and evil spirits. We find several references in the Old Testament to this very problem, such as "discern between good and evil;"[2] "discern between good and bad;"[3] "discern between the unclean and clean;"[4] "discern between their right hand and their left hand;"[5] "discern between the righteous and the wicked;"[6] and "discern both good and evil."[7]

We have discussed many ways to make this differentiation. The key behaviors to look for revolve around the following criteria:

- ◉ The spirit should gently advise you without attempting to manipulate you or violate your free will.

- ◉ Its message should benefit the soul more than the body. Advice for building up your self-image is acceptable. Focusing on power, money, fame, or controlling others is not.

- ◉ The spirit must do more than believe in God. Demons also believe in the Creator. High-level spirit guides always acknowledge the *sovereignty* of God.

- ◉ You should always feel compassion and love as a result of this contact. The love should be unconditional.

We can receive Rhema directly internally by way of an internal vision, a still voice, our conscience, and a "calling." Indirect internal Rhema can be obtained from hearing distant voices, dream contacts with spirit guides, and messages from OBEs.

Direct external sources of Rhema are automatic writing and the physical manifestation of a guide. Indirect external avenues to Rhema come from true prophets and Holy Scriptures.

The chart on page 69 summarizes discerning criteria when faced with communication from a spirit.

Opening Up the Third Eye

We are actually all spirits who just happen to occupy a physical body in order to function on the Earth plane. Our trip to this world was by way of dimensional doors through hyperspace until our soul entered a physical body during birth. Let us not forget our spiritual heritage and a link to spirit realms by way of an inner eye, or Third Eye, located on the center of the forehead just above the eyebrows.

Negative Entity	Spirit Guides
Chooses for you	Leaves choice for you
Imprisons	Empowers
Promotes dependency	Promotes independence
Intrudes	Respects
Urges	Supports
Excludes	Includes
Flatters	Informs
Commands	Suggests
Demands	Guides
Tests	Nudges
Insists on obedience	Encourages growth and development
Often claims ultimate authority	Recognizes a higher power
Offers shortcuts	Offers integration

This Third Eye can be refocused or activated in a passive observing manner, so that while in our corporeal frame we can still see the world through this inner eye. An example of a common and natural use of our Third Eye is a subtle presence detected in the corner of your sight. As you turn your head you can feel a certain presence that is trying to get your attention. This may be an astral object or person. Sometimes our inner eye overlaps with the corner of our physical eye.

We all have Third-Eye encounters, but few of us pay attention to them. It is our beliefs that are programmed to reject these experiences as anything but imaginary. In preparing to activate your Third Eye there are simple exercises you can practice, such as the following:

☉ Relax yourself and maintain direct eye contact with the eyes of your pet. Notice a feeling of deep inner peace as you gaze into its eyes.

- ◎ Now try looking at your own face in a mirror with subdued lighting and keeping this focus without laughing or distracting yourself for four minutes. Spend at least two of these minutes gazing at your own eyes.

- ◎ Select a relaxing part of your home and practice meditation, hypnosis, or contemplation with your eyes both open.

What we are doing with these simple exercises is conditioning the physical eyes to overlap with the inner eye. As the physical eyes view the material world, the Third Eye sees the Astral plane which gives impressions beyond physical reality. We are attempting to bring both of these visions together. It is far easier to achieve this when both physical eyes are open.

Here is a more detailed technique using the mirror gazing I alluded to earlier:

1. With subdued lighting and no interruptions, breathe deeply and watch your face in a mirror. It is ideal to practice this when you are a bit tired physically and mentally, but not too fatigued.

2. Stay in a relaxed state and focus with your physical eyes on one spot between your eyes, a single eye or on your forehead. Refrain from attempting to focus in on both eyes. Your head should be motionless and uninterrupted.

3. Shortly you may feel a warmth on the back of your neck. It is critical at this time that you do not move your head or blink your eyes. This will only divert attention away from your inner eye.

4. This warm feeling is your spirit energy being activated by guides. Now visualize an inner door you are opening while keeping your focus on the area on which you chose to concentrate in the mirror.

5. Be open to notice a change in your image in the mirror. This may be a slight change, but it represents an overlapping of your physical and inner eyes.

6. Imagine a bright white light around your body as you continue gazing into the mirror. The image may change to that of another person, an extraterrestrial, or even someone of the opposite sex. Do not be alarmed. You may see yourself from a prior life, the face of a spirit guide, or an ET studying our race.

7. Refrain from making judgments. Just focus on one spot and relax your sight again. Keep observing any other faces that come before your Third Eye.

8. This exercise should not take longer than 10 minutes. Take a break and repeat it as often as you like.

You can also practice this exercise with a friend seated across a table and very close to you. If you do not see a changing of your face in either case it means that you merely looked at your face, or your friend's, through your physical eyes. Do not be disappointed but simply repeat this exercise until you do register these facial alterations.

Once you master this simple technique you can expand your psychic abilities by watching people and their moving faces throughout the day. Another application is by using photographs or videotapes. You will begin to superimpose other faces on these images with practice.

When you are noticing people with this skill, it is not unusual to receive psychic data about who they really are. You may obtain glimpses of their past life personas, or another aspect of their true personalities that they may be trying to hide from you. Always be open to receive whatever your inner eye gives you.

If you see many faces of the same person, it often indicates the person is unhappy and considers him- or herself unworthy. These additional faces represent an attempt to mask his or her sadness and low self-image. Another possibility is that this individual has several attached entities, or *subpersonalities* and each one of them is acknowledging its presence in this person's aura. This concept of subpersonalities is important, so let us discuss it in detail.

Subpersonalities

Our subconscious mind retains the memories of all of our past, parallel, and future lives, including its sojourn on the Soul plane and other dimensions. Occasionally, Earthbound spirits attach themselves to our auras due usually to traumatic deaths in their former lives and fear of entering the white light (Higher Self) to journey to the Soul plane.

These discarnate entities (there are usually more than one) can significantly affect our moods, behaviors, attitudes, and personality traits.

They do not voluntarily, as a rule, make themselves known to us. Specific spirit releasement and integration techniques can be implemented to remove these subpersonalities and guide them into the white light.[8]

A subpersonality may also be a remnant of one of our own previous lives. Whatever their origin, subpersonalities are never stable and function more like shadow personalities, immature and trapped in the unhappy emotions that created them. A subpersonality dooms an individual to relive a trauma. Left untreated, people who have subpersonalities can exhibit bizarre and unsettling behavior, such as overeating, drug or alcohol abuse, or a tendency to enter into abusive relationships. Conventional therapists would describe these as the "inner child" or a condition called Dissociative Identity Disorder (which was previously called Multiple Personality Disorder).

Very often we allow these subpersonalities to attach themselves to our auras when we are subjected to physical or emotional trauma, such as physical or sexual abuse, the loss of a job, a sudden ending to a long-term relationship, or negative projection techniques, such as black magic.

When a subpersonality represents a fragment of one of our own past lives, it is necessary to regress the host to a past life to relive the exact moment a subpersonality was born. Frequently, this moment is the death scene. I often ask my patients to remove the daggers, bullets, or other deadly objects. Then I invite each subpersonality to rejoin its past-life persona, review the moment of death, and move on to the Soul plane, into the white light.

Spirit guides can be quite helpful in pointing out the presence of these subpersonalities and assisting in their eventual integration and removal.

As a result of integration and cleansing techniques, dysfunctional behaviors stop immediately. My patients describe the effect as having a burden lifted or a blockage removed. They return to normal life, feeling stronger than ever.

A former patient of mine named Gwen had such a phenomenon happen to her when she was 17 years old. She had a perfectly normal life until September 1995. Then she started hearing voices and became obsessively interested in knives. She would "play" with a hunting knife she had purchased, and she cut herself several times.

Gwen's parents brought her to my Los Angeles office, believing that their daughter was psychotic and suicidal. A superconscious mind tap, however, revealed that an entity named Lowell had attached itself to Gwen.

It seems that Lowell had been a hunter in England during the Middle Ages. He was also very fond of knives. He was beheaded for poaching on the king's land.

Lowell was a troubled spirit who had wandered the Astral plane as a ghost for several hundred years. He selected Gwen's consciousness to attach to only because his wife in his English life was also named Gwen.

As part of his integration, I tried to use a chakra laser technique to attach his severed head to his body. The technique involves visualizing colored lights, or healing rays, emanating from key points of the body. When that failed, I instructed him to carry his detached head into the light, which he did. Gwen never heard from Lowell again, and the voices, as well as her fascination with knives, disappeared as quickly as they had appeared. Her spirit guides assisted me throughout this process.

Lucid Sight

You can easily eliminate headaches resulting from mirror gazing by placing one hand on your heart and the other on your forehead. Next, remove your hand from your forehead and place it on the back of your head. This should relieve the discomfort and prevent it from recurring. This technique can be applied to other approaches as well.

A vision of the same face but younger indicates a spiritually evolved person who has successfully integrated all personality aspects. It is your spirit guides who continually monitor your progress with inner eye watching, as well as any other psychic development skill.

Another exercise to activate the Third Eye is known as *lucid sight.* This amounts to seeing a person's aura. While focusing on a person's face for a time with the mirror gazing technique I previously presented, you can see a glowing outline of that individual as you move your line of vision away from that person's face.

Sometimes you see a dull milky aura of them. At other times you note the entire surroundings beginning to glow by itself. When this happens you are now looking into the Astral plane. It is not unusual to observe your own aura and dancing colored lights representing Astral plane inhabitants, possibly spirit guides. The entire field of vision becomes so bright that there is no need for artificial light if this takes place at night.

When you practice the OBE techniques I present in Chapter 6, this type of inner eye vision will become commonplace. All forms of visualization methods function to attract astral and etheric energies toward us. This facilitates activation of our Third Eye.

Agitation of the Third Eye is one basic step to balancing your chakras. This in turn places you on a path of true enlightenment. Try this method to both see and clear the aura and further activate your inner eye:

Relax, apply protection, and tell yourself you wish to clear your aura. Stand up and breathe in deeply. As you exhale, visualize a circle of energy in the form of a white light above your head. Sense this energy moving in a clockwise direction as it moves down your body.

All negativity is now being removed from your aura and sent to the ground beneath your feet, where it will be neutralized. Now take in a few deep breaths and relax.

To clear another person's aura, have your subject stands with his or her feet apart and arms hanging loosely. Do not touch your subject, but apply the following procedures approximately two inches from his or her skin surface:

With your thumbs touching and your hands spread out, move your hands from the top of your subject's head until you reach the floor. Remember not to touch your subject.

Now go back and repeat this procedure clockwise until you have encircled your subject. Last, do the arms, inner legs, and under each foot. Have your subject shake his or her body and sip some water. The aura is now cleansed.

The next step is to begin seeing the aura. This is most commonly observed as a white glow. The following exercise will help you perceive this layer of the aura:

Relax and inwardly direct yourself toward seeing your subject's aura. Breathe gently while facing your subject and clear your mind. Do not stare, especially at the eyes. Look through or around your subject.

Place your attention around the head and shoulder region. As you defocus your eyes and gaze, a white glow will appear. If this glow is still present when you look away completely, it is an optical illusion and must be ignored. Only the glow surrounding a person is a true representation of the person's aura.

These two methods will train you to see the colors of the aura:

Stare at a card that is green, mauve, blue/green, pink/red, yellow, or blue. These are the colors of the inner center of the astral body (a less material body that surrounds the physical body). When you can see this color with your eyes closed, quickly open your eyes and look at your subject's head. The color on the card will be superimposed on your subject's head. Do this exercise with each of the other colors.

With your subject you can use either light shining through stained glass, or colored light bulbs.

Do not use these two exercises regularly once you have mastered the art of seeing auric colors. They are designed for training your mind to see colors quickly. These colors may take the appearance of light shining through a prism or stained glass. It is most common to observe these auric colors as fluctuating, moving, fading, and deepening in no particular order. They often appear as a momentary glow or flash of color, as they are constantly moving and changing.

When learning how to see auras, the following recommendations will speed up your progress:

◎ Look at your subject with blurred eyes. It is best not to wear your glasses.

◎ Relax yourself with meditation or hypnosis prior to observing auras.

◎ Look at the head and shoulder region first. These locations are the easiest places to observe the aura.

◎ Have your subject sit in front of a light-colored or white background. Ask your subject to close his eyes and to concentrate on sending you energy.

◎ While your subject is concentrating, close your eyes and ask your Higher Self for assistance. Open your eyes and begin gazing at your subject's forehead. Occasionally close your eyes, as you may first see the outline of the aura when your eyes are closed.

◎ Ask your subject to concentrate on shaping the aura into a peak at the top of his head. Your subject should also focus entirely on one color.

Figure 3 represents a summary of the effects of aura colors.

Some colors affect the body because of their lower frequencies, while others influence the brain due to their higher frequencies. The following chart summarizes these effects:

Physical	Green, light blue	Restful
	Red	Stimulating
	Orange	Revitalizing
Emotional	Turquoise, sky blue	Restful
	Orange	Stimulating
	Peach	Revitalizing
Mental	Indigo	Restful
	Yellow	Stimulating
	Emerald green	Revitalizing
Spiritual	Blue	Restful
	Violet, purple	Stimulating
	Gold	Revitalizing

Figure 3. The Effects of Aura Colors on Our Conscious and Physical Body

Figure 4 on page 77 lists the various colors you are likely to observe in auras and their generally accepted meanings.

When you begin receiving impressions upon activation of the inner eye, there are many possible ways in which you will see the world around you. It is not uncommon to feel a slight pressure on the Third Eye area of your forehead (between your eyes and just above the eyebrows). There is no danger and sometimes this is accompanied by fatigue. Activating the Third Eye requires expenditure of psychic energy and the more you practice the less energy drain you will experience.

At other times you may notice mustaches and beards on clean-shaven men, or even women! Glasses, bandanas, hats, earrings, and other items from their astral selves or past lives may be viewed by you at this time. If you do not attempt to focus too hard, you will facilitate this process and observe these other faces being superimposed one on top of the other.

Color	Effect
Indigo	Altered states of consciousness, integration, and purification. Too much of this color leads to depression.
Silver	A high degree of psychic development.
Red	This color represents pure energy and is subdivided as follows:
Basic red	Courage and strength.
Brick red	Anger.
Crimson	Loyalty.
Deep red	Sensuality.
Pink	Soothingness, optimism, and cheerfulness.
Brown	This is a stabilizing, earthy, and grounding color.
Dull brown	Low energy.
Gold	Intuition and knowing. This is a very spiritual color and amplifies psychic abilities.
Purple	Spiritual power. The deeper the purple, the greater the psychic significance.
Violet	Stimulates dream activity and psychic perception of past lives.
Blue	Intellectual development, creative expression, imagination, and idealism.
Orange	Optimism, vitality, job, and a balance of the mental and physical. Often preferred by salespeople, speakers, promoters, and media personalities.
Yellow	Mental activity, wisdom, creativity, and emotions.
Yellow-gray	Fear.
Green	Compassion, balance, growth, ingenuity, and a calming effect.
Pale green	Healing powers.
Green-gray	Envy and pessimism.
Black	Depression and death. This is rarely seen.
White	Purity and deep spirituality. White represents all the colors of the visible spectrum.

Figure 4. The Meaning of Aura Colors

Other people report seeing shadows and beings of light. When you access your Higher Self prior to practicing these exercises (see Chapter 4), the superconscious component of your mind will advise you which of these entities are inhabitants of the Astral plane, which are merely visitors (astral voyagers) and which are spirit guides.

If you are still having difficulty with Third Eye activation techniques, practice them again following the completion of trying the various self-hypnosis methods presented throughout this book. The altered states of consciousness (ASC) represented by self-hypnosis function as a gateway into other dimensions. This works to activate our inner eye, as well as all other psychic abilities.

As you become expert on establishing ASC, you may experience amnesia of the experience itself. This is actually a medium-level hypnotic trance and it is not difficult to simply suggest to yourself that you recall everything you perceive. For those of you who have mastered the art of *lucid dreaming* (being aware that you are dreaming while in the dream state), this will be second nature.

Building Blocks to Spirit Guide Contact

The following 11 criteria are what I refer to as "building blocks" in preparing yourself for spirit guide contact. I have included questions for you to consider in order to facilitate your growth and to assist you in locating possible weaknesses that might inhibit this otherworldly communication. Consider these carefully.

1. **Balance.** This is a state of equilibrium, of inner and outer harmony. You must be centered to be in balance. Spiritual balance is natural.
   Questions to consider:
   ◎ Does your imbalance affect others? How?
   ◎ What do you need to do to establish balance?
   ◎ Are you willing to make changes?
   ◎ What obstacles currently exist in your life that contribute to this lack of balance?

2. **Individuality.** The sum total of your personality traits and other characteristics makes you unique from others and represents your individuality.

Questions to consider:

◎ Are you afraid of doing something different?

◎ What is special about you?

◎ Do you have a unique trait that you have been inhibited to express?

3. **Discipline.** You must maintain self-control and stick to your training exercises to develop psychically. Without this self-discipline you will become out of balance and your psychic talents will suffer and you will delay contact with your guide.

Questions to consider:

◎ Why do you fail?

◎ Do you have difficulty planning a goal?

◎ Have you sabotaged your efforts in the past?

◎ Have you built a solid base for yourself?

4. **Cooperation.** This principle is based on giving and receiving in equal amounts. Because you will be affecting others as a result of your guide contact, this is a most important building block. It results in shared energy as well as shared experiences.

Questions to consider:

◎ What do you want from this relationship?

◎ What changes are you willing to make?

◎ How difficult is it to be the real you?

◎ Are you giving enough or too much?

◎ How hard is it for you to share?

5. **Wisdom.** When you exhibit sound judgment and can differentiate between right and wrong, you are showing wisdom. It is not enough to acquire knowledge. You must put it to practical use. Wisdom is based on experience as well as knowledge.

Questions to consider:

◎ What mistakes have you repeated?

◎ Do you consider all options when making decisions?

◎ What have you learned from life?

6. **Vision.** This building block is a natural ability to visualize, prepare for the future, and imagine. I refer to this as global assessment.

   Questions to consider:

   ◎ Can you identify your karmic obligations and relationships?

   ◎ Do you listen to and follow your inner voice?

   ◎ Do you ignore opportunities to grow and tune in to others?

7. **Creativity.** Being creative involves producing something from your imagination and thoughts. It is a way of transforming ideas into reality. We use our right brain in the creative process. The right brain is how we receive spirit guide contact.

   Questions to consider:

   ◎ What creative talents do you have?

   ◎ What ideas would you like to see become a reality?

   ◎ What has prevented you from expressing your talents?

8. **Control.** This principle deals with regulation and taking charge of your life. When you are in control your mind removes obstacles, and your spiritual growth, as well as your physical body, is recharged and facilitated.

   Questions to consider:

   ◎ Are you ready to take control of your life?

   ◎ Can you move beyond your limitations?

   ◎ Is there anything or anyone you fear?

9. **Release.** To release is to set free from confinement and restraint. When you liberate yourself from worry, grief, pain, and obligations, you are releasing yourself and in a better position to contact spirit guides.

   Questions to consider:

   ◎ Do you know what is holding you back?

   ◎ Do you have confidence in your ability to obtain this release?

   ◎ Can you confront negativity without fear?

10. **Power.** The energy and force to act on your convictions is your power. It is not something to be feared, unless you misuse it. This is your psychic empowerment.

Questions to consider:

- ◎ Have you given up any of your power?

- ◎ How can you better express your power?

- ◎ Can you sense the inner strength you possess?

11. **Success.** When you attain goals by achievement and recognition, you have exhibited success.

Questions to consider:

- ◎ What do you desire to be considered successful?

- ◎ Are you prepared to make sacrifices to attain goals?

- ◎ Who has helped and hindered your previous attempts at success?

Additional Questions to Answer Prior to Your Inner Spirit Guide Contact

It is always important to examine your thoughts, motives and actions to identify both your strengths and weaknesses. That is why I posed questions with each of the building blocks in the previous section.

You will find it far easier and more profound to experience spirit guide contact when you have definite goals and at least some ideas as to how you may attain these objectives. Consider these questions as you focus in on your karmic purpose, which is simply why you chose your current life and how you can best grow spiritually:

- ◎ Are there any creative processes at which you wish to be better?

- ◎ Do you eat the kind of food that creates health and energy in your body? Do you ingest any food that works against your physical or spiritual balance?

- ◎ Are you aware of any obstacles that are in the way of your total success?

- ◎ If you could be, do, have, or become absolutely anything, what would it be?

- ◎ What are your three most important goals?

- ◎ Do you regularly take steps towards achieving your goals?

- ◎ Do you take time to set goals and evaluate your progress and behavior regularly?

◉ Are there any intellectual tasks you wish to perform better?

◉ Do you take time to notice all the beauty in the world around you?

◉ Are there any functions of your work life at which you wish to be more competent?

◉ Do you have any physical conditions that are currently limiting you in any way?

◉ Do you exercise regularly?

◉ Do you stop to examine how much you have to be thankful for?

As you prepare for your initial spirit guide contacts, let go of any fear concerning this communication. We are all spirits. The only difference between us and a guide is that they don't occupy a physical body and are more spiritually evolved. Even if you encounter spirits that are not from the light, you can counsel them and call on high-level guides to assist them into the light.

Souls who committed suicide, or died by traumatic means, are the most likely candidates for your encounters, if not with a high-level guide. Simply focus your attention on a brilliant white light and surround them with it. Ask your Higher Self and theirs for assistance, along with spirit guides. When you sense a loving energy, you know that you have acted as a catalyst in bringing these troubled souls to a more enlightened state. They will now venture on to the Soul plane and you will have earned positive karma for your kindness. In my book *Peaceful Transition* I present several scripts to assist you with this process.

The true form of a spirit guide is that of colored lights or twinkling, bright white light. They have no gender, as duality does not exist in their realm. These guides travel at the speed of light and require a raising of our consciousness to view them. As our frequency raises, they lower theirs and assume a form with which we can identify and feel comfortable. This is not a compromise to their spiritual growth, merely an adjustment to their receiver function.

There are many levels of learning in the spiritual realms. Keep an open mind and express love at all times so that you can benefit from these guide contacts. Learn how to eliminate fear and more spiritually create your own universe, as God has created His. Use self-hypnosis to foster this process and become part of the God energy complex from which we all originated.

◎◎◎◎◎◎◎◎◎◎◎◎

CHAPTER 4

Basic Hypnotic Techniques for Contacting Spirit Guides

In discussing the use of hypnosis to contact spirit guides we must understand how the mind works. The unawake or unaware component of the mind is referred to as the *unconscious mind*. This is divided into light sleep and deep sleep. Freud used to term "unconscious" incorrectly, as he was referring to the *subconscious mind* that we will deal with shortly.

Our consciousness is divided into two main sections. One is called the *conscious mind proper*, or simply the conscious mind for short. The other is the subconscious mind. When we exhibit an analytical, critical, and logical left brain function, we are using our conscious mind.

The subconscious is, in reality, the soul or spirit we possess and is electromagnetic radiation equivalent to a radio or television signal. This component is our creative, emotional, and right-brain division. When we reincarnate into a new body, it is the subconscious that actually survives clinical death, along with the physical body. We attempt to purify and perfect our subconscious by way of reincarnation and the karmic cycle.

There is a perfect component of our subconscious known as the Higher Self or *superconscious mind*. This component originates from the God energy and continually advises us on how to perfect the subconscious, along with our spirit guides. You will achieve perfection of the soul when you eventually merge with this superconscious mind (represented as the white light).

We normally associate the conscious mind with the term "self." It is included with all of our day-to-day decision making and rational thought processes. The subconscious functions more as a computer and stores every piece of data received from our five senses. Our soul also has memories of past and future lives by its ability to tap into its *Akashic Records*. The Akashic Record are the memories of all events stored around the spiritual body of the Earth. We can tap into these by way of Spirit Guides or self-hypnosis.

There is quite an overlap between the conscious and subconscious minds. We require both of them to live. Information is continually flowing from the sense organs to the brain, being stored in both the physical brain and the energy level we refer to as the subconscious. It is the conscious mind that reviews this data and makes decisions based, in part, upon the recommendations of your subconscious. Your ultimate response to any situation is based on previous experience and censorship provided by the conscious mind.

Spirit guide contact cannot come through the conscious mind because the latter is far too critical. We must set the conscious mind aside and deal directly with the subconscious in order to access these beings from other dimensions. Hypnosis is this process of doing just that. Other methods such as yoga, meditation, dreams (a form of hypnosis and an OBE), biofeedback and creative hobbies (also a form of hypnosis) can also achieve this goal.

Neurologically, we speak of the brain in terms of brain waves. The conscious mind is represented by *beta waves* on the electroencephalograph (EEG) of 14 to 30 cycles per second, where the subconscious mostly exhibits *alpha waves* of eight to 13 cycles per second. *Theta waves* of four to seven cycles per second indicate deeper states of the subconscious (reverie) and light sleep. We see *delta waves* of .5 to 3.5 cycles per second in deep levels of sleep, which is a form of our unconscious (unawake or unaware) mind.

Figure 5 on page 85 reflects this relationship and depicts physical characteristics associated with each brain wave.

Hypnosis is a rather natural and simple process that allows us to shift from beta to alpha and place ourselves in a position to contact spirit guides. We experience approximately four hours of *natural* hypnosis daily. All daydreams are examples of hypnosis as are reading, watching television, driving on long trips, creative states, jogging, just as you awaken, (*hypnopompic*) and before you go to sleep (*hypnogogic*).

In addition to the four hours of waking hypnosis via daydreams, we must consider the three hours of nighttime dreams (REM stage) of our sleep cycle. All dreams represent natural hypnosis and OBEs. This adds

	Brain Waves	Mental Characteristics	Physical Characteristics	Graph of Brain Waves
14 to 30 cycles per second B E T A	100 95 90 85 80 75 70 65 60 55 50	wide awake state excitement, frustration aware of all senses very alert actively aware active thought patterns comfortably alert consciously aware normal thought patterns easy thoughts less active thoughts	extreme tension, uptight high metabolic behavior hands moist and clammy accelerate work ability hyperactive high degree of stamina comfortable, restful state good observation state physically at rest beginning to realize increased composure	
8 to 13 cycles per second A L P H A	45 40 35 30 25	pre-drowsiness increased susceptibility passive awareness total sensory withdrawal low alphagenic state	releasing all body feeling passive awareness numb, quiet deep realization complete passivity	
4 to 7 cycles per second T H E T A	20 15 10	drowsiness beginning unconscious unconscious	unaware unaware unconscious	
.05 to 3.5 cycles per second D E L T A	5 0	deep sleep state death	deep sleep state	

Figure 5

up to seven hours daily of entirely natural levels of hypnosis, which is 2,500 hours per year for the average person! Is it no wonder why this relaxed state feels so unusual? Most people who experience hypnosis do not regard it as a different state, just more relaxed.

You may view hypnosis as a connection between the physical body and the nonphysical subconscious and Higher Self. Some apply the term altered state of consciousness (ASC) to this state. The hypnotic state is characterized by a deep level of focused concentration.

The subconscious mind can best be influenced in a passive or relaxed state, such as in hypnosis. This restful quieting of the mind cleanses it, opening it to pure, more elevated thoughts from your psychic energy source, the Higher Self. Hypnosis builds both mental vigor and enthusiasm because it removes all fear and the negative thoughts that act as roadblocks to energy, inspiration, and accomplishment. It facilitates spirit guide contact.

To develop the art of self-hypnosis, all you need to do is practice some very simple exercises. Always go at your own pace and repeat these procedures as frequently as you desire until the relaxed levels and other experiences are attained.

Your environment or REM in which you practice may have a great effect on your ability to enter into self-hypnosis. I recommend a quiet room free of distractions and unnecessary sounds. Keep the lighting subdued and sit in a comfortable chair (a recliner is ideal) or lie down on a bed or couch. If you prefer to sit or lie on the floor, make sure the carpet is thick and you have a pillow available.

Dress in loose, light, and comfortable clothing. Either remove or adjust all ties, belts, shoes, and so on, so that they do not apply distracting pressure to your body. Keep the temperature of the room a few degrees above room temperature. It is not unusual for your body temperature to drop a few degrees (this is perfectly safe), so this added room temperature assists in keeping you physically comfortable.

Before beginning your practice sessions, close your eyes and empty your mind of all unnecessary thoughts. Breathe slowly and deeply and focus all of your attention on relaxing your entire body as directed by the scripts I will present shortly.

Think of yourself as becoming calmer and more relaxed and you will notice sensations of heaviness, especially in the arms and legs. This technique will eliminate any sleeping problems that may have bothered you. Other advantages of hypnosis may be summarized as follows:

- Facilitates spirit guide contact.
- Increased relaxation and the elimination of tension.
- Increased and focused concentration.
- Improved memory ("hypernesia").
- Improved reflexes.
- Increased self-confidence.
- Pain control.
- Improved sex life.
- Increased organization and efficiency.
- Increased motivation.
- Improved interpersonal relationships.
- Slowing down the aging process.
- Facilitating a better career path.
- Elimination of anxiety and depression.
- Overcoming bereavement.
- Elimination of headaches, including migraines.
- Elimination of anxiety and depression.
- Strengthening one's immune system to resist any disease.
- Elimination of habits, phobias, and other negative tendencies (self-defeating sequences).
- Improving decisiveness.
- Improving the quality of people, and circumstances in general, that you attract into your life.
- Increasing your ability to earn and hold onto money.
- Overcoming obsessive-compulsive behavior.
- Improving the overall quality of your life.
- Improved psychic awareness—ESP, meditation, astral projection (out-of-body experience), telepathy, superconscious mind taps, and so on.

◎ Elimination of the fear of death by viewing one's past and future lives.

◎ Attracting a soulmate into your life.

◎ Establishing and maintaining harmony of body, mind, and spirit.

Please bear in mind that there is no sudden switch from the conscious state to the subconscious hypnotic level. What occurs is a gradual transition from beta to alpha. You will not be able to detect the precise moment when you attain the self-hypnotic state.

What you will notice is a gradual lessening of your awareness of the physical environment. You will not fall asleep and can quickly and easily return to beta functioning should an emergency arise, or your privacy becomes interrupted. As you develop skill with your own mind, you will be able to go into a trance much more quickly. Even surroundings that were once too distracting to handle will now be tolerable for practicing self-hypnosis.

One of the most efficient methods to assure successful experiences with self-hypnosis (all hypnosis is self-hypnosis) is to develop a mindset that you can achieve this natural state of mind. As you continue practicing the techniques presented in this book, your life will improve dramatically and you will be well on your way to psychic empowerment. The key is to eliminate all forms of cynical and negative thinking and take charge of your life. This may be facilitated through spirit guide contact by way of hypnosis.

Applying the trance state to spirit guide contact, we may say that this frame of mind sets aside one level of consciousness (willpower, ego, or conscious mind) to allow another level of consciousness (spirit guide or Higher Self via the subconscious) to come through.

There are two very different forms a trance may take. The mediumistic trance is characterized by the withdrawal of the conscious mind (ego) from the physical body and allowing a spirit guide to communicate directly with you. Another type of this category results in a partial withdrawal of the ego during this process. These are passive states during which the individual's memory is either limited or nonexistent.

The second trance category is referred to as a Shamanic trance. In this type, the individual's ego withdraws from the physical body, but the latter is left protected. A more active process ensues in that the soul leaves the physical body to communicate with spirit guides in other dimensions and returns to the physical body with complete memories of these experiences. I will present techniques to do this in Chapter 6.

You can develop any trance state with relative ease by using visualizations and guided imagery approaches. These methods help focus the mind with images, while at the same time calming it. You can now become more aware of the inner realms (subconscious and Higher Self) of your mind.

To maximize your trance levels, you need to develop creative imagination, visualization, and concentration skills. The result will be an increase in your perception of the spiritual dimensions and spiritual growth.

Creative imagination enables your subconscious to create scenes and images associated with the information received from the spirit guides. These three-dimensional representatives are equivalent to a daydream or night dream, during which you lose your awareness of the ordinary world around you. You are now more receptive to communication from the higher spiritual realms.

The ability to create a mental image or picture and hold it within your mind is what we mean by visualization. This life-like representation allows you to identify with the object or experience.

Concentration refers to your ability to maintain the image you created in your mind without wandering on to another thought or impression. It implies the technique of putting aside all mundane and distracting thoughts, feelings, and impressions that would compete with the initiate image you created.

Your soul gains entrance into these spiritual dimensions by using these three abilities characteristic of a trance: creative imagination, visualization, and concentration. This results in direct spiritual perceptions by the subconscious, rather than symbols or metaphors that require translation and interpretation.

The exercises in this book will train you to enter trance states. Whether it be meditation or self-hypnosis approaches, the trance state will have certain basic characteristics. These are:

1. A generalized feeling of relaxation.
2. A sense of time moving quickly. You will actually have no idea how much real time elapsed.
3. Focused concentration.

4. A lack of movement in your body.

5. Your eyes may move back and forth (rapid eye movement or REMs).

Are Trance States Possession?

In order to exhibit possession, certain characteristics would have to be present. A possessed individual experiences a sudden and extreme change in consciousness with no memory of what took place during that state of mind. In addition, a new personality with traits totally different from that person would be manifested. These do not occur during hypnotic trances.

Your fears concerning possession are groundless for the previously mentioned reasons and two additional factors. First, techniques are preceded by white light protection, which makes it impossible for a negative being or any other possessing entity to take over your body. Second, hypnotic trances are a normal and natural state of mind, occurring for 7 hours of our 24-hour daily cycle. Without these natural alpha levels our body would die.[1]

Here is a simple progressive relaxation self-hypnosis exercise that trains you to systematically relax each part of your body. As with all self-hypnosis and meditations, I highly recommend making a tape of these exercises.

Now listen very carefully. I want you to imagine a bright white light coming down from above and entering the top of your head, filling your entire body. See it, feel it, and it becomes reality. Now imagine an aura of pure white light emanating from your heart region, again surrounding your entire body, protecting you. See it, feel it, and it becomes reality. Now only your Higher Self, Masters and guides, and highly evolved loving entities who mean you well will be able to influence you during this or any other hypnotic session. You are totally protected by this aura of pure white light.

Now I want you to concentrate on the muscle groups that I point out to you. Loosen them, relax them while visualizing them. You will notice that you may be tense in certain areas and the idea is to relax yourself completely. Concentrate on your forehead. Loosen the muscles in your forehead. Now your eyes. Loosen the muscles around your eyes. Your eyelids relax. Now your face, your face relaxes. And your mouth...relax the muscles around your mouth, and even the inside of your mouth. Your chin; let it sag and feel heavy. And as you relax your muscles, your breathing continues...regularly...and...deeply...deeply within yourself. Now your neck, your neck relaxes. Every muscle, every fiber in your neck relaxes. Your shoulders relax...your arms...your elbows...your forearms...your wrists...your hands...and your fingers relax. Your arms feel loose and limp; heavy and loose and limp. Your whole body begins to feel loose and limp. Your neck muscles relax; the front of your neck; the back muscles. Keep breathing deeply and relax. Now your chest. The front part of your chest relaxes and the back part of your chest relaxes. Your abdomen...the pit of your stomach, that relaxes. The small of your back, loosen the muscles. Your hips...your thighs...your knees relax...even the muscles in your legs. Your ankles...your feet...and your toes. Your whole body feels loose and limp. And now as you feel the muscles relaxing, you will notice that you begin to feel heavy and relaxed and tired all over. Your body begins to feel...very...very...tired and you are going to feel...drowsier ...and...drowsier, from the top of your head right down to your toes. Every breath you take is going to soak in deeper and deeper and deeper, and you feel your body getting drowsier and drowsier.

- Allow all outside thoughts during this relaxation phase to drift passively through your mind.

- Suggest to yourself that at any time you may experience a spirit guide contact, and this communication would be terminated if your physical body felt in any way uncomfortable.

Alright now. Sleep now and rest. You did very, very well. Listen very carefully. I'm going to count forward now from 1 to 5. When I reach the count of 5 you will be back in the present, you will be able to remember everything you experienced and reexperienced. You'll feel very relaxed, refreshed and you'll be able to do whatever you have planned for the rest of the day or evening. You'll feel very positive about what you've experienced and very motivated about your confidence and ability to play this tape again, to experience self-hypnosis. Alright now. One, very, very deep. Two, you're getting a little bit lighter. Three, you're getting much, much lighter. Four, very very light. Five, awaken. Wide awake and refreshed.

Here is another simple self-hypnosis exercise that allows you to free your body of tension, as well as attain a deeper level of hypnosis:

Take a deep breath and let it out slowly.
Close your eyes.

Lie back comfortably in the chair.

Let yourself go...loose, limp, and slack.

Let all the muscles of your body relax completely.

Breathe in and out...nice and slow.

Concentrate on your feet and ankles and let them relax.

Soon you will begin to have a feeling of heaviness in your feet.

Your feet are beginning to feel as heavy as lead.

Your feet are getting heavier and heavier.

Let yourself go completely.

Now let all of the muscles in your legs relax totally and completely.

Your legs are beginning to feel heavier and heavier.

Let yourself go completely.

Give yourself up totally to this very pleasant...relaxed, comfortable feeling.

Let your whole body go loose, limp, and slack.

Your whole body is becoming as heavy as lead.

Let the muscles of your stomach completely relax.

Let them become loose, limp, and slack.

Next the muscles of your chest and back.

Let them go completely loose, limp, and slack, and as you feel heaviness in your body, you are relaxing more deeply.

Your whole body is becoming just as heavy as lead.

Let yourself sink down deeper in the chair.

Let yourself relax totally and completely.

Let all of the muscles in your neck and shoulders relax.

Let all of these muscles go loose, limp, and slack.

Now the muscles in your arms are becoming loose, limp, slack, and heavy.

As they relax, they are getting heavier and heavier.

As though your arms are as heavy as lead.

Let your arms go.

Let your whole body relax completely.

Your whole body is deeply and completely relaxed.

Now a feeling of complete relaxation is gradually moving over your whole body.

All of the muscles in your feet and ankles are completely relaxed.

Your calf and thigh muscles are completely relaxed.

All of the muscles in your legs are loose, limp, and slack.

And as you relax...your sleep is becoming deeper and more relaxing.

The feeling of relaxation is spreading through all of your body.

All of the muscles of your body are becoming loose, limp and slack. Totally relaxed.

Your body is getting heavier and heavier.

You are going deeper and deeper into relaxation.

Whenever you desire to reenter this wonderfully relaxing state of self-hypnosis, all you will have to do is say the number 20 three times in succession. Twenty, 20, 20 and feel yourself sinking down into a deep relaxation.

When you are totally relaxed, you will be able to give yourself any suggestions you desire.

Now stay in this peaceful state and allow your spirit guides to maximize your level of relaxation and spiritual growth.

Play new age music for 3 minutes.

Alright now. Sleep, now, and rest. You did very, very well. Listen very carefully. I'm going to count forward now from 1-5. When I reach the count of 5 you will be back in the present, you will be able to remember everything you experienced and reexperienced. You'll feel very relaxed, refreshed and you'll be able to do whatever you have planned for the rest of the day or evening. You'll feel very positive about what you've experienced and very motivated about your confidence and ability to play this tape again, to experienced self-hypnosis. Alright now. One, very, very deep. Two, you're getting a little bit lighter. Three, you're getting much, much lighter. Four, very very light. Five, awaken. Wide awake and refreshed.

This technique is another deepening method that utilizes counting and breathing approaches to train you to experience an even more relaxed alpha state:

Now I want you to notice the tension in your chest muscles...the tension in your shoulders and upper arms. And I want you to pay particular attention to how...the moment I say "Let go"...all that tension disappears immediately...and you tend to sag limply down into the chair. Now...Let go.

I am going to count slowly up to 5...and as I do so...you will take five very deep breaths.

And with each deep breath that you take...each time you breathe out...you will become more and more relaxed...and your trance will become deeper and deeper.

One...breathe deeply...more and more deeply relaxed...deeper and deeper into relaxation.

Two...deeper deeper...deeper and deeper relaxed...deeper and deeper in hypnosis.

Three...breathing even more deeply...more and more deeply relaxed...more and more deeply relaxed.

Four...very, very deep breath...and deeper and deeper relaxed...your trance depth is becoming even deeper and deeper.

Five...very, very deep breath...very, very deeply relaxed...very, very deeply relaxed.

Once again...I want you to take one very deep breath...and fill your chest...and hold it until I say...Let go.

Then...let your breath out as quickly as possible...and as you do so...you will feel yourself sagging limply back into the chair...and you will become twice as deeply relaxed as you are now...twice as deeply relaxed. Now, take that very deep breath...fill your chest...hold it...(15-second pause)...hold it...(15-second pause)...hold it...(20- to 30-second pause) Let go.

Visual Imagery

You must clear your mind and relax in order to center your awareness and become receptive to spirit guide contact. There are several ways to do this. One of the simplest methods is the use of visual imagery. Imagery is a window on your inner world; a way of viewing your own ideas, feelings, and interpretations. It is a rich, symbolic, and highly personal language.

Imagery per se does not require that you be able to visualize objects, people, or energy beings. You may perceive things in your "mind's eye," but you can also hear with your inner ear, feel, taste, and experience other sensations with your imagination or subtle bodies.

Some people imagine in vivid visual images with color, sound, smell, and sensation, while others may experience sounds, songs, or thoughts in their heads without any pictures. Some will be more aware of senses or feelings that guide them and let them know when they are close to something meaningful. It doesn't really matter how you imagine—just that you learn to recognize and work with your own imagery. Imagery is a vehicle to this understanding, which may come through inner pictures, words, thoughts, sensations, or feelings.

Concentration is the first step in improving your ability to visualize. The following exercise will help you develop your visualizations skills:

Relax and think of a situation in your life that you would like to change. It must be something within your power, but something you have procrastinated about dealing with. Visualize a solution to your problem and focus on this image.

Use your psychic energy to create minute details of this plan of action. Concentrate on the actions of others in your plan. Hold this picture in your mind for as long as you can. Soon your Higher Self will assist you in this endeavor.

Feel yourself right in the middle of this plan, directing it, and reaping its rewards. Keep the plan simple but direct, and execute it forcefully.

These visualization exercises will open your channels to your psychic abilities:

Relax and imagine yourself on a deserted beach at noon. See yourself writing your name in the sand and watching the waves wash it away. Smell the salt air and listen to the sound of the waves against the rocks as you walk up the shoreline. Feel the peacefulness and listen to the sound of the seagulls as they look for food.

Move to an inlet of a small lake and stand by a shallow pool of water. Look at your reflection in this pool and see the many facets of your soul. Observe that you can be loving, jealous, angry, creative, happy, weak and strong.

Keep looking at yourself and pinpoint the problems that can be corrected. See yourself changing and merging with the happy and strong you. See images of the dysfunctional you as you splash the water. Watch as these images disappear.

Here are some additional helpful hints concerning visual imagery with hypnosis:

1. Images you can focus on, such as a quiet lake, moonbeams across the water, a rose, and a flickering candle, work well.

2. For breathing techniques, observe your breath as it moves through your body. Note any feelings and sensations as you visualize your consciousness slowly moving from the top of your head all the way down to your feet. Do this for 15 minutes to half an hour.

3. Do not try to change things or analyze them while you practice self-hypnosis. Just become aware of them. As your hypnosis practice continues, you will find more space in your mind. That is, thoughts and images will intrude less frequently during your session of practicing self-hypnosis. The habitual patterns may loosen. Do not become attached to the calmness or the peace you experience during self-hypnosis; just be aware of them as changing states of mind. Thoughts or images will probably always arise, but the periods of stillness will become longer. What will change is your ability to relate to whatever arises. It is possible to learn to be non-judgmental—neither praising nor condemning, but just being.

4. Whatever approach you use to initiate self-hypnosis will become easier with continued practice and patience.

This is a basic psychic development visualization and mind-expanding technique.

Imagine yourself taking the form of an eagle. You are flying several hundred feet above the Earth, completely free and uninhibited. Feel yourself soaring, gliding, climbing upward to your Higher Self. Floating freely in the air, you can observe the world unfolding below you. See the colors of the planet, the blues and greens, the Earth tones.

Sense the majesty of the heavens and the panorama of the living universe. Soar and glide to the rhythm of life. Ride the wind and soar higher and higher. You have freed yourself from the earthly bonds that once shackled your mind to convention, self-doubt, and confusion. Feel the quiet radiance of life surrounding you; hear the harmony that is you in tune with creation, be still, observe, and know.

Glide upward—ever upward—toward understanding, toward light, and toward beauty. Beauty surrounds you in this sanctity of space. This is where other worlds exist beyond the confines of your everyday mind. Just as a seed contains the promise of fulfillment, your mind already contains the promise of greater gifts.

As you let go of fixed ideas, doubts, and other negative influences, you open the way for love, patience, and gentleness. Your Higher Self guides you to enjoy the rewards of your new reality.

Be receptive to the guidance of your Higher Self. Your Higher Self guides you and protects you, even when you are not consciously aware of it. Grow in the silence of your spiritual self. See the white light all around you.

Be still and listen. Your Higher Self already knows your needs and guides you to live a clear new way each day. It will guide you to action by giving you gifts of the spirit.

When you talk with someone, listen—really listen—with your inner ear as well as your outer ears. You may hear things being said at the inner level that are not spoken at the outer levels. Listen also to your inner voice and respond to it.

When you see a person or an event, look—really look—and perceive it with your inner vision. See and understand the workings behind the scenes. Open yourself to all the impressions; look deeper than the surface.

Now create a picture or vivid symbol of yourself using and applying your psychic gifts. Bring your accomplished ideals and goals together into a specific image. Visualize your goals as already accomplished.

Now slowly return from your upward flight. Return as a floating feather. Circle gently, and land softly on the beach. Bring something positive and helpful back with you. Hear the waves and recall the thoughts, feelings, symbols, and ideas from your journey. You are developing your gifts and learning to use them daily as you open yourself up to information and psychic energy from your Higher Self.

Alright now. Sleep now and rest. You did very, very well. Listen very carefully. I'm going to count forward now from 1-5. When I reach the count of 5 you will be back in the present, you will be able to remember everything you experienced and reexperienced. You'll feel very relaxed, refreshed and you'll be able to do whatever you have planned for the rest of the day or evening. You'll feel very positive about what you've experienced and very motivated about your confidence and ability to play this tape again, to experience self-hypnosis and improve your visualization skills.

Alright now. One, very, very deep. Two, you're getting a little bit lighter. Three, you're getting much much lighter. Four, very very light. Five, awaken. Wide awake and refreshed.

Always remember that visual imagery involves to some extent creating images in your mind. Whether these be shapes with color, odors, tastes, sounds, or landscapes, most of us can experience real or imaginary events in the mind's eye. In order to facilitate this skill, you must put analysis, judgment, and expectations aside. It is not necessary to create visual images to communicate with spirit guides. This skill is desirable, but not required.

Balancing Energy Centers Within Our Auras

The aura is an electromagnetic field that all living things possess. It is an extension of the soul and can be photographed by Kirlian photography. This energy field we call the aura is seen as a series of colors, radiates light and constantly vibrates.

An inner center of auric colors are pink/red, blue/green, blue/mauve, and yellow. They represent health, balance, and spirit energy. The aura is actually a complete record of the spiritual and physical status of the soul and its physical body. Each color has special meanings depending on where it is found and depending on its particular shade.

The aura may be seen psychically as an oval-shaped ring of light that either pulses or appears as a swirling pattern of several colored lights. This energy field is composed of seven interwoven rings of light and each component represents something else.

The seven aura rings are as follows:

- Ring 1 represents physical health.
- Ring 2 represents the emotions.
- Ring 3 represents the intellect.
- Ring 4 represents the subconscious, especially the imagination and intuition.
- Ring 5 represents the Higher Self.
- Rings 6 and 7 are not visible on most people and represent advanced cosmic aspects of the soul's energy.

Within the aura there are special energy centers (quite different from *chakras* that I will discuss shortly), each having their own color and moving in a clockwise direction.

These are labeled as follows:

1. The *inspiration center* is located in the upper part of the head, and is blue.

2. The *communication center* is located in the lower head and neck, and is mauve.

3. The *emotional center* is located in the heart aura, and is pink laced with red.

4. The *courage center* is located in the solar plexus region, and is yellow.

5. The *creativity center* is located in the tailbone, and is green. This center includes the feet and legs.

The following exercise will help you see whether these centers are in balance:

1. Relax, apply protection, and ask your Higher Self to tune into the blue of inspiration. Check the blue in its own center and follow the blue line moving down into the communication center. Check the blue energy moving through the mauve and down to the emotional center. Check the blue as it spirals around the emotional center and then moves down to the courage center. Check as it spirals around the courage center and moves down to the creativity center, including the legs and feet.

    If you sense any imbalance in blue energy, focus on the blue energy from your Third-Eye area and keep the focus until you sense that your blue energy is back in balance.

2. Repeat this procedure with mauve, beginning in the communication center. Check the mauve in its own center first, then travel upward to check inspiration, down to communication, down and around emotion, down and around courage, down and around creativity, including the legs and feet, and back to the communication center.

    If you sense an imbalance, pause, then send mauve from your mid-forehead center to the point affected until the imbalance is corrected.

3. The next center is emotions (pink/red). Follow the same procedure. Repeat the procedure for courage (yellow), then creativity (green).

4. Next, from your mid-forehead to 12 inches above your head send a beam of all colors. Sweep down past all centers to below your feet and back up to above your head. Switch off the contact by sensing the colors fading. End your trance as usual.

Chakras

Chakras are energy centers in your astral body through which you are connected with your Higher Self. There are seven major chakras in your body that run from the top of your head to the base of your spine and there are several semimajor ones in your hands, feet, knees, and ankles. There are also thousands of minor chakras throughout your entire body.

The first, base chakra, is located at the base of the spine and associated with the color red. The second, sacral or sexual chakra, is located about three or four inches below the navel and is seen as orange. The third, solar plexus chakra, is located at the bottom front of the rib cage and is yellow. The fourth, heart chakra, is located in the middle of the chest and is seen as green. The fifth, throat chakra, is located in the throat and is associated with the color blue. The sixth, Third Eye or brow chakra, is located in the middle of the forehead and is seen as indigo. The seven, crown chakra, is located at the top center of the head and many people associate it with either violet or white, or a combination of the two with violet at the bottom and white on the top.

Chakras actually receive energy from both our Higher Self and spirit guides. This may be in the form of communication or energy work to build up the immune system or accelerate our spiritual growth.

The first three chakras represent the lower chakras. Initiating an OBE from any of these energy centers will result in a trip to the lower Astral plane. Chakras four through seven are known as the higher chakras. When you leave the body through one of them, you are assured a voyage to the more pleasant upper Astral plane.[2] Figure 6 illustrates the location of these seven chakras.

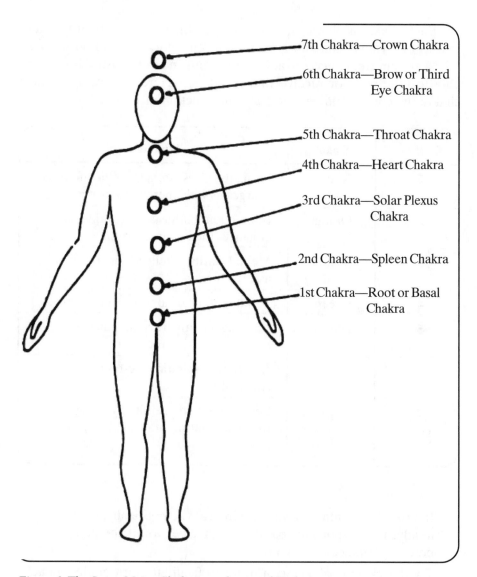

7th Chakra—Crown Chakra

6th Chakra—Brow or Third Eye Chakra

5th Chakra—Throat Chakra

4th Chakra—Heart Chakra

3rd Chakra—Solar Plexus Chakra

2nd Chakra—Spleen Chakra

1st Chakra—Root or Basal Chakra

Figure 6. The Seven Major Chakras on the Astral Body.

Each chakra is characterized by one of the seven colors of the rainbow as I previously stated. Each of the seven colors of the rainbow transmits a certain frequency, or rate of vibration, and our physical bodies are able to tune in to or receive that frequency. Here is a listing of each chakra, its corresponding color and the function of each color.

Chakra	Color	Functions
1	Red	Sexuality, gives strength to the life force, charges us with energy and protects us.
2	Orange	Interaction, enthusiasm, confidence, enhances the immune system.
3	Yellow	Mental clarity, intellect, cheerfulness, assertiveness
4	Green	Balance and harmony, peace, security.
5	Blue	Calming, creativity, communication, patience, seeking the truth.
6	Indigo	Intuition, inspiration, ecstasy, deeper spirituality.
7	Violet	Spiritual growth, sensitivity, imagination, the synchronization of the left and right brain.

In order to maintain harmony, physically, emotionally, mentally, and spiritually, it is important to expose ourselves to all the colors of the rainbow and balance our chakras.

Try this chakra balancing in order to facilitate spirit guide contact:

Take a deep breath...fill your chest...and hold it until I tell you to "Let go."

Now I want you to notice the tension in your chest muscles...the tension in your shoulders and upper arms. And I want you to pay particular attention to how...the moment I say "Let go"...all that tension disappears immediately...and you tend to sag limply down into the chair. Now... Let go.

I am going to count slowly up to five...and as I do so...you will take five very deep breaths.

And with each breath that you take...each time you breathe out...you will become more and more relaxed...and your trance will become deeper and deeper...breathe deeply...more and more deeply relaxed...deeper and deeper in relaxation... breathe deeper...deeper and deeper relaxed...becoming deeper and deeper in hypnosis...breathing even more deeply...more and more deeply relaxed...more and more deeply relaxed... very, very deep breath...deeper and deeper and deeper relaxed...your trance depth is becoming even deeper and deeper...very, very deep breath...very, very deeply relaxed...very, very deeply relaxed.

Once again...I want you take one very deep breath...fill your chest...and hold it until I say...Let go.

Then...let your breath out as quickly as possible...and as you do so...and you will become twice as deeply relaxed as you are now...twice as deeply relaxed as you are now...twice as deeply relaxed. Now, take that very deep breath...fill your chest...hold it...(15 seconds pause)...hold it...(15 seconds pause)...hold it...(20 to 30 seconds pause) Let go.

Now listen very carefully, I want you to image a bright white light coming down from above and entering the top of your head, filling your entire body. See it, feel it, and it becomes reality. Now imagine an aura of pure white light emanating from your heart region, again surrounding your entire body, protecting you. See it, feel it, and it becomes reality. Now only your Higher Self, Masters and guides, and highly evolved loving entities who mean you well will be able to influence you during this or any other hypnotic session. You are totally protected by this aura of pure white light.

In a few moments, I am going to count from 1 to 20. As I do so you will feel yourself rising up to the superconscious mind level where you will be able to receive information from your Higher Self and masters and guides. You will also be able to overview all of your past, present and future lives. Number 1, rising up. Two, 3, 4, rising higher. Five, 6, 7, letting information flow. Eight, 9, 10, you are halfway there. Eleven, 12, 13, feel yourself rising even higher. Fourteen, 15, 16, almost there. Seventeen, 18, 19, and 20. Now you are there. Take a moment and orient yourself to the superconscious mind level.

Play new age music for 1 minute.

Focus on the first chakra at the base of your spine. Begin breathing in and out from this basal chakra.

Notice how as you exhale, heat energy is felt at the first chakra, and it grows stronger with each breath. Visualize this energy as a ball of red fire which grows brighter as it gets warmer. Perceive your consciousness being centered in the middle of this red ball of energy.

Focus on how this affects you physically, mentally, emotionally, and spiritually. Feel this red ball of energy radiate out to all parts of the body.

Stay with the image and note how this cleanses and balances your first chakra.

Play new age music for 1 minute.

Now focus on the second chakra by the spleen. Begin breathing in and out from this chakra. Notice how as you exhale, heat energy is felt at the second chakra, and it grows stronger with each breath. Visualize this energy as a ball of orange fire which grows brighter as it gets warmer. Perceive your consciousness being centered in the middle of this orange ball of energy.

Focus on how this affects you physically, mentally, emotionally, and spiritually. Feel this orange ball of energy radiate out to all parts of your body.

Play new age music for 1 minute.

Now focus on the third chakra at the solar plexus. Begin breathing in and out from this chakra.

Notice how as you exhale, heat energy is felt at the third chakra, and it grows stronger with each breath. Visualize this energy as a ball of yellow fire which grows brighter as it gets warmer. Perceive your consciousness being centered in the middle of this yellow ball of energy.

Focus on how this affects you physically, mentally, emotionally, and spiritually. Feel this yellow ball of energy radiate out to all parts of the body.

Stay with the image and note how this cleanses and balances your third chakra.

Play new age music for 1 minute.

Now focus on the fourth chakra by your heart. Begin breathing in and out from this chakra.

Notice how as you exhale, heat energy is felt at the fourth chakra, and it grows stronger with each breath. Visualize this energy as a ball of green fire which grows brighter as it gets warmer. Perceive your consciousness being centered in the middle of this green ball of energy.

Focus on how this affects you physically, mentally, emotionally, and spiritually. Feel this green ball of energy radiate out to all parts of the body.

Stay with the image and note how this cleanses and balances your fourth chakra.

Play new age music for 1 minute

Now focus on the fifth chakra at the throat. Begin breathing in and out from this chakra.

Notice how as you exhale, heat energy is felt at the fifth chakra, and it grows stronger with each breath. Visualize this energy as a ball of blue fire which grows brighter as it gets warmer. Perceive your consciousness being centered in the middle of this blue ball of energy.

Focus on how this affects you physically, mentally, emotionally, and spiritually. Feel this blue ball of energy radiate out to all parts of the body.

Stay with the image and note how this cleanses and balances your fifth chakra.

Play new age music for 1 minute.

Now focus on the sixth chakra at the Third Eye. Begin breathing in and out from this chakra.

Notice how as you exhale, heat energy is felt at the sixth chakra, and it grows stronger with each breath. Visualize this energy as a ball of indigo fire which grows brighter as it gets warmer. Perceive your consciousness being centered in the middle of this indigo ball of energy.

Focus on how this affects you physically, mentally, emotionally, and spiritually. Feel this indigo ball of energy radiate out to all parts of the body.

Stay with the image and note how this cleans and balances your sixth chakra.

Play new age music for 1 minute.

You have now balanced each chakra, except the crown chakra which is balanced by the Higher Self. Allow your Higher Self to balance this seventh chakra by inhaling again and see this energy leave from the top of your head or crown chakra, where it now appears as violet. Exhale gently and perceive this violet aura surrounding your entire body. Notice how this violet color changes to white and pulsates around your entire physical body creating a wonderful relaxing and balanced feeling.

Play new age music for 1 minute.

Alright now. Sleep now and rest. You have done very well. Listen very carefully. I'm going to count now from 1-5. When I reach the count of 5 you will be able to remember everything you experienced and reexperienced. You'll feel very relaxed, refreshed and you'll be able to do whatever you have planned for the rest of the day or evening. You'll feel very positive about what you've experienced and very motivated about your confidence and ability to play this tape again, to experience your Higher Self and balance your chakras. Alright now. 1, very, very deep. 2, you're getting a little bit lighter. 3, you're getting much, much lighter. 4, very, very light. 5, awaken. Wide awake and refreshed.

This next exercise will align the four upper chakras (energy centers) of the astral body and help you to maximize your communication with your spirit guide. I refer to this as the *higher chakras link*:

Now listen very carefully. I want you to imagine a bright white light coming down from above and entering the top of your head, filling your entire body. See it, feel it, and it becomes reality. Now imagine an aura of pure white light emanating from your heart region, again surrounding your entire body, protecting you. See it, feel it, and it becomes reality. Now only your Higher Self, masters and guides, and highly evolved loving entities who mean you well will be able to influence you during this or any other hypnotic session. You are totally protected by this aura of pure white light.

In a few moments, I am going to count from 1 to 20. As I do so you will feel yourself rising up to the superconscious mind level where you will be able to receive information from your Higher Self and masters and guides. You will also be able to overview all of your past, present and future lives. One, rising up. Two, 3, 4, rising higher. Five, 6, 7, letting information flow. Eight, 9, 10, you are halfway there. Eleven, 12, 13, feel yourself rising even higher. Fourteen, 15, 16, almost there. Seventeen, 18, 19, and 20. Now you are there. Take a moment and orient yourself to the superconscious mind level.

Play new age music for 1 minute.

You are now in a deep hypnotic trance and from this superconscious mind level, you are in complete control and able to access this limitless power of your superconscious mind. I want you to be open and flow with this experience. You are always protected by the white light.

Focus your attention on your Third Eye region of your forehead. This is located between your eyes and is the 6th chakra.

Imagine a glowing white light as you inhale being drawn into this Third Eye area and creating a sensation of warmth. Hold this focus for a count of eight. Now exhale.

As you inhale again see this glowing white light being drawn up to the crown chakra located at the top of the head. See a rainbow bridge being formed here. Hold this focus of the rainbow bridge for a count of eight at the crown chakra, exhale, repeat this procedure two more times.

Visualize the rainbow bridge moving into the Third Eye chakra and finally into the throat (5th) chakra. As you inhale feel this warm sensation permeating the throat. Hold this focus of the rainbow bridge in the throat chakra for a count of 8, exhale.

Imagine this rainbow bridge moving from the throat chakra into the heart (4th) chakra. This is the area in the middle of the chest at the level of the heart. As you inhale feel this warm sensation permeating the heart chakra. Hold this focus for a count of 8, exhale.

Finally, inhale deeply and hold your breath for a count of 10. As you hold your breath visually link up the rainbow bridges in your heart, throat, Third Eye and crown chakras with a band of glowing white light. Feel this link as a warm, tingly sensation. Exhale slowly and repeat this procedure two more times.

Play new age music for 2 minutes.

You have activated your higher spiritual centers for receiving communication from your spirit guides.

Alright now. Sleep now and rest. You did very, very well. Listen very carefully. I'm going to count forward now from 1 to 5. When I reach the count of 5 you will be back in the present, you will be able to remember everything you experienced and reexperienced. You'll feel very relaxed, refreshed and you'll be able to do whatever you have planned for the rest of the day or evening. You'll feel very positive about what you've experienced and very motivated about your confidence and ability to play this tape again, to experience your higher chakras link. Alright now. One, very, very deep. Two, you're getting a little bit lighter. Three, you're getting much, much lighter. Four, very, very light. Five, awaken. Wide awake and refreshed.

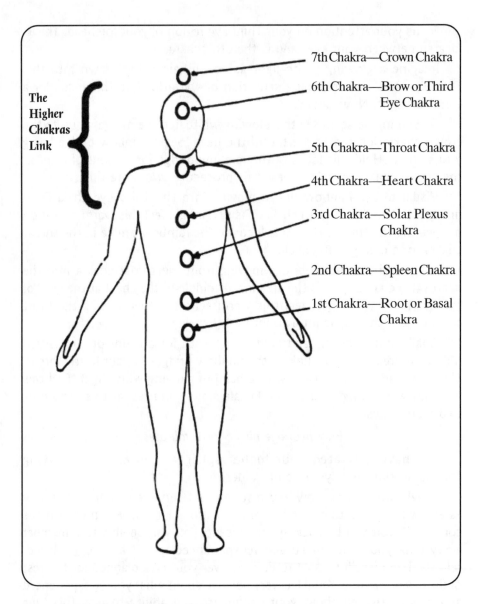

Figure 7. The Higher Chakras Link

Here are some exercises designed to help you remove fears and free your psychic energy.

Now listen very carefully. I want you to imagine a bright white light coming down from above and entering the top of your head, filling your entire body. See it, feel it and it becomes reality. Now imagine an aura of pure white light emanating from your heart region, again surrounding your entire body, protecting you. See it, feel it, and it becomes reality. Now only your Higher Self, Masters and guides and highly evolved loving entities who mean you well will be able to influence you during this or any other hypnotic session. You are totally protected by this aura of pure white light.

Mentally see yourself at the foot of a mountain. Begin a gradual ascent now. And as you wind your way slowly along that mountain path, become aware of a heaviness, a tiredness, a sense of anger, futility, and pain. Your climb is slower and you feel those burdens you are carrying, burdens for which you had not even realized you asked, but that you are carrying nevertheless. And the sun grows hotter as it climbs higher in the sky. And you travel on. Soon you come to rest by a small crevice in the rocks. And suddenly a stream appears. And the stream widens, water rushing down the rocks. You shed your clothes and stand beneath the waterfall. Feel the clear, cool water pouring down all over you. Let the gentle stream of water wash away all your fears, all your sorrows, all your anxiety.

Now stepping out from under the waterfall, you rest for a while, letting yourself dry off in the sun. Let the sunlight stream down upon you and fill every cell and tissue until you feel light and refreshed and renewed. When you are ready you can return to your usual awareness, relaxed, refreshed, and filled with energy.

Now reflect on those fears or habits that you would like to release. Write each fear, habit, or negative feeling or experience on a separate piece of paper.

Imagine yourself taking the pieces of paper one at a time and reading them aloud. Then burn each one, saying, "As this paper burns, my fear is destroyed." You may want to see the negative energy transformed into positive energy. As you burn each paper, you may say, "his fire is transforming my worry into careful attention." When you have finished burning all the papers, sit quietly and reflect on what you have said and done. Feel yourself released from fears and negative energy and filled with love and joy.

Play new age music for 4 minutes.

Alright now. Sleep now and rest. You did very, very well. Listen very carefully. I'm going to count forward now from 1-5. When I reach the count of 5 you will be back in the present, you will be able to remember everything you experienced and reexperienced. You'll feel very relaxed, refreshed and you'll be able to do whatever you have planned for the rest of the day or evening. You'll feel very positive about what you've experienced and very motivated about your confidence and ability to play this tape again, to experience your psychic energy. Alright now. One, very, very deep. Two, you're getting a little bit lighter. Three, you're getting much, much lighter. Four, very very light. Five, awaken. Wide awake and refreshed.

This next exercise is what I refer to as a sanctuary technique:

Now listen very carefully. I want you to imagine a bright white light coming down from above and entering the top of your head, filling your entire body. See it, feel it and it becomes reality. Now imagine an aura of pure white light emanating from your heart region, again surrounding your entire body, protecting you. See it, feel it and it becomes reality. Now only your Higher Self, masters and guides and highly evolved entities who mean you well will be able to influence you during this or any other hypnotic session. You are totally protected by this aura of pure white light.

Relax, breathe deeply, and send a warm feeling into your toes and feet. Let this feeling break up any strain or tension, and as you exhale let the tension drain away. Breathe deeply and send this warm feeling into your ankles. It will break up any strain or tension, and as you exhale let the tension drain away. Breathe deeply and send this feeling into your knees, let it break up any strain or tension there, and as you exhale let the tension drain away. Send this warm sensation into your thighs so any strain or tension is draining away. Breathe deeply and send this warm feeling into your genitals and drain away any tension.

Send this warm feeling into your abdomen now; all your internal organs are soothed and relaxed and any strain or tension is draining away. Let this energy flow into your chest and breast; let it soothe you and as you exhale any tension is draining away. Send this energy into your back now. This feeling is breaking up any strain or tension and as you exhale the tension is draining away. The deep, relaxing energy is flowing through your back, into each vertebra, as each vertebra assumes its proper alignment. The healing energy is flowing into all your muscles and tendons, and you are relaxed, very fully relaxed. Send this energy into your shoulders and neck;

this energy is breaking up any strain or tension and as you exhale the tension is draining away. Your shoulders and neck are fully relaxed. And the deep relaxing energy is flowing into your arms; your upper arms, your elbows, your forearms, your wrists, your hands, your fingers are fully relaxed.

Let this relaxing energy wash up over your throat, and your lips, your jaw, your cheeks are fully relaxed. Send this energy into your face, the muscles around your eyes, your forehead, your scalp are relaxed. Any strain or tension is draining away. You are relaxed, most completely relaxed.

And now float to your space, leave your physical body and move between dimensions and travel to your space, a meadow, a mountain, a forest, the seashore, wherever your mind is safe and free. Go to that space now. And you are in your space, the space you have created, a space sacred and apart.

Here, in this space, you are free from all tension and fears, and are in touch with the calm, expansive power within you. Here in this space you have access to spiritual information and energy. Here is the space where you can communicate with your spirit guides. Your flow is in harmony with the flow of the universe. Because you are part of the whole creation you have access to the power of the whole of creation. Here you are pure and free. This is your personal sanctuary.

Here, in this space, you can recreate your day, a day that has been difficult for you. Conjure up each thought, each act, each word, and every fear. See them all very clearly.

Play new age music for 1 minute.

And now formulate each word, each act, each thought you enjoyed, that you consider important, anything you feel positive about. Reconstruct each happy thought, fleeting smile, pleasant experience. And let these images grow. Let them become larger and larger. Let them spill over into your consciousness. You are bathed in the joy of the remembered experience.

Play new age music for 2 minutes.

You have done very well. Now I want you to further open up the channels of communication by removing any obstacles and allowing yourself to receive information and experiences that will directly apply to and help better your present circumstances. Allow yourself to receive more advanced and more specific information from your spirit guides to raise your soul's energy and improve your karmic subcycle. Do this now.

Play new age music for 3 minutes.

Alright now. Sleep now and rest. You did very, very well. Listen very carefully. I'm going to count forward now from 1 to 5. When I reach the count of 5 you will be back in the present, you will be able to remember everything you experienced and reexperienced. You'll feel very relaxed, refreshed and you'll be able to do whatever you have planned for the rest of the day or evening. You'll feel very positive about what you've experienced and very motivated about your confidence and ability to play this tape again, to experience your sanctuary. Alright now. One, very, very deep. Two, you're getting a little bit lighter. Three, you're getting much, much lighter. Four, very, very light. Five, awaken. Wide awake and refreshed.

The Superconscious Mind Tap

We have discussed the Higher Self and included it in several exercises so far in a general way. The ultimate source of our soul's energy is its perfect component known as the Higher Self, or superconscious mind. By accessing your Higher Self you have awareness and knowledge not available to you during your routine waking activities. Guided meditation, hypnosis, and dreams are the main paths to your Higher Self.

When you complete your karmic cycle, your soul will merge with your Higher Self and you will then ascend to the higher planes to reunite with God. The best way to contact your Higher Self is to practice centering and clearing exercises along with visualizing techniques. A superconscious mind tap is simply training the subconscious mind (Higher Self). This self-hypnosis exercise is the main technique I utilize in my office.

The superconscious mind tap is particularly valuable in our discussion because it:

- ◎ Trains you to raise the quality of your own soul's (subconscious mind's) frequency vibrational rate.

- ◎ Promotes contact and communication with lost loved ones and spirit guides.

- ◎ Overviews past and future lives with spirit guides or anyone in your life today.

- ◎ Facilitates your ability to function as a trance channel.

Here is the self-hypnotic script I use with my patients to train them to contact their Higher Selves. As with all such scripts, this works best if you make a tape.

Now listen very carefully. I want you to imagine a bright white light coming down from above and entering the top of your head. Filling your entire body. See it, feel it and it becomes reality. Now imagine an aura of pure white light emanating from your heart region. Again surrounding your entire body. Protecting you. See it, feel it and it becomes reality. Now only your spirit guides, Higher Self, and highly evolved loving entities who mean you well will be able to influence you during this or any other hypnotic session. You are totally protected by this aura of pure white light.

In a few moments I am going to count from 1 to 20. As I do so you will feel yourself rising up to the superconscious mind level where you will be able to receive information from your Higher Self and spirit guides. You will also be able to overview all of your past, present and future lives. Number 1 rising up. Two, 3, 4, rising higher. Five, 6, 7, letting information flow. Eight, 9, 10, you are halfway there. Eleven, 12, 13, feeling yourself rising even higher. Fourteen, 15, 16, almost there. Seventeen, 18, 19, number 20 you are there. Take a moment and orient yourself to the superconscious mind level.

Play new age music for 1 minute.

You may now ask yourself any question about any issue. Or, you may contact any of your spirit guides or departed loved ones from this level. You may explore your relationship with any person. Remember, your superconscious mind level is all knowledgeable and has access to your Akashic Records.

Now slowly and carefully state your desire for information or an experience and let this superconscious mind level work for you.

Play new age music for 8 minutes

You have done very well. Now I want you to further open up the channels of communication by removing any obstacles and allowing yourself to receive information and experiences that will directly apply to and help better your present lifetime. Allow yourself to receive more advanced and more specific information from your Higher Self and Masters and guides to raise your frequency and improve your karmic subcycle. Do this now.

Play new age music for 8 minutes.

Alright now. Sleep now and rest. You did very, very well. Listen very carefully. I'm going to count forward now from 1-5. When I reach the count of 5 you will be back in the present, you will be able to remember everything you experienced and reexperienced, you'll feel very relaxed and refreshed, you'll be able to do whatever you have planned for the rest of the day or evening. You'll feel very positive about what you've just experienced and very motivated about your confidence and ability to play this tape again to experience the superconscious mind level. Alright now. One, very very deep. Two, you're getting a little bit lighter. Three, you're getting much much lighter. Four, very very light. Five, awaken. Wide awake and refreshed.

As with all self-hypnosis and meditations, I highly recommend making a tape of these exercises. If you would like professionally recorded tapes of these techniques, simply contact my office.

Here is a superconscious mind tap script to prepare you for a spirit guide contact:

Now listen very carefully. I want you to imagine a bright white light coming down from above and entering the top of your head, filling your entire body. See it, feel it, and it becomes reality. Now imagine an aura of pure white light emanating from your heart region, again surrounding your entire body, protecting you. See it, feel it, and it becomes reality. Now only your Higher Self, masters and guides, and highly evolved loving entities who mean you well will be able to influence you during this or any other hypnotic session. You are totally protected by this aura of pure white light.

In a few moments, I am going to count from 1 to 20. As I do so you will feel yourself rising up to the superconscious mind level where you will be able to receive information from your Higher Self and Masters and guides. One, rising up. Two, 3, 4, rising higher. Five, 5, 6, 7, letting information flow. Eight, 9, 10, you are halfway there. Eleven, 12, 13, feel yourself rising even higher. Fourteen, 15, 16, almost there. Seventeen, 18, 19, and 20. Now you are there. Take a moment and orient yourself to the superconscious mind level.

Play new age music for 1 minute.

You are in a deep hypnotic trance and from this superconscious mind level, you are in complete control and able to access this limitless power of your superconscious mind. I want you to be open and flow with this experience. You are always protected by the white light.

At this time I would like you to ask your Higher Self to incorporate the following affirmations and suggestions into my soul's growth. Trust your Higher Self and your own ability to allow any thoughts, feelings or impressions to come into your subconscious mind concerning these goals. Do this now.

Play new age music for 1 minute.

I am of pure light and pure energy.

My time is my own.

I am a free and powerful being.

I draw to myself success and happiness.

I draw to myself an ideal relationship.

I draw to myself sexual energy and bliss.

My body heals and balances itself.

I clear my mind and self of everything I no longer need.

I have endless inner strength and knowledge.

I create my own positive reality.

I love myself completely and unconditionally.

I have no fear.

I am in complete control of my destiny.

I am able to be fully focused and centered in the present moment.

I am connected with my Higher Self and the universe.

I am patient with my own progress and that of others.

I draw loving and supportive relationships.

I have enough time to accomplish my goals.

I love and believe in myself.

I am at peace with myself and the universe.

I feel safe, secure and protected.

Every day in every way, I am more confident in my ability to handle anything.

I am now attracting only the highest level of spirit guide to assist both my Higher Self and my overall consciousness in spiritual contact and growth.

Take a few moments now and visualize yourself incorporating each one of these suggestions and affirmations into your consciousness.

Play new age music for 4 minutes.

Alright now. Sleep now and rest. You did very, very well. Listen very carefully. I'm going to count forward now from 1-5. When I reach the count of 5 you will be back in the present, you will be able to remember everything you experienced and reexperienced. You'll feel very relaxed, refreshed and you'll be able to do whatever you have planned for the rest of the day or evening. You'll feel very positive about what you've experienced and very motivated about your confidence and ability to play this tape again, to experience your Higher Self and grow spiritually. Alright now. One, very, very deep. Two, you're getting a little bit lighter. Three, you're getting much much lighter. Four, very, very light. Five, awaken. Wide awake and refreshed.

Here is a method using the sanctuary that I introduced earlier to meet a spirit guide.

Sit back, relax, breathe deeply, and send a warm feeling into your toes and feet. Let this feeling break up any strain or tension, and as you exhale let the tension drain away. Breathe deeply and send this warm feeling into your ankles. It will break up any strain or tension, and as you exhale let the tension drain away. Breathe deeply and send this feeling into your knees, let it break up any strain or tension there, and as you exhale let the tension drain away. Send this warm sensation to your thighs so any strain or tension is draining away. Breathe deeply and send this warm feeling into your genitals and drain away any tension.

Send this warm feeling into your abdomen now; all your internal organs are soothed and relaxed and any strain or tension is draining away. Let this energy flow into your chest and breast; let it soothe you and as you exhale any tension is draining away. The deep, relaxing energy is flowing through your back, into each vertebra, as each vertebra assumes its proper alignment. The healing energy is flowing into all your muscles and tendons, and you are relaxed, very fully relaxed. Send this energy into your shoulders and neck; this energy is breaking up any strain or tension and as you exhale the tension is draining away. Your shoulders and neck are fully relaxed. And the deep relaxing energy is flowing into your arms; your upper arms, your elbows, your forearms, your wrists, your hands, your fingers are fully relaxed.

Let this relaxing energy wash up over your throat, and your lips, your jaw, your cheeks are fully relaxed. Send this energy into your face, the muscles around your eyes, your forehead, your scalp are relaxed. Any strain or tension is draining away. You are relaxed, more completely relaxed.

And now float to your space, leave your physical body and move between dimensions and travel to your space, a meadow, a mountain, a forest, the seashore— wherever your mind is safe and free. Go to that space now. And you are in your space, the space you have created, a space sacred and apart. Here, in this space, you are free from all tension and in touch with the calm, expansive power within you. Here in this space you have access to spiritual information and energy. Here is the space where you can communicate with your spirit guides. Your flow is in harmony with the flow of the universe. Because you are part of the whole creation you have access to the power of the whole of creation. Here you are pure and free. This is your personal sanctuary.

Wherever your sanctuary is, I would like you to place a pool in its surroundings. Stand at this pool and request an audience with a high-level spirit guide. Suddenly a magnificent being surrounded by a brilliant white light rises up out of the water from this pool. This is your spirit guide.

This guide greets you with unconditional love and complete acceptance. You accompany your guide to a small room where you place your defense mechanisms in a lead-lined box. This part of your consciousness will remain in this box throughout the duration of this encounter.

Now you feel safe and protected as your guide envelops your body in a white light and devoid of your ego you make no judgments or attempt to analyze this contact.

At this time ask your guide the following questions:

- What fears or other blocks do I have that are preventing me from growing spiritually?
- What message do you have for me that will assist me at this time?
- What is my karmic purpose?
- What talents or skills do I possess that I have not been using that I may activate now to achieve spiritual growth?

You may ask your guide any other questions at this time. Let the answers to your queries flow into your subconscious for a few moments.

Play new age music for 6 minutes.

Now return to the room with the lead-lined box and retrieve your conscious mind. Bid farewell to your guide, after thanking him or her, and watch as this spiritual advisor returns to the pool and dives in.

Play new age music for 1 minute.

Alright now. Sleep now and rest. You did very, very well. Listen very carefully. I'm going to count forward now from 1-5. When I reach the count of 5 you will be back in the present, you will be able to remember everything you experienced and reexperienced. You'll feel relaxed, refreshed and you'll be able to do whatever you have planned for the rest of the day or evening. You'll feel very positive about what you've experienced and very motivated about your confidence and ability to play this tape again, to experience your spirit guide. Alright now. One, very, very deep. Two, you're getting a little bit lighter. Three, you're getting much, much lighter. Four, very very light. Five, awaken. Wide awake and refreshed.

Try this exercise to further prepare you to meet a spirit guide.

Now listen very carefully. I want you to imagine a bright white light coming down from above and entering the top of your head, filling your entire body. See it, feel it and it becomes reality. Now imagine an aura of pure white light emanating from your heart region, again surrounding your entire body, protecting you. See it, feel it and it becomes reality. Now only your Higher Self, masters and guides and highly evolved loving entities who mean you well will be able to influence you during this or any other hypnotic session. You are totally protected by this aura of pure white light.

In a few moments, I am going to count from 1 to 20. As I do so you will feel yourself rising up to the superconscious mind level where you will be able to receive information from your Higher Self and masters and guides. You will also be able to overview all of your past, present and future lives. One, rising up. Two, 3, 4, rising higher. Five, 6, 7, letting information flow. Eight, 9, 10, you are halfway there. Eleven, 13, feel yourself rising even higher. Fourteen, 15, 16 almost there. Seventeen, 18, 19, and 20. Now you are there. Take a moment and orient yourself to the superconscious mind level.

Play new age music for 1 minute.

You are now in a deep hypnotic trance and from this superconscious mind level, you are in complete control and able to access this limitless power of your superconscious mind. I want you to be open and flow with this experience. You are always protected by the white light.

At this time I would like you to ask your Higher Self to assist you in preparing to meet a spirit guide of the highest level of spiritual development.

Select one very positive quality you would like to incorporate into your life at this time. This might be joy, peace, love or something to that effect. As you focus on this goal create an image of how your life would be different. Keep the images and other aspects of this change in your life steadily in your mind.

Play new age music for 3 minutes.

Now I want you to focus in on opening each and every one of your chakras to receive the perfect energy from your Higher Self and spirit guide.

Perceive this energy represented by a brilliant white light entering your right brain, then flowing in your left brain and finally radiating in both brain hemispheres simultaneously. Feel an awareness of your desired positive quality as this is occurring. Do this now.

Play new age music for 4 minutes.

Alright now. Sleep now and rest. You did very, very well. Listen very carefully. I'm going to count forward now from 1-5. When I reach the count of 5 you will be back in the present, you will be able to remember everything you experienced and reexperienced. You'll feel very relaxed, refreshed and you'll be able to do whatever you have planned for the rest of the day or evening. You'll feel very positive about what you've experienced and very motivated about your confidence and ability to play this tape again, to experience your Higher Self and prepare for a meeting with a spirit guide. Alright now. One, very, very deep. Two, you're getting a little bit lighter. Three, you're getting much, much lighter. Four, very very light. Five, awaken. Wide awake and refreshed.

We can utilize the superconscious mind tap to specifically attract a high-level spirit guide for an enlightening communication. Here is such an exercise:

Now listen very carefully. I want you to imagine a bright white light coming down from above and entering the top of your head. Filling your entire body. See it, feel it, and it becomes reality. Now imagine an aura of pure white light emanating from your heart region. Again surrounding your entire body. Protecting you. See it, feel it, and it becomes reality. Now only your Higher Self, Masters and guides, and highly evolved loving entities who mean you well will be able to influence you during this or any other hypnotic session. You are totally protected by this aura of pure white light.

In a few moments I am going to count from 1 to 20. As I do so you will feel yourself rising up to the superconscious mind level where you will be able to receive information from your Higher Self and Masters and guides. You will also be able to overview all of your past, present and future lives. One, rising up. Two, 3, 4, rising higher. Five, 6, 7, letting information flow. Eight, 9, 10, you are halfway there. Eleven, 12, 13, feel yourself rising even higher. Fourteen, 15, 16, almost there. Seventeen, 18, 19, and 20 you are there. Take a moment and orient yourself to the superconscious mind level.

Play new age music for 1 minute.

You are now in a deep hypnotic trance and from this superconscious mind level there exists a mechanism to invite a spirit guide communication.

You are in complete control and able to access this limitless power of your superconscious mind. I want you to be open and flow with this experience. You are always protected by the white light.

At this time I would like you to ask your Higher Self to assist you in attracting a high-level spirit guide. Trust your Higher Self and your own ability to allow a highly evolved spirit guide or master to communicate with your subconscious now.

Play new age music for 6 minutes.

You have done very well. Now I want you to further open up the channels of communication by removing any obstacles and allowing yourself to receive information and experiences from this spirit guide that will directly apply to and help better your present lifetime. Allow yourself to receive more advanced and more specific information from your Higher Self and masters and guides to raise your frequency and improve your karmic subcycle. Do this now.

Play new age music for 4 minutes.

Alright now. Sleep now and rest. You did very, very well. Listen very carefully. I'm going to count forward now from 1 to 5. When I reach the count of 5 you will be back in the present, you will be able to remember everything you experienced and reexperienced. You'll be very relaxed and refreshed, you'll be able to do whatever you have planned for the rest of the day or evening. You'll feel very positive about what you've just experienced and very motivated about your confidence and ability to play this tape again to experience a spirit guide contact. Alright now. One, very, very deep. Two, you're getting a little bit lighter. Three, you're getting much, much lighter. Four, very, very light. Five, awaken. Wide awake and refreshed.

Using Your Dreams to Meet a Spirit Guide

The state of mind you are in just prior to falling asleep is referred to as a *hypnogogic* level and is an example of natural hypnosis. We can utilize this alpha brain wave state to invite a spirit guide into our dream world.

Whether you call it the Astral plane or dream world, this dimension is a natural habitat for spirit guides. I am referring only to the upper Astral plane. There is far greater freedom in dream world, because our every thought and emotion creates a reality.

Each dream begins with psychic energy that the individual transforms into a reality just as functional and real as physical reality. There is form within dream reality, but the potential form exists, within psychic energy, long before its materialization. We can use our dreams to improve health, gain inspiration, restore vitality, solve problems and contact a spirit guide. These can all be accomplished because the conscious mind (ego) cannot function on dream world.

To understand the mechanism of dream world you need to know that the waking consciousness is not the ego. The ego is only that portion of waking consciousness that deals with physical manipulation. Waking consciousness can be taken into the dream state, but the ego cannot, as it would falter and cause failure there. When you take your consciousness into the dream state, you will meet with various conditions, some you can manipulate, some you cannot. Some dream locations will be of your own making, and others will be strange to you because they belong to other dimensions of reality.

Here is a simple exercise on programming your dreams to establish communication with a spirit guide:

> While in hypnosis, just before going to sleep, say to yourself, "I would like to contact a high-level spirit guide who will offer me spiritual advice and facilitate my spiritual growth. My Higher Self will also be involved with this meeting and I will recall this encounter when I wake up in the morning."

Keep a cassette player ready to record or a pen and pad by your bed. When you awaken, dictate or write down what you remember of the dream. Keep practicing this, night after night, and you will recall these dreams in more and more detail.

Another helpful hint is to imagine an actual spirit guide contact while you are lying in bed and just about to fall asleep. Focus on each detail and allow your "stream of consciousness" (Higher Self) to assist you with this visualization. This method has the advantage of bridging both the waking and dream world, which trains your mind to send out a stronger signal that is more likely to attract a spirit guide.

Pay attention to your dream tonight and try to recall it tomorrow morning. During your waking hours, watch and be internally attentive to any seemingly foreign ideas that may "pop into" your mind. At the same time be externally attentive to events—a remark that hits you in a different way, words or phrases from the morning paper that may catch your attention, anything around or outside the house that may seem to be telling you something—anything that may convey a message from a spirit guide.

Meeting an Angel

I have previously discussed angels by pointing out that these messengers of God were never human and represent the divine energy of the Creator of our universe.

There are four factors that determine whether we will have a face-to-face contact with our angels:

1. Such contact must be part of God's plan.

2. We must truly understand what angels are and do, as well as what they will not or cannot do.

3. Our motives for wanting such an encounter must be pure.

4. We must be prepared for an encounter.

Angels will use whatever medium is most likely to attract our attention. Very often they will utilize our dreams to help us. Here is a self-hypnosis exercise to invite a communication with an angel.

Now listen very carefully. I want you to imagine a bright white light coming down from above and entering the top of your head, filling your entire body. See it, feel it, and it becomes reality. Now imagine an aura of pure white light emanating from your heart region, again surrounding your entire body, protecting you. See it, feel it, and it becomes reality. Now only your angels, High Self, and highly evolved loving entities who mean you well will be able to influence you during this or any other hypnotic session. You are totally protected by this aura of pure white light.

In a few moments, I am going to count from 1 to 20. As I do so you will feel yourself rising up to the superconscious mind level where you will be able to receive information from your angel protectors. One, rising up. Two, 3, 4 rising higher. Five, 6, 7, letting information flow. Eight, 9, 10, you are halfway there. Eleven, 12, 13, feeling yourself rising even higher. Fourteen, 15, 16, almost there. Seventeen, 18, 19, and 20, you are there. Take a moment and orient yourself to the superconscious mind level.

Play new age music for 1 minute.

You may contact any of your angels from this level. You may explore your relationship with any person. Remember, your superconscious mind level is all knowledgeable and has access to your Akashic Records. Let your Higher Self send out the appropriate energy to attract one of your angels.

Now slowly and carefully state your desire for information or an experience and let this superconscious mind level work for you. Feel the healing energy and love coming from your Guardian Angel.

Play new age music for 8 minutes.

You have done very well. Now I want you to further open up the channels of communication by removing any obstacles and allowing yourself to receive information and experiences that will directly apply to and help better your present lifetime. Allow yourself to receive more advanced and more specific information from your angels to raise your frequency and improve your karmic subcycle. Do this now.

Play new age music for 8 minutes.

Alright now. Sleep now and rest. You did very, very well. Listen very carefully. I'm going to count forward now from 1-5. When I reach the count of 5 you will be back in the present, you will be able to remember everything you experienced and reexperienced. You'll feel very relaxed, refreshed, and you'll be able to do whatever you have planned for the rest of the day or evening. You'll feel very positive about what you've just experienced and very motivated about your confidence and ability to play this tape again to experience your angels. Alright now. One, very, very deep. Two, you're getting a little bit lighter. Three, you're getting much, much lighter. Four, very, very light. Five, awaken. Wide awake and refreshed.

Some additional things you can do to facilitate contact with your Guardian Angel are:

1. Use meditation and prayer to request their assistance on a regular basis.

2. Get in touch with nature. Take long walks, hike, go to the seashore, the mountains, and so on.

3. Read books about angels.

4. Surround yourself with pleasant music. Practice singing, as angels are very attracted to this.

5. Develop your creativity in some way. Angels love to inspire any type of creative endeavor.

6. Practice self-hypnosis and meditation for your own spiritual growth. This is the surest way to attract an angel and expand your awareness at the same time.

Healing Through Spirit Guide Contact

When we increase our faith in our Higher Self and spirit guides, one noticeable change in our awareness is accelerated healing. Relaxation represents the initial step in healing. Hypnosis has been used throughout history to discipline our mind and harness spirit guide contact for healing.

Hypnosis sets the conscious mind aside so it can no longer worry and retard the natural process of healing. In order to heal you must *feel* and hypnosis heals us through this sensory mechanism assisted by the Higher Self and spirit guides. You must encourage and allow the Higher Self and spirit guides to do their work.

Spirit guides can heal us directly by also working through our senses. Sometimes you perceive a brief image in your mind's eye, or activate your inner eye for a brief moment. Do not be inhibited to ask your guide to assist you directly at any time.

Integration of the soul and its energy components (aura, chakras, and so on) with the physical body is necessary for true healing to take place. The only real resistance to this process is fear, fear of pain or of the consequences of an illness.

Resistance is the main way the ego asserts itself because it is always threatened by change. You need to request your guide to send strength and healing energy and ask for this resistance to be lifted. This is best done in self-hypnosis. Some of my patients experience a sensation of something being lifted off their body when I conduct such a hypnotherapy session.

The language and actions of spirit guides are based on love. Always present your requests to them with pure motives and in a loving fashion. Other approaches, more often than not, are simply rejected. Spirit guides will do just about anything you ask in the name of love and light.

A process of integration within our consciousness and physical body sometimes requires time to manifest. During our dream state (a natural level of hypnosis) the guide will communicate with us as images and perform a form of psychic surgery on our astral body to bring about this healing.

There is an old saying in metaphysics: "as above, so below." This means that upon arising, any healing initiated to our astral body will be felt in our physical body as well. This is a form of integration. Although we may be healed this way, another universal law states that any harm felt by our astral body will *not* affect our physical form. We have a built-in protection mechanism in the multidimensional universe.

Forgiveness and compassion not only represent cornerstones to spiritual growth, but healing as well. Both of these qualities evolve out of understanding. Contact with our guides through hypnosis clearly shows us the truth and in that truth we can let go of the illusion of separation, of guilt, of anger, and, most especially, of being a victim. Forgiveness and compassion accelerate this process.

Each of us is highly susceptible to hypnosis because we experience this natural state for seven hours daily. Practicing the self-hypnosis exercises presented throughout this book affords us the perfect opportunity to establish contact with our spirit guides and request healing from these highly evolved and often perfect beings of light.

As with all of the scripts I present, I suggest you make a tape of these exercises to facilitate your mastery of the method given. Try this technique I refer to as the Five Elements to contact spirit guides and effect healing:

Now listen very carefully. I want you to imagine a bright white light coming down from above and entering the top of your head, filling your entire body. See it, feel it, and it becomes reality. Now imagine an aura of pure white light emanating from your heart region, again surrounding your entire body, protecting you. See it, feel it, and it becomes reality. Now only your Higher Self, masters and guides, and highly evolved loving entities who mean you well will be able to influence you during this or any other hypnotic session. You are totally protected by this aura of pure white light.

In a few moments, I am going to count from 1 to 20. As I do so you will feel yourself rising up to the superconscious mind level where you will be able to receive information from your Higher Self and Masters and guides. You will also be able to overview all of your past, present, and future lives. One, rising up. Two, 3, 4, rising higher. Five, 6, 7, letting information flow. Eight, 9, 10, you are halfway there. Eleven, 12, 13, feel yourself rising even higher. Fourteen, 15, 16, almost there. Seventeen, 18, 19, and 20. Now you are there. Take a moment and orient yourself to the superconscious mind level.

Play new age music for 1 minute.

You are now in a deep hypnotic trance and from this superconscious mind level, you are in complete control and able to access this limitless power of your superconscious mind. I want you to be open and flow with this experience. You are always protected by the white light.

Imagine that you are in a rainforest. You are walking barefoot across the forest floor. Feel the cool, green vegetation underneath your feet. Notice the trees all around you. Hear the rustling of the leaves as a breeze blows gently through the trees. Inhale the woody aroma. Feel the warmth and the strength of the spirit of the tree as it becomes a part of your energy.

Now, summon the spirit guide of the wood element, the tiger. Feel the presence of the tiger as she approaches you. Inhale the strength of the tiger's energy into your abdomen. The tiger is telling you to look up at the sky and see a beautiful sunset. As the sky darkens, begin to see the planet Jupiter. Inhale the wisdom of Jupiter and feel it cleansing your soul.

Play new age music for 1 minute.

As you continue to walk through the rainforest, you come to a clearing. There is a campfire in the middle of the clearing. Feel the warmth of the fire and see the orange and red flames. Inhale the love and joy of the flames glowing in your heart. Feel the excitement as the spirit of the fire becomes a part of your soul. Now, summon the spirit guide of the fire element, the horse. See a beautiful, golden horse coming towards you, his mane dancing in the firelight. Feel the presence of the horse as he approaches you. Inhale the love of the horse energy into your heart. The golden horse is telling you to look up and see the planet Mars. Inhale the wisdom of Mars, and feel it opening your heart.

Play new age music for 1 minute.

Leaving the clearing and going deeper into the woods, notice the soft, warm, moist earth beneath your bare feet. Hear the sounds of birds singing. Smell the sweet, fragrant blossoms of the rainforest flowers. The air is becoming thick with a warm mist and the earth's aromas. Inhale the earth scent, drawing its power into your stomach. Now, summon the spirit guide of the earth element, the bear. Feel the presence of the bear as she approaches you. Inhale the nurturing of the bear's spirit, deep within your belly. The bear is telling you to look up and see the planet Saturn. Inhale the wisdom of Saturn, and feel it nourishing your essence.

Play new age music for 1 minute.

Continuing to go even deeper into the rainforest, you come to a cave. Notice the cool dry air and a metallic aroma. Entering the cave, going deeper and deeper, you notice a glimmer of light up ahead. Approaching the light, you see brilliant white diamonds sparkling in the rocks. Inhale the cool spirit of the diamonds deep into your lungs, feeling the white light of the diamond energy. Now, summon the spirit guide of the metal element, the dove. Look up and notice an opening in the ceiling of the cave. Feel the presence of the white dove as he approaches the opening.

Inhale the spirit of the dove's power of forgiveness deep within your lungs, allowing whatever sorrow you may feel to be released. The white dove is telling you to look up and see the planet Venus. Inhale peace and serenity from Venus, and feel it expanding within your lungs.

Play new age music for 1 minute.

Leaving the cave, go back to the cool night air of the rainforest. Off in the distance, hear the sound of a waterfall. Feel the cold wet air against your skin and face. Smell the salty air and inhale the mystic power of the blue water, deep down into the lower part of your abdomen. Now, summon the spirit guide of the water element, the turtle. Feel the presence of the turtle as she approaches you. Inhale the turtle's creative life force deep within your lower back. The turtle is telling you to look up and see the planet Mercury. Inhale the knowledge of your life's purpose from Mercury, and the power to pursue it.

Play new age music for 1 minute.

Thank each one of your spirit guides for their wisdom and healing energy.

Alright now. Sleep now and rest. You did very, very well. Listen very carefully. I'm going to count forward now from 1 to 5. When I reach the count of 5 you will be back in the present, you will be able to remember everything you experienced and reexperienced. You'll feel relaxed, refreshed and you'll be able to do whatever you have planned for the rest of the day or evening. You'll feel very positive about what you've experienced and very motivated about your confidence and ability to play this tape again, to experience your spirit guides. Alright now. One, very, very deep. Two, you're getting a little bit lighter. Three, you're getting much, much lighter. Four, very, very light. Five, awaken. Wide awake and refreshed.

CHAPTER 5

Channeling

When you mention to most people the concept of communicating with spirit guides, the term that most often surfaces is channeling. Channeling is defined as connecting with a spirit guide or your own Higher Self (the perfect component of your own soul's energy) and communicating this information verbally.

Some people consider channeling a bridge or link with the higher planes. Although your soul may not travel beyond the Soul plane until your energy is perfect, you can receive information from a high-level spirit guide at any time.

Channeling involves expanding your consciousness and achieving a trance state. When you have done this, you are now receptive to the guidance from these perfect entities. You now become a vehicle through which higher energies can direct you to facilitate your spiritual growth and that of others.

Without realizing it, you have channeled many times in your life. This experience is a result of moments of creativity, inner guidance, crisis, and times of inspiration. Your spirit guides were with you during these and other times in your life. They may not have revealed themselves to you, but a connection with the spiritual realms was made.

Think for a moment of episodes in your life when you were led in a certain direction that provided growth. It may have been a boost of energy when you needed it most. You may have had a great idea that manifested itself in reality as a positive experience or reward. This could have taken the form of a financial backing from an unexpected course for a project or a personal debt.

During channeling you steadily build up a connection with your spirit guide. This gives you a constant link with the higher planes and will result in more frequent and accurate experiences of inner guidance and intuitive insight.

This technique opens your soul up to receive love, the most important force in the universe. Love, for example, is the only message your guardian angels carry. You now can become more confident, powerful, assertive and empowered. An increase in your patience, understanding and compassion will be noted.

It is through channeling that you can learn what your karmic purpose is. In other words, why you are here. You will come to know the meaning of life, and how to globally assess your place in the universe.

You can learn to heal yourself and others through channeling. This method has been responsible for wisdom, philosophy, scientific discoveries, and great works of art. The first discipline you must develop to savor these benefits is to learn to trust your inner guidance and messages.

Do not expect channeling to solve all of your problems. You will only change, as a result of this method, in ways you want to change yourself. You are solely responsible for the actions necessary to make these changes a reality. Your growth lessons and opportunities will be accelerated by channeling.

Channeling will, most definitely, assist you in clarifying your karmic purpose. As a result of following this higher road, you may experience popularity, fame, and fortune. These will not have the same importance as before, so do not be concerned about your newfound abundance swaying you from your spiritual growth.

Always surround yourself with white light and clearly state that you only invite a high-level guide prior to channeling. Naturally, you do not want to attract troubled spirits or negative entities and you won't if you follow my recommendations.

In channeling, your consciousness does not leave the physical body. This is quite different than OBEs and teleportation methods that I will present in Chapter 6. All you are doing is making room, so to speak, in your physical body for another being to speak through you. You can terminate this process at any time.

Speaking in tongues, or *glossalalia*, is considered by the Catholic Church as a miraculous transient gift of speaking in foreign languages.

The word "tongue" is used in both the Old and New Testaments to mean language. This ability is identified with the ecstatic utterances of the Hellenistic religion and the phenomenon of ecstatic prophecy. According to Christian scholars this characteristic manifested the presence and power of the Holy Spirit. We can see from this summary that speaking in tongues represents a form of channeling.

Fear is the only obstacle to channeling. Empower yourself and let your desire for personal growth, healing, and any other worthwhile goal send out a strong signal to attract a high-level guide. When you master this technique, you will see results in your life that are beyond your wildest imagination. An accelerated level of psychic empowerment is one advantage of channeling. You can also help others by functioning as a vehicle for the dissemination of spiritual wisdom.

Absolutely anyone can learn to channel. Spirit guides will assist you throughout this process. All you need to do is open yourself up to receive love and the spiritual energy of a higher dimensional being. Channeling is something you do daily when you enter daydream states and other examples of self hypnosis. Here you are channeling the perfect energy of your Higher Self. That is particularly common when practicing the superconscious mind-tap exercise I presented in Chapter 4.

Receiving spiritual guidance during your dream states represents another form of channeling. When you acknowledge a sudden inspirational thought, intuition, or hunch, you are functioning as a conscious channel. All creative endeavors and inventive ideas result from channeling. People have been channeling since ancient times.

I cannot overemphasize the importance of developing the ability to access your Higher Self. My superconscious mind tap method is simple and quite powerful. It assists you in eliminating fear, protects you, sends out a strong signal to attract high-level guides and allows you to maximize this contact.

Your Higher Self functions as a screening agent and will see to it that only positive light beings become your channels. When it comes time to change the guide you are channeling to one more appropriate for your current level of spiritual development, your Higher Self will assist you in bringing in the new light being to speak through your physical body.

Another advantage of bringing the Higher Self into this equation is that your superconscious can more easily help you with expressing the guide's message and understanding its content.

Whatever you call these guides (ascended masters, archangels, light beings, spirit guides or other labels), each of us can establish a direct link with their energy and channel their essence without any harm or discomfort to our own essences or physical bodies.

Channeling requires patience and practice, not "special psychic abilities." One simple method to begin channeling is to simply relax yourself, access your Higher Self and request a high-level guide to communicate through you. I will present a detailed script of such a technique later on in this chapter.

It doesn't really matter which type of guide you desire to channel. The technique is identical; the difference is only in who you request. I provide detailed lists of the various types of guides to give you a menu from which to select. You are encouraged to read other books in the bibliography and other sources to expand this classification. The more you know about spirit guides, the easier it will be to request the light being most suited for your spiritual growth.

Later on, as you log in many channeling hours, the appropriate guides will come through your physical body when needed. They will come to you in more and expanded ways and *always* leave you feeling loved unconditionally. The more you shed your fears and acknowledge yourself as a spiritual being, the easier it will be to open yourself up to the wisdom and love available to you from spirit guides.

Here is a more advanced protection technique that you might want to use in your initial channeling sessions. This works to allay fears and affords you powerful spiritual protection. It is not necessary to practice with this method, but I provide it for those who feel additional protection is desirable:

Focus on your subconscious mind as a beam of light of average intensity is burrowing down into the Earth where it discovers a certain mineral. This mineral begins to glow, becoming radiant and brighter with brilliant white and colored lights as its components.

This mineral light now radiates warmth and enters the bottom of your feet, moves up your legs and continues rising up into your body permeating every fiber and cell.

Perceive this loving and healing light illuminating your entire body and surrounding it with a protective aura of white and colored lights. Feel this revitalizing energy from the mineral recharging your soul's core and removing all fears, energy blockages, and any unwanted energies from any source.

Finally see this example of the God energy shoot up out of the top of your head and showering your entire body and aura with protective light. Only your Masters and guides, Higher Self, and loving spiritually evolved entities can communicate with you in any way. You are totally protected and ready to act as a channel.

Channels and Mediums

Many people confuse mediums with channels. There is quite a difference between the information obtained from these disciplines. A medium functions as a channel for the soul of one who has recently died, or crossed into spirit. The information received from this less-than-perfect and often troubled being is usually of a personal nature for those left behind. It is an attempt to reconnect with the family and friends from its recent sojourn on the Physical plane.

Mediums receive information from a variety of spirits few of whom can be considered true spiritual guides. Psychic abilities such as clairvoyance, clairaudience, and others are often exhibited by the medium. The data received are meant for a limited audience.

Channeling, on the other hand, is characterized by the channeler functioning as the direct voice of a high-level guide. Rarely are psychic gifts, such as clairvoyance, demonstrated. In addition, many of the spirits channeled never lived on this planet.

Most commonly, there is only one personality who comes through on a regular basis. This entity attempts to teach to a wide audience. The information given is usually *not* of a personal nature and has the aura of great significance for societal and planetary growth, not merely for individual evolvement.

We can see classic examples of channeling in the late Jane Roberts's *Seth*. Seth claimed to have arisen as individual components of energy materialized within the Earth plane. He had past lives with Jane Roberts and her husband, Robert.

The Michael guide channeled by Jessica Lansing (a publicist who began channeling the Michael entity in October of 1970) stated it originated from the "mid-Causal plane" and was composed of a thousand fragments of a being like itself. Others state that they represent a "group form" residing in hyperspace or from other planets.

Most of the themes from channeled entities relates to our multidimensional universe existing as a living being and that love is its most important component. We are also taught that we create our own reality by way of our subconscious minds and fear is the only true obstacle to our ascensions.

We maintain a connection with God through the Higher Self and spirit guides. An eventual reuniting with the God energy complex is our destiny once we perfect our soul. Because each component of the universe, including our planet, is a living spiritual being, it behooves us to show proper respect in all parts of the world in which we live. What goes around comes around.

Be wary of channeling from entities who act in a materialistic, arrogant, and egotistical manner. These are the beings who most commonly forecast world cataclysms and urge you to give away your possessions, stockpile food and water, and pray for survival from Armageddon. Do not listen to these lower-level spirits. The future is brighter than you can possibly imagine at this time.

Qualities of a Good Channel

To be prepared to channel, certain characteristics should be a part of your personality. You may not possess all of these at this time. Those qualities that you do have may need more focus and development. I present these here so you can have a model to assist your own preparation to be an effective channel.

A good channeler is enthusiastic, willing, and dedicated to this discipline. He or she values truth, is independent, intelligent, intuitive and can easily recognize higher wisdom. This person is hard-working, sincere, kind, likes to daydream and have vivid imagination.

Another quality good channelers have is the tendency to see the potential in others, rather than who others currently are. They also have the innate ability to anticipate the needs of others. A very important quality they possess is the desire to help others.

One advantage reported by frequent channelers is a greater sense of stability in their lives. They feel more grounded and in charge of their world. You need not fear losing your identity or stability as a result of channeling.

What It Feels Like to Channel

When you are functioning as a channel, you are in a state of consciousness that allows you to receive communication from a spirit guide. Think of a time in your life when inspiration seemed to flow effortlessly. This is what channeling feels like.

You may have been counseling a family member or friend and found yourself saying things you hadn't originally planned to say. A moment of deep prayer or meditation, appreciating the beauty of nature or a child, and a sudden impulse to state something profound at an unexpected time are other examples of channeling.

The feeling of responding to an inner voice that appears to originate from a higher source than your normal thoughts is how a trance channeler feels during a reading. You notice subtle changes in your perception of the world around you. Answers to previously considered difficult questions now come easily.

Many people who routinely channel feel a warmth in their hands or an absence of some physical sensation. You may note a tingling at the top of your forehead (Third Eye region) or in your neck. Even the tone and rhythm of your voice may appear different; often it is deeper and slower.

While channeling, your attention is directed inward. This allows you to receive messages from the spiritual planes. At the same time it dulls your awareness toward thinking, worrying and other mundane activities. Sounds around you may even appear to be amplified.

Your mind is directed to a place, within just a few minutes, where you connect with a spirit guide in channeling. Meditation and self-hypnosis states take longer to achieve this effect. Channeling does not require a still and calm mind, as do self-hypnosis and meditation. Your spirit guide plays an important role in establishing and maintaining the state of channeling.

There are two main types of channels. The unconscious channels have no memory of the communication received from their spirit guide. The conscious channels remain partially or completely aware (conscious) of the messages given to them during a reading. Some of these conscious channels are unable to recall this communication an hour or so after this link to their spirit guides.

It is recommended to remain conscious during a channeling experience. This way you will recall everything (usually) that transpired. Another advantage to this approach is being aware of and surrounded by a richness of energy that is beyond words when experiencing the spirit guide's world and your own at the same time.

You will always raise your own soul's energy (frequency vibrational rate or fvr) when you remain conscious during a channeling session. Many images, sensations and emotions permeate your very being during a channeling. Sometimes symbols or wave patterns will be given to you that you must interpret. These are more commonly experienced when you ask your spirit guide the nature of reality or questions concerning God.

Receiving Messages From Spirit Guides

The process of channeling consists of receiving information from a higher being supervised by your Higher Self through your soul (subconscious) and finally to your conscious mind. You then translate these messages through words and concepts with which you are most familiar.

A flow and synchronization must be established between your right brain (intuitive) and left brain (analytical). This is done with less difficulty in a relaxed trance state, even if this is a very light trance. You are actually utilizing both hemispheres of your brain simultaneously during a channeling.

Telepathy, as we have discussed previously, is often chosen by a spirit guide as their mode of transmitting information. Other times metaphors, colors, and symbolic figures are used. Some guides discuss previous lifetimes, others are philosophical or poetic. A guide may choose to challenge you to find your own answers through a series of questions directed at you. This spiritual being may discuss the higher truths in the universe or initiate a discourse about your soul's purpose.

The vocabulary you possess will often attract a certain type of spirit guide. Artistic guides prefer to deal with artists, scientific guides find scientists, and so on. Spirit guides select the method that will get their messages across to you in the simplest fashion. It will often be in a form that seems most natural to you.

Practice will increase the chances of your guide's message coming in clearly. Your own spiritual growth and consciousness expansion will assist you in becoming a better channel. Accessing your own Higher Self is the fastest way I know to achieve this.

You may have, in the past, been exposed to a trance channeler or medium. There are several types of these individuals. *Clairvoyant* ("clear seeing") mediums actually visually detect a spirit guide but cannot hear this entity. These psychics are able to "see" within the body and diagnose disease. This form of *medical clairvoyant* was best illustrated by the late Edgar Cayce. Cayce was one of the world's most influential and best-known phychics and soul healers, possessing the remarkable innate ability, while he was in a hypnotic trance, to medically diagnose individuals he had never even met. I describe his work in detail in my book *Soul Healing*.

Some psychics have the capability of observing the contents of closed safes, boxes and rooms physically blocked from their current vision. We call this *X-ray clairvoyance*. Also included in this category is the ability to see into the past (*retrognition*) and future (*precognition*). *Psychometry* (being able to tell the history of an object by simply touching or hold it) and crystal gazing (*scrying*) are additional clairvoyant gifts.

When a medium can hear what is being communicated by a guide but cannot see them, we use the term *clairaudience* ("clear hearing"). This type of psychic actually hears sounds and voices from other dimensions.

Mediums are *clairsentient* ("clear sensing") when they receive spirit contact through their other senses, such as taste, touch, smell, and their emotions. A "feeling" that a spirit guide was Greek is an example of this mechanism. A clairsentient might feel the pain of sorrow experienced by a spirit, or the bliss of a high-level guide. This psychic may also feel hot, cold, or any other sensation.

Last, physical mediums create physical evidence of their spirit communication. They have been known to produce a substance called *ectoplasm* (a whitish substance that emanates from the medium's mouth during a channeling), rappings, knocks, or other physical phenomena.

The most important quality a medium or channeler must develop is their ability to concentrate on one thing at a time for several minutes without becoming distracted. Spirit guides inform us that the psychic center for all of these other worldly talents is situated at the position of the Third Eye—between and slightly above the two eyebrows. That is why I presented an exercise to activate the Third Eye in Chapter 3.

Inviting Communication With a Spirit Guide

Spirit communication by way of channeling is unique and this contact may be initiated in one of several ways. You may have your first experience supervised by a high-level guide, or make this connection through your own individual efforts. It is always easiest to make these contacts through the use of cassette tapes, and I encourage you to make tapes of the scripts I present. You may also contact my office for a list of tapes professionally recorded by me (see page 254).

One of the first signs you will notice when you successfully channel a guide is a difference in their vibratory presence. You will actually sense the vibrations of a spirit guide, and it will be significantly different from your own. These guides normally exhibit a vibration beyond your normal range of perception, but adjust their fvr to be within our range of detection. At first it may take awhile for you to distinguish between yourself and your guide. You may notice subtle changes in your body, in your posture, or in your breathing. You may observe a subtle change in the rhythm, speed, or pattern of your voice, or other variations in your being.

You must bear in mind that this link between your guide and you becomes stronger with each succeeding contact. At times you may not see or hear this being of light, but detect colors, lights, or fragrances. It is not uncommon for you to enter into an altered state of consciousness (ASC) and exhibit an OBE.

I have previously discussed the importance of focused concentration in preparing you for this communication. The exercises presented in Chapter 3 should be mastered before going on with this experience. It is critical that you eliminate as much distracting thoughts as possible and develop a state of "inner listening."

Initially the data you receive during a channeling session may appear just out of your reach. When that happens simply ignore it and allow further communication to be established. Your guide will see to it that you receive any concept or instruction that your guide feels will assist your spiritual growth. You will always feel uplifted and positive as a result of these sessions.

Do not be surprised if your ego (defense mechanism) tries to disrupt this process. Doubts may arise, or you may find yourself analyzing the data you receive. In the beginning your guide will assist you in developing a state of heightened awareness. Through a trial-and-error mechanism your guide will fine tune a procedure compatible with you that will permit this transmission with the highest level of clarity.

This entire process can be facilitated by your developing a mindset of feeling comfortable and at ease with your spirit guide. The greater the significance of the guide's message to you, the better the spiritual link. This level of harmony and oneness with your guide is never dangerous (white light protection techniques assures this), and allows you to comprehend things about yourself that you may never have contemplated.

It is not uncommon to respond with a sense of familiarity to these experiences and wonder why you never considered them before. I highly suggest that you not look for hidden, disguised, obscure, vague, or cryptic messages. Guidance from these entities may present themselves as a visualization, inner message, an energy level change, or other sensation.

From the guide's universe there is no past, present or future per se. Your guide is always present and will respond to your request for a communication. It is natural to question whether you are contacting your Higher Self or a guide. This is a good question because all channeling is transmitted through your soul (subconscious) in the presence of your Higher Self. Your mind (right brain) receives these messages by way of your soul and that is one reason why these experiences seem so familiar. Our dreams, intuition, and other psychic manifestations are often the presentation of spirit guides.

There is no test to determine the true source of this contact. All you will note is a knowingness concerning the origin of the messages you receive. You must remember that your Higher Self is perfect and its wisdom can be as profound and enlightening as that of any high-level guide.

Some people use the principle of obtaining a guide's name to differentiate between contact originating from their Higher Self or a spirit guide. This may or may not work. Spirit guides identify each other by energy patterns, and coming up with a name is not so easy. They could give you one of their names from a previous life on Earth, or none at all. Quite simply, do not attach much significance to establishing the name of your guide, especially in the early stages of your channeling.

There are certain times when you should refrain from channeling. For instance, when you are in an emotional or physical crisis, physically exhausted, or chronically depressed, it is best to establish a balance in your mind-body relationship prior to channeling. Reserve spirit contact for times when you are healthy, well rested, and positive. This will assure a better connection with your guide and it will maximize any subsequent benefits from this communication.

Before I present a channeling exercise, let me summarize the mechanism of spirit guide contact.

The easiest way to understand channeling is to think of a radio station signal. That signal or frequency is actually electromagnetic radiation, identical to your soul. If you are trying to receive a certain radio station, by adjusting the dial you can separate two competing signals so that one comes in more clearly.

This is how we can establish a communication with a spirit guide. There are many signals (spirit guides) in the Astral plane and beyond. By fine tuning your psychic abilities (the dial in my analogy), you can receive the signal (spirit guide) that you are looking for, or that wants to communicate with you.

It is during the dream (REM) cycle at night that most of this contact is made. The techniques presented in this book are designed to assist you in establishing this communication during normal waking hours.

Sleep is a natural state of mind for channeling. We tune in to our subconscious and superconscious minds as part of the process of dreaming, which occurs three hours every night.

Daydreams are simply waking levels of natural trance states. During this state you are relaxed, focused, more creative, and less aware of the passing of each moment of time. These altered states of consciousness are when most of your insights, creative inspirations, and problem-solving talents surface. You are also more balanced and centered at this time.

Automatic Writing

We can channel spirit guides through a technique known as automatic writing. This method consists of one-hand writing information that has nothing to do with our conscious mind thoughts. In other words, you could be watching television, listening to music, or engaged in a conversation with someone, and these distractions will in no way affect your automatic writing.

In order to do this exercise, place a writing tablet with blank paper in front of you and a pen or pencil in your normal writing hand. Hold the pen or pencil directly over the paper as if you were about to write a letter:

Take a deep breath...fill your chest...and hold it until I tell you to "Let go."

Now I want you to notice the tension in your chest muscles...and the tension in your shoulders and upper arms. And I want you to pay particular attention to how...the moment I say "Let go"...all that tension disappears immediately...and you tend to sag limply down into the chair. Now...Let go.

I am going to count slowly up to 5... and as I do so...you will take five very deep breaths. One, very, very deep. Two, you're getting a little bit lighter. Three, you're getting much, much lighter. Four, very, very light. Five, awaken. Wide awake and refreshed.

And with each deep breath that you take...each time you breathe out...you will become more and more relaxed...and your trance will become deeper and deeper...breathe deeply...more and more deeply relaxed...deeper and deeper into relaxation...breathe deeper...deeper and deeper relaxed...becoming deeper and deeper in hypnosis... breathing even more deeply...more and more deeply relaxed...more and more deeply relaxed...very, very deep breath...deeper and deeper relaxed...your trance depth is becoming even deeper and deeper...very, very deep breath...very, very deeply relaxed...very, very deeply relaxed.

Once again...I want you to take one very deep breath...fill your chest...and hold it until I say... Let go.

Then...let your breath out as quickly as possible...and as you do so...you will become twice as deeply relaxed as you are now...twice as deeply relaxed. Now, take that very deep breath...fill your chest...hold it...(15-second pause)...hold it...(15-second pause)...hold it...(20- to 30-second pause) Let go.

Now listen very carefully. I want you to imagine a bright white light coming down from above and entering the top of your head, filling your entire body. See it, feel it, and it becomes reality. Now imagine an aura of pure white light emanating from your heart region, again surrounding your entire body, protecting you. See it, feel it, and it becomes reality. Now only your Higher Self, masters and guides, and highly evolved loving entities who mean you well will be able to influence you during this or any other hypnotic session. You are totally protected by this aura of pure white light.

In a few moments, I am going to count from 1 to 20. As I do so you will feel yourself rising up to the superconscious mind level where you will be able to channel information from your Higher Self and Masters and guides. One, rising up. Two, 3, 4, rising higher. Five, 6, 7, letting information flow. Eight, 9, 10, you are halfway there. Eleven, 12, 13, feel yourself rising even higher. Fourteen, 15, 16, almost there. Seventeen, 18, 19, and 20. Now you are there. Take a moment and orient yourself to the superconscious mind level.

Play new age music for 1 minute.

You are now in a deep hypnotic trance and from this superconscious mind level, you are in complete control and able to access this limitless power of your superconscious mind. I want you to be open and flow with this experience. You are always protected by the white light.

At this time I would like you to ask your Higher Self to assist you in attracting a spirit guide to enter your consciousness and communicate with you through automatic writing. Trust your Higher Self and your own ability to allow any thoughts, feelings, or impressions to come into your subconscious mind from a spirit guide.

Now clear your mind and breathe deeply. Soon you will feel your hand move. Do not focus on this action. Under no circumstances attempt to use your conscious mind to direct this hand. Let this process continue.

Play new age music for 6 minutes.

Alright now. Sleep now and rest. You have done very well. Listen very carefully. I'm going to count forward now from 1 to 5. When I reach the count of 5 you will be able to remember everything you experienced and reexperienced. You'll feel very relaxed, refreshed and you'll be able to do whatever you have planned for the rest of the day or evening. You'll feel very positive about what you've experienced and very motivated about your confidence and ability to play this tape again, to experience automatic writing and spirit guide channeling. Alright now. One, very, very deep. Two, you're getting a little bit lighter. Three, you're getting much, much lighter. Four, very, very light. Five, awaken. Wide awake and refreshed.

This exercise should be terminated when your hand containing the pen or pencil stops moving. Do not become discouraged if you are not successful the first few times you try this technique. Your ability to concentrate and relax greatly affect the results of automatic writing and any alpha method. Remember how to get to Carnegie Hall: practice, practice, practice.

Automatic writing has been used by spiritualists for centuries to communicate with departed souls and spirit guides. Many writers, artists, and scientists have utilized automatic writing for inspiration and ideas.

A Channeling Exercise

The following exercise will allow you to relax yourself and prepare for any channeling, meditative, or self-hypnosis experience:

Lie down comfortably, close your eyes and begin to relax. Allow yourself to become more and more relaxed. Breathe very deeply and send a warm feeling into your toes and feet. Let this feeling break up any strain or tension and as you exhale let the tension drain away. Breathe deeply and send this warm feeling into your ankles. It will break up any strain or tension and as you exhale let the tension drain away. Breathe deeply and send this feeling into your knees, let it break up any strain or tensions there and as you exhale let the tension drain away. Send this warm sensation into your thighs so any strain or tension is draining away. Breathe deeply and send this warm feeling into your genitals and drain away any tension.

Send this warm feeling into your abdomen now; all your internal organs are soothed and relaxed and any strain or tension is draining away. Let this energy flow into your chest and breast; let it soothe you and as you exhale any tension is draining away. Send this energy into your back now. This feeling is breaking up any strain or tension and as you exhale the tension is draining away. The deep relaxing energy is flowing through your back, into each vertebra as each vertebra assumes its proper alignment. The healing energy is flowing into all your muscles and tendons and you are relaxed, very fully relaxed. Send this energy into your shoulders and neck; this energy is breaking up any strain or tension and as you exhale the tension is draining away. Your shoulders and neck are fully relaxed. And the deep relaxing energy is flowing into your arms; your upper arms, your elbows, your forearms, your wrists, your hands, your fingers are fully relaxed.

Let this relaxing energy wash up over your throat, and your lips, your jaw, your cheeks are fully relaxed. Send this energy into your face, the muscles around your eyes, your forehead, your scalp are relaxed. Any strain or tension is draining away. You are relaxed, most completely relaxed.

Now, listen very carefully. I want you to imagine a bright white light coming down from above and entering the top of your head, filling your entire body. See it, feel it, and it becomes reality. Now imagine an aura of pure white light emanating from your heart region, again surrounding your entire body, protecting you. See it, feel it, and it becomes reality. Now only your Higher Self, Masters and guides, and highly evolved loving entities who mean you well will be able to influence you during this or any other hypnotic session. You are totally protected by this aura of pure white light.

In a few moments, I am going to count from 1 to 20. As I do so you will feel yourself rising up to the superconscious mind level where you will be able to receive information from your Higher Self and Masters and guides. One, rising up. Two, 3, 4, rising higher. Five, 6, 7, letting information flow. Eight, 9, 10, you are halfway there. Eleven, 12, 13, feel yourself rising even higher. Fourteen , 15, 16, almost there. Seventeen, 18, 19, and 20. Now you are there. Take a moment and orient yourself to the superconscious mind level.

Play new age music for 1 minute.

You are now in a deep hypnotic trance and from this superconscious mind level, you are in complete control and able to access this limitless power of your superconscious mind. I want you to be open and flow with this experience. You are always protected by the white light.

At this time I would like you to ask your Higher Self to assist you in attracting a high-level spirit guide for the purpose of allowing this entity to channel its wisdom and healing energy through your physical body. At all times you will be perfectly safe and surrounded by the white light of the Higher Self. Trust your Higher Self and your own ability to allow any thoughts, feelings or impressions to come into your subconscious mind concerning this high-level guide.

Now imagine a doorway in front of you that leads to the location of your guide. Slowly walk through this doorway and sense the beauty and love in this realm.

Raise your frequency to its highest level with the assistance of your Higher Self and request the presence of your guide. Feel the love and see its light as it approaches you.

Now ask your guide to assist you in preparing your physical body to channel. Tell this being of light that you are committed to serve the universe and wish to have him or her speak verbally through you.

Now imagine a beam of light connecting your throat to that of the guide. Open up your throat chakra and receive the light energy of your guide.

Make any adjustments to your soul's energy with the help of your Higher Self to facilitate this connection.

At this time allow your guide to enter your aura and speak through you. Ask your guide to assist you in this goal and feel its presence getting stronger and stronger.

Now allow your guide to enter completely within your aura. Ask this spirit any questions you may have telepathically, or just let it speak through you.

Play new age music for 6 minutes.

You have done very well. Now I want you to further open up the channels of communications with your guide.

Allow yourself to receive more advanced and more specific information from this being to raise your frequency and improve your karmic subcycle. Do this now.

Play new age music for 4 minutes.

Thank your guide and ask him or her to strengthen the connection between you both, so it will be easier to channel this spirit again.

Alright now. Sleep now and rest. You did very, very well. Listen very carefully. I'm going to count forward now from 1 to 5. When I reach the count of 5 you will be back in the present, you will be able to remember everything you experienced and reexperienced. You'll feel very relaxed, refreshed, and you'll be able to do whatever you have planned for the rest of the day or evening. You'll feel very positive about what you've experienced and very motivated about your confidence and ability to play this tape again, to experience your spirit guide, and function as a channel. Alright now. One, very, very deep. Two, you're getting a little bit lighter. Three, you're getting much, much lighter. Four, very, very light. Five, awaken. Wide awake and refreshed.

If you are unsure as to how to ask questions or what to ask, see the last exercise at the end of Chapter 6.

Channeling brings you into contact with high-level spirit guides and your Higher Self. One result of this communication and experience is an acceleration in your growth and psychic empowerment. Your channeled beings will assist you in bringing more confidence, awareness of your karmic purpose and joy into your life. These changes are often slow and cumulative, so be patient.

Another advantage of channeling is that it provides you with still another tool to search the universe and deep within your own consciousness to find answers. Do not expect channeling to immediately solve your problems without requiring any effort on your part.

You are still responsible for your growth and dealing with the world in which you live. Channeling never violates the free will universal law. It simply provides you with an opportunity to work out your karma and add quality to the universe with easy joy and love, rather than frustration, disappointment and struggle.

Do not ask guides for lottery numbers, stock picks, football scores, and the like. These light beings have no interest in such materialism and work only with those who are motivated to use their wisdom for spiritual growth. Let us not forget that your abundance will increase as you follow your spiritual path. I refer to this as *karmic capitalism*.

It is advisable to concentrate on establishing a link with high-level guides with your channeling efforts, rather than developing your psychic abilities. Refer back to my comparison of mediums and channelers (page 133).

As you channel your guide may be replaced by another light being. This is done to afford you the expertise of a specialist or one that is more compatible with your level of growth. Several guides representing different areas of expertise may be channeled through you. This is less common but still possible.

Spirit guides being channeled are interested in bringing a higher consciousness to our planet. They may affect healing through your physical body. If this occurs you will grow even more spiritually. Channeling assists you in becoming more grounded, more centered, and more able to deal effectively with your daily life.

You are in no danger of losing your personal identity when channeling, as long as you practice the grounding and protection techniques presented throughout this book. What you are more likely to notice is a greatly improved self-image and an ability to define your personal boundaries with others more easily than ever before. You will know yourself as a more powerful, balanced, clear-thinking person while these guides are with you.

By expressing an interest in metaphysics, reading books on this discipline, attending seminars and workshops and discussing this topic with those close to you, a clear signal is being sent to the spirit realm to bring an appropriate guide to you for channeling. All you need do now is set aside practice time regularly and continue living a good, moral life filled with love and sharing. An inner voice will direct you to a spirit guide to assist you with your growth.

The contact you eventually establish with your guide as a channel may take place gradually. This light being most often comes to you in your dream state. Another method they use is to direct you to a certain book or movie or connect you with a like-minded soul on a similar path.

You may experience a desire to make new friends, engage in certain hobbies, and become motivated to expand your consciousness in an upward direction. Certain "coincidences" (actually synchronicities, or meaningful occurrences without apparent cause) become evident in your life. For example, you may be browsing in your local bookstore and a book on spirit guide contact just happens to fall from the shelf right in front of you.

Do not be surprised to find yourself knowing things that you didn't know before. This is often due to connecting with other dimensions. In addition to contacting your guides in dreams, metaphysical disciplines such as astrology, numerology, tarot card, Runes, and the like introduce them to you.

You have an innate ability to contact spirit guides and connect directly with them in moments of inspiration, inner guidance, and creativity. An advanced form of inner wisdom and knowingness will be seen as the higher vibration from this spirit flows through your very essence.

One goal of your guide is to foster your own ability to become more confident and independent, while projecting love, compassion, and understanding: a true child of the universe.

Channeling your guide will assist you in finding answers to everything from mundane everyday issues to the most challenging spiritual questions. You can use channeling for healing, teaching, and expanding your creativity in all areas of your life. You can bring through great knowledge, wisdom, inventions, works of art, philosophy, poetry, and discoveries of all kinds.

Although channeling will not assure you fame or love from others, it will increase your understanding of others in a more compassionate way. You will undoubtedly place yourself more directly on a spiritual path and may, indeed, experience fame, recognition, and popularity. These now will not have the same importance as before.

Spirit guides are mostly interested in people who have spiritual interests, perseverance, and enthusiasm to serve mankind. They expect you to also take your commitment to this work seriously.

The experience of channeling is different for each of us. Some feel as if they had fallen asleep and have no memories at all of what information they received. These states are referred to as *unconscious channeling.*

Conscious channelers remember much, if not all, of the communication from their guides. For these receivers it is like a dream, because the memory fades quickly if not reviewed immediately. Most fall somewhere between these two modes of channeling. To increase the likelihood of remaining conscious during your channeling, get plenty of rest and eat a light meal prior to establishing communication with your guide.

Do not be alarmed if you feel somewhat disassociated throughout your experience. I include self-hypnosis exercises to prepare you for this state for that very reason. This characteristic of viewing your world from both the perspective of your guide and your own is a form of dual consciousness that will be covered in greater detail in Chapter 6.

Oftentimes you will sense images, feelings, or thoughts from your own consciousness at the same time you receive those from your guide. This is perfectly natural, so do not concern yourself with it. There are no right or wrong ways to channel. Just go along with the flow. Remember, we often observe channeling in our lives as insights, inspirational thoughts, creative ideas, and guidance in any form.

CHAPTER 6

◎②◎②◎②◎②◎②◎②◎

Advanced Hypnotic Techniques
for Contacting Spirit Guides

Telepathy

Spirit guides communicate with us by telepathy. In order for us to receive a guide's message, this communication must be encoded from the energy of the spiritual being's dimension to that of ours. Whether we receive their telepathic message as visual imagery, symbols, or inner thoughts, some form of translation is required before our physical brain can understand this data.

Many view telepathy as a phenomenon in which thought is transmitted as energy. We, as receivers, must somehow decipher this energy frequency so that our brain can make sense of it. Regardless of the mechanism of telepathy, it is a most psychically empowering experience that can enlighten us and give evidence to the concept of the permanence of the soul, also a form of electromagnetic radiation energy.

The following exercises will train you in telepathic communication. This skill will come in handy when you meet a spirit guide. When you have mastered this technique, a signal is sent out into the spirit guide's realm and this entity is now more likely to communicate with you so that you will recall this contact.

This first exercise is practiced when you are alone and relaxed:

Take a deep breath...fill your chest...and hold it until I tell you to "Let go."

Now I want you to notice the tension in your chest muscles...the tension in your shoulders and upper arms. And I want you to pay particular attention to how...the moment I say "Let go"...all that tension disappears immediately...and you tend to sag limply down into the chair. Now...Let go.

I am going to count slowly up to five...and as I do so...you will take five very deep breaths.

And with each deep breath that you take...each time you breathe out...you will become more and more relaxed...and your trance will become deeper and deeper.

One...breathe deeply...more and more deeply relaxed...deeper and deeper into relaxation.

Two...breathe deeper...deeper and deeper relaxed...becoming deeper and deeper in hypnosis.

Three...breathing even more deeply...more and more deeply relaxed...more and more deeply relaxed.

Four...very, very deep breath...deeper and deeper relaxed...your trance depth is becoming even deeper and deeper.

Five...very, very deep breath...very, very deeply relaxed...very, very deeply relaxed.

Once again...I want you to take one very deep breath...fill your chest...and hold it until I say..."Let go."

Then...let your breath out as quickly as possible...and as you do so...you will feel yourself sagging limply back into the chair...and you will become twice as deeply relaxed as you are now...twice as deeply relaxed. Now, take that very deep breath...fill your chest...hold it...(15-second pause)...hold it...(15-second pause)...hold it...(20- to 30-second pause)...Let go.

Now I want you to create a message you would like to send to a friend or loved one. Simplify this message into one or two sentences and focus all of your attention on this telepathic data and the person to whom you are transmitting it.

Create a mental image of this receiver. If necessary, gaze at a photo of that person. Add some visual imagery to your message as you concentrate on this information and this person mentally receiving it.

As you create this imagery, intensely focus all of your concentration first on the message, next on the related visualizations and finally on the person successfully receiving this communication.

Play new age music for 4 minutes.

Alright now. Sleep now and rest. You did very, very well. Listen very carefully. I'm going to count forward now from 1 to 5. When I reach the count of 5 you will be back in the present, you will be able to remember everything you experienced and reexperienced. You'll feel very relaxed, refreshed, and you'll be able to do whatever you have planned for the rest of the day or evening. You'll feel very positive about what you've experienced and very motivated about your confidence and ability to play this tape again, to experience telepathy. Alright now. One, very, very deep. Two, you're getting a little bit lighter. Three, you're getting much, much lighter. Four, very, very light. Five, awaken. Wide awake and refreshed.

For this next exercise you will practice receiving telepathic communication from a friend or loved one. It is ideal to have the same person you used in the previous exercise play the role of telepathic sender. Ask this individual to practice with the previous exercise while you focus on receiving that person's message.

Take a deep breath...fill your chest...and hold it until I tell you to "Let go."

Now I want you to notice the tension in your chest muscles...the tension in your shoulders and upper arms. And I want you to pay particular attention to how...the moment I say "Let go"...all that tension disappears immediately...and you tend to sag limply down into the chair. Now...Let go.

I am going to count slowly up to five...and as I do so...you will take five very deep breaths. One, very, very deep. Two, you're getting a little bit lighter. Three, you're getting much, much lighter. Four, very, very light. Five, awaken. Wide awake and refreshed.

And with each deep breath that you take...each time you breathe out...you will become more and more relaxed...and your trance will become deeper and deeper...breathe deeply...more and more deeply relaxed...deeper and deeper into relaxation...breathe deeper...deeper and deeper relaxed...becoming deeper and deeper in hypnosis...breathing even more deeply...more and more deeply relaxed...more and more deeply relaxed...very, very deep breath...deeper and deeper relaxed...your trance depth is becoming ever deeper and deeper...very, very deep breath...very, very deeply relaxed...very, very deeply relaxed.

Once again...I want you to take one very deep breath...fill your chest...and hold it until I say...let go.

Then...let your breath out as quickly as possible...and as you do so...you will feel yourself sagging limply back into the chair...and you will become twice as deeply relaxed as you are now...twice as deeply relaxed. Now, take that very deep breath...fill your chest...hold it...(15-second pause)...hold it...(15-second pause)...hold it (20- to 30-second pause) Let go.

Imagine a television screen or movie screen in your mind's eye. Now visualize the sender of this telepathic message onto your mental screen and focus all of your concentration on this person.

Remain totally receptive to receiving this message, as in a few moments words that represent the sender's message will appear on this mental screen. Be patient as you allow this entire message to be spelled out onto your mental screen, in your mind's eye.

Play new age music for 4 minutes.

Alright now. Sleep now and rest. You did very, very well. Listen very carefully. I'm going to count forward now from 1 to 5. When I reach the count of five you will be back in the present, you will be able to remember everything you experienced and reexperienced. You'll feel very relaxed, refreshed, and you'll be able to do whatever you have planned for the rest of the day or evening. You'll feel very positive about what you've experienced and very motivated about your confidence and ability to play this tape again, to experience telepathy. Alright now. One, very, very deep. Two, you're getting a little bit lighter. Three, you're getting much, much lighter. Four, very very light. Five, awaken. Wide awake and refreshed.

Precognition

One of the many advantages of spirit guide contact is receiving information about the future. We use the term *precognition* to describe awareness of future events before they occur in the Physical plane. This principle is commonly seen as intuition and hunches. I use the term *age progression* to describe this phenomenon.

This simple exercise will train you to master the technique of seeing into the future:

Now listen very carefully. I want you to imagine a bright white light coming down from above and entering the top of your head, filling your entire body. See it, feel it, and it becomes reality. Now imagine an aura of pure white light emanating from your heart region, again surrounding your entire body, protecting you. See it, feel it, and it becomes reality. Now only your Higher Self, Masters and guides and highly evolved loving entities who mean you well will be able to influence you during this or any other hypnotic session. You are totally protected by this aura of pure white light.

In a few moments, I am going to count from 1 to 20. As I do so you will feel yourself rising up to the superconscious mind level where you will be able to receive information from your Higher Self and masters and guides. One, rising up. Two, three, four, rising higher. Five, six, seven, letting information flow. Eight, nine, 10, you are halfway there. Eleven, 12, 13, feel yourself rising even higher. Fourteen, 15, 16, almost there. Seventeen, 18, 19, and 20. You are there. Take a moment and orient yourself to the superconscious mind level.

Play new age music for 1 minute.

I would like you to create a mental screen, such as on a television set or movie screen, within your mind to project events from the future.

Select a topic or situation that will occur in the near future and that excites you. An example would be a newspaper headline you imagine yourself reading.

Using your mental screen, visualize your entire day during which this event will occur. Imagine yourself showering, eating breakfast, working, and so on. Carry this imagery to the end of the day.

For example, see yourself buying a newspaper on the way home from work or an errand. Now visualize yourself sitting down and reading the headline.

Play new age music for 4 minutes.

Alright now. Sleep now and rest. You did very, very well. Listen very carefully. I'm going to count forward now from 1 to 5. When I reach the count of 5 you will be back in the present, you will be able to remember everything you experienced and reexperienced. You'll feel very relaxed, refreshed and you'll be able to do whatever you have planned for the rest of the day or evening. You'll feel very positive about what you've experienced and very motivated about your confidence and ability to play this tape again to experience precognition. Alright now. One, very, very deep. Two, you're getting a little bit lighter. Three, you're getting much, much lighter. Four, very, very light. Five, awaken. Wide awake and refreshed.

Jot down your results in a journal. For other types of events try to place yourself in as real a situation as you can relative to the event and where you are likely to be.

Try this exercise several times. Choose more important situations as you become more proficient with this technique.

Probable Future Paths

The future is not etched in stone. In fact, the new physics demonstrates that there are an infinite number of parallel universes that exist alongside ours. Many refer to these parallel universes as probable futures, or paths in the multidimensional universe.

We all have the ability to create any path we so desire and select the ideal probable future through the use of our free will. Spirit guides often will not inform us about our future options until we are spiritually ready to handle that data in such a way as to enhance our growth.

For example, let us suppose that a relationship in which you are currently involved is destined to end on all probable futures. If your guide told you that now, you might choose to end it prematurely, thus denying yourself and the other person valuable learning opportunities. This is especially important if you shared past lives with that individual and had significant karmic lessons to master.

In the previous example a spirit guide is more likely to assist the individual in finding the higher purpose of this relationship and to develop the ability to trust his or her own judgment, rather than have it decided by outside beings.

If you totally want to change your current future path, you must change yourself. The future is determined to a great degree by your motives and actions. You can always better this path by undergoing spiritual growth.

From this spirit guide's perspective, this mechanism is far more complicated. They live in a world of simultaneous time in which all past, present, and future events are taking place now. We only observe events in the physical world step by step.

A spirit guide can overview all probable future paths and assist you in making appropriate choices. The problem occurs in seeing far into our future. It is easier for a guide to comment on a short-term future event because the number of probabilities are fewer. Each time we make a decision additional paths are created. Because the number of possibilities increases the further you look into the future, a far distant event is harder to predict because of these geometrically enhanced probable paths.

We must always consider our free will. Free will allows us to select one of many options, which, in turn, creates many other probable paths. Spirit guides view our future in two distinct ways. Our intentions produce a certain series of probable futures, while the actions we take form other options. The latter is easier to predict, but the former involves timing and this complicates the picture. By delaying taking a certain action, you can greatly alter its outcome. The reverse is also true.

Here is an exercise to determine probable futures and select your ideal path:

Now listen very carefully. I want you to imagine a bright white light coming down from above and entering the top of your head, filling your entire body. See it, feel it, and it becomes reality. Now imagine an aura of pure white light emanating from your heart region, again surrounding your entire body, protecting you. See it, feel it, and it becomes reality. Now only your Higher Self, masters and guides and highly evolved loving entities who mean you well will be able to influence you during this or any other hypnotic session. You are totally protected by this aura of pure white light.

In a few moments, I am going to count from 1 to 20. As I do so you will feel yourself rising up to the superconscious mind level where you will be able to receive information from your Higher Self and Masters and guides. One, rising up. Two, three, four, rising higher. Five, six, seven, letting information flow. Eight, nine, 10, you are halfway there. Eleven, 12, 13, feel yourself rising even higher. Fourteen, 15, 16, almost there. Seventeen, 18, 19, and 20. You are there. Take a moment and orient yourself to the superconscious mind level.

Play new age music for 1 minute.

Now I would like you to visualize a series of five doors, each with the word "future" printed on it in large bold letters. These doors are labeled Future 1 through 5.

Think of a situation or upcoming event you would like to explore. Gather the actual factors you currently have available on this circumstance and review them in your mind.

Now open the door labeled "Future 1" and perceive how this situation will unfold. Observe as many details as you can. Refrain from becoming emotionally involved with this option.

Play new age music for 3 minutes.

Repeat this procedure for the door labeled "Future 2," "Future 3," "Future 4," and "Future 5." Choose the door that best meets your needs and focus on the number of that door.

Play new age music for 3 minutes.

You have just created your own reality.

Alright now. Sleep now and rest. You have done very well. Listen very carefully. I'm going to count forward now from 1 to 5. When I reach the count of five you will be back in the present, you will be able to remember everything you experienced and reexperienced. You'll feel very relaxed, refreshed, and you'll be able to do whatever you have planned for the rest of the day or evening. You'll feel very positive about what you've experienced and very motivated about your confidence and ability to play this tape again, to experience precognition. Alright now. One, very, very deep. Two, you're getting a little bit lighter. Three, you're getting much, much lighter. Four, very, very light. Five, awaken. Wide awake and refreshed.

We can use precognition approaches to maximize contact with spirit guides. In addition, this skill prepares you for challenges and allows you to change these events or maximize experiences. You can avoid negative circumstances in life by taking advantage of this natural psychic ability. Precognition also offers the opportunity to solve problems. A third advantage of precognition is that it helps you to expand your psychic awareness and attract high-level spirit guides.

You can apply these techniques to empower yourself, not by manipulating or controlling the future, but by selecting a probable future path that will function to enhance your karmic purpose. The future represents probabilities, not predestined fate. Let your spirit guides assist you in custom designing your own destiny.

Out-of-Body Experiences

Sometimes spirit guides prefer that we meet them in their world on the upper Astral plane, or another component of the fifth dimension. We can facilitate contact with them by mastering the art of leaving the body. I refer to this as *astral voyaging*.

The following effects are commonly reported by those who are empowered enough to venture out of their physical body:

- Sensations of leaving and reentering the physical body.

- The experience of dual consciousness when near the physical body. Dual consciousness is being aware of both the physical and astral bodies at the same time.

- Colors are perceived more vividly, as are objects.

- Scenes of unexplainable beauty are noted. These are often unrelated to the physical environment.

- Feelings of "tuggings" at the back of the head when the OBE is too long in duration. This precedes the return to the physical body.

- The astral world is usually somewhat different from the physical world.

- The presence of the Higher Self, departed loved ones and spirit guides.

It is perfectly safe to leave the physical body. I have personally astral voyaged at least 1,000 times and have trained several thousand patients in this technique. Let us not forget that every night we leave the physical body for three hours during our nightly dream (REM) cycle.

During an OBE our consciousness, as represented by the soul, is disengaged from our physical body. This subconscious retains its powers as an independent and completely functional nonbiological being, much like a spirit guide. The difference lies in our lower level of spiritual evolution.

Our soul functioning in an astral body maintains a connection with its physical counterpart through a pulsating *silver cord*. This silver cord functions like an umbilical cord carrying energy originating from the Higher Self to our physical form. The most common connection observed is from the solar plexus of the physical body to the back of the astral head. Most astral voyagers do not detect this cord, because they would have to turn around to observe it. At the moment of death this silver cord is severed.

There is absolutely nothing to fear while astral voyaging, because our soul is under the continued protection afforded by our Higher Self (white light) and spirit guides. In working with over 11,000 patients I have *never* observed any form of harm resulting from an OBE.

All that is required to have an OBE is motivation for this experience and conscientious practice. You must overcome fear to leave the body and recall this adventure. There is absolutely no possibility of being stranded on the Astral plane, or other dimensions in which you may find yourself. You retain an awareness of the physical body, too, (*dual awareness*) and will immediately reunite with it if it is disturbed in any way.

To properly orient yourself to this new dimension (most commonly known as the Astral plane), remain still and focus in on any bright object in your environment. You can always return to the physical body immediately by simply thinking of blinking your eyes or moving one of your fingers.

By mastering OBEs you can:

◎ Erase negative karma and shorten the karmic cycle.

◎ Overcome the fear of death.

◎ Enjoy instant recall of your past lives.

◎ Call on spirit guides to assist you in your spiritual growth.

◎ Discover what happens to the soul between lifetimes.

◎ Obtain evidence that the world beyond is just another dimension of existence.

◎ Learn to assist others with their spiritual growth by channeling information from spirit guides.

◎ Establish better communication with your Higher Self.

Astral Sex

Another way in which a spirit guide can assist us is with astral sex. We all experience times of loneliness, frustration, and depression. Sex on the Astral plane can be very helpful in not merely providing us with a sexual outlet, but in improving our Physical plane relationships as well.

As I stated in *Astral Voyages:*

"The actual experience of sex in dream world with your dream lover is like nothing you have experienced on the Physical plane. First, your throat chakra expands and a tingly sensation is produced throughout your entire dream body.

"The next phase is a face-to-face position with your dream lover, lining up both of your now expanded throat chakras. What results is an exchange of light energy that is quite difficult to describe. As a white light descends over both of you, beams of light enter the chakras one by one. Each of these energy centers open wide to receive this onrushing energy. All blockages are eliminated and a complete purification of your dream body unfolds. Finally, your first chakra creates a sudden surge of Kundalini energy that rises like an oil well gushing through your own chakra.

"This results in a burst of energy encompassing the entire room. Your dream body quivers in response to this energy surge. Next, your dream lover moves closer to you until both of your bodies are touching. A whirlpool of light energy emanating from both of your crown chakras swirls around your bodies, which now function as one unit.

"Slowly, your astral lover moves away from you and decreases this energy flow. Soon you again regain your previous vibratory rate. He or she will most likely gently kiss you and disappear. Your physical body is likely to respond with a sensation of feeling completely energized and very stimulated to engage in Physical plane sex with your mate."

In order to facilitate your astral voyaging, here are some recommendations that will assure your success:

- ◎ Warm weather favors astral voyagers. Keep your room a few degrees above room temperature.

- ◎ Do not attempt astral projection during a thunderstorm. The weather should be dry and clear with high barometric pressure. Remember the sound of thunder is associated with the physical plane and will retard your OBE.

- ◎ Wear very loose clothing or none at all.

- ◎ Make your initial attempts in complete darkness, or in very dim light.

- ◎ Make sure there is dead silence.
- ◎ Practice alone.
- ◎ Time your trials late at night, right before you normally retire.
- ◎ Get yourself in a comfortable position. Lie on your right side for best results. Absolutely never lie on your left side. (The ancient Egyptians initiated this principle but never explained their rationale.)

One common complaint reported by novice astral voyagers is that of amnesia and paralysis just before leaving their physical body. Although these temporary effects are quite harmless, they do generate fear of OBEs. Fear is the one emotion that will block an OBE (as well as spiritual growth and spirit guide contact). This is easily prevented by practicing the superconscious mind tap I presented in Chapter 4. White light protection properly administered makes it practically impossible to experience amnesia or paralysis.

A simple yoga breathing exercise will prepare you for your initial controlled astral voyage. Try this method:

Lie down in a comfortable position. Establish a steady and rhythmic breathing pattern. Imagine your breath rising up the body through the bones of the legs and finally forced out of them.

Repeat this step but now focus on the bones of the arms, then the skull, the stomach and genitals. Visualize your breath rising up the backbone as you inhale, and descending down it as you exhale.

Now send your breath (as in the previous step) to your forehead, back of head, base of the brain, heart, solar plexus, navel region, and genitals.

Finally, exhale all of your breath from your lungs and relax.

Now try this single contemplation technique just before going to sleep:

1. Relax your entire body while lying in bed and rotate your eyeballs upward towards your Third Eye region of your forehead. This should cause a slight strain on the muscles surrounding the eyes.

2. Focus on an inner black screen and perceive only darkness. Do not drift off to sleep yet.

3. Listen for a faint high whistle in the top of your head, or any other unusual sounds. Create one if one does not occur by itself.

4. Imagine a tingling sensation spreading from your Third Eye region down throughout your physical body. Keep focusing on your black inner screen during this time. Request an audience with your spirit guide on another dimension as you do this.

5. Visualize this sound as part of a wave with luminous white color to it on your inner black screen. Watch this wave rise and carry your astral body with it resulting in a complete separation from its physical counterpart.

6. Now remove all thoughts and images of the inner black screen, and merely keep a vague awareness centered around your Third Eye region, and concentrate on the image of your guide, if you have seen it before.

Most commonly you will drift off to sleep following step 6 and find yourself out-of-the body in a lucid-dreamlike state of awareness. Repeat these steps several times if you experience your mind wandering. Focused concentration is a prerequisite for successful astral voyaging.

It is always recommended to focus on an actual location or guide prior to falling asleep. Being emotionally involved facilitates this process. Maintain a detailed image of your guide as you drift asleep. An imaginary image is less desirable, but better than no image at all.

This next exercise uses self-hypnosis to guide you out-of-the body:

Now listen very carefully. I want you to imagine a bright white light coming down from above and entering the top of your head, filling your entire body. See it, feel it, and it becomes reality. Now imagine an aura of pure white light emanating from your heart region, again surrounding your entire body, protecting you. See it, feel it, and it becomes reality. Now only your Higher Self, Masters and guides, and highly evolved loving entities who mean you well will be able to influence you during this or any other hypnotic session. You are totally protected by this aura of pure white light.

Let yourself relax completely...and breathe quietly...in...and out.

And as you do so...you will gradually sink into a deeper, deeper sleep.

And as you sink into this deeper, deeper sleep...I want you to concentrate on the sensations you can feel in your left hand and arm.

You will feel that your left hand is gradually becoming lighter and lighter.

It feels just as though your wrists were tied to a balloon...as if it were gradually being pulled up...higher and higher...away from the chair.

It wants to rise up...into the air...towards the ceiling.

Let it rise...higher and higher.

Just like a cork...floating on water.

And, as it floats up...into the air...your whole body feels more and more relaxed...heavier and heavier...and you are slowly sinking into a deeper, deeper sleep.

Your left hand feels even lighter and lighter.

Rising up into the air...as if it were being pulled up towards the ceiling.

Lighter and lighter...light as a feather.

Breathe deeply...and let yourself relax completely.

And as your hand gets lighter and lighter...and rises higher and higher into the air...your body is feeling heavier and heavier...and you are falling into a deep, deep sleep.

Now your whole arm, from the shoulder to the wrist, is becoming lighter and lighter.

It is leaving the chair...and floating upwards...into the air.

Up it comes...into the air...higher and higher.

Let it rise...higher and higher...higher and higher.

It is slowly floating up...into the air...and as it does so...you are falling into a deeper, deeper trance.

Recall a spiritually uplifting moment in your life. It may have been a feeling of reverence during a religious service or that you felt in a planetarium looking up at the stars. Ask your spirit guide to communicate with you at this time.

Visualize a floating sensation spreading throughout your entire body. Continue breathing deeply and feel your soul leaving your body through the top of your head, as it rises up beyond the Earth plane to the Astral plane.

Note the warm feeling now spreading and permeating throughout your entire body. Stay with this feeling for three minutes.

Experience a feeling of total love and peace. Let yourself immerse your complete awareness in a sense of balance and centering of your soul's energy. Again request contact with your spirit guide.

Play new age music for 4 minutes.

Alright now. Sleep now and rest. You did very, very well. Listen very carefully. I'm going to count forward now from 1-5. When I reach the count of 5 you will be back in the present, you will be able to remember everything you experienced and reexperienced. You'll feel very relaxed, refreshed and you'll be able to do whatever you have planned for the rest of the day or evening. You'll feel very positive about what you've experienced and very motivated about your confidence and ability to play this tape again, to experience astral voyaging. Alright now. One, very, very deep. Two, you're getting a little bit lighter. Three, you're getting much, much lighter. Four, very, very light. Five, awaken. Wide awake and refreshed.

A *body dissociation* occurs when you lose awareness of your physical body. This form of mental detachment is harmless, as are all of the exercises presented in this book. Practicing this approach will further condition you to experience astral voyaging:

Now listen very carefully. I want you to imagine a bright white light coming down from above and entering the top of your head, filling your entire body. See it, feel it, and it becomes reality. Now imagine an aura of pure white light emanating from your heart region, again surrounding your entire body, protecting you. See it, feel it, and it becomes reality. Now only your Higher Self, Masters and guides, and highly evolved loving entities who mean you well will be able to influence you during this or any other hypnotic session. You are totally protected by this aura of pure white light.

In a few moments, I am going to count from 1 to 20. As I do so you will feel yourself rising up to the superconscious mind level where you will be able to receive information from your Higher Self and masters and guides. One, rising up. Two, three, four, rising higher. Five, six, seven, letting information flow. Eight, nine, 10, you are halfway there. Eleven, 12, 13, feel yourself rising even higher. Fourteen, 15, 16, almost there. Seventeen, 18, 19, and 20. You are there. Take a moment and orient yourself to the superconscious mind level.

Play new age music for 1 minutes.

Visualize now a peaceful scene either real or imagined. Focus all of your concentration on this experience so that you feel all of the accompanying sensations of fulfillment and comfort in your body and mind. Exaggerate this feeling of peace and tranquility as you expand upon this perception. Allow yourself to feel happier and more blissful than you have ever felt.

Play new age music for 4 minutes.

Now focus on your right arm and observe how this arm is drifting further and further away from your body which is relaxing, releasing and letting go...Now notice that both your hands and arms feel far, far away from your body...Now your body is feeling as if it belongs to someone else, going further and further away. Now your head drifts away and you are left with your mind feeling tranquil and serene...Everything happening by itself. There is a feeling of coolness, stillness, and quiet. In the state of calmness, you feel free of agitation, unruffled, quiet and placid. Stay with this feeling of being completely detached from your physical body.

Play new age music for 4 minutes.

Alright now. Sleep now and rest. You did very, very well. Listen very carefully. I'm going to count forward now from 1 to 5. When I reach the count of 5 you will be back in the present, you will be able to remember everything you experienced and reexperienced. You'll feel very relaxed, refreshed and you'll be able to do whatever you have planned for the rest of the day or evening. You'll feel very positive about what you've experienced and very motivated about your confidence and ability to play this tape again, to experience body dissociation. Alright now. One, very, very deep. Two, you're getting a little bit lighter. Three, you're getting much, much lighter. Four, very, very light. Five, awaken. Wide awake and refreshed.

Here is a guide imagery approach to astral voyaging:

Now listen very carefully. I want you to imagine a bright white light coming down from above and entering the top of your head, filling your entire body. See it, feel it, and it becomes reality. Now imagine an aura of pure white light emanating from your heart region, again surrounding your entire body, protecting you. See it, feel it, and it becomes reality.

Now only your Higher Self, masters and guides, and highly evolved loving entities who mean you well will be able to influence you during this or any other hypnotic session. You are totally protected by this aura of pure white light.

In a few moments, I am going to count from 1 to 20. As I do so you will feel yourself rising up to the superconscious mind level where you will be able to receive information from your Higher Self and masters and guides. One, rising up. Two, 3, 4, rising higher. Five, 6, 7, letting information flow. Eight, nine, 10, you are halfway there. Eleven, 12, 13, feel yourself rising even higher. Fourteen, 15, 16, almost there. Seventten, 18, 19, and 20. You are there. Take a moment and orient yourself to the superconscious mind level.

Play new age music for 1 minute.

You are about to embark on an imaginary journey, during which your awareness will be introduced to perceptions that are quite different from anything you have encountered before.

You absolutely have the ability to voyage to the Astral plane or beyond.

Your silver cord will always remain attached to your physical body—protecting you and transmitting communication from your Higher Self to your subconscious.

Continued practice will ensure your success. Your voyages will only be to the upper Astral plane or beyond. There is no possibility of ending up on the lower Astral plane.

Your Higher Self and masters and guides are always with you, advising and protecting you. Only positive entities will be a part of this experience.

Now raise your vibrations spreading throughout your body from the bottom of the spine to the top of the head. Feel the vibrations accentuate this ascension. Do this now.

Play new age music for 2 minutes.

Your astral body is now separating itself from the physical. See yourself in your mind's eye leave your body through the top of your head. See it happening in your mind and feel it happening in your body.

See your astral body float just about your physical body. Now stand next to your physical body and observe it. Move out of this room and rise up into the air. Fly around your local area. Do this now.

Play new age music for 2 minutes.

Now continue rising up into the atmosphere as you venture on to a dimension of your choosing. For this first voyage select from one of the following:

- Upper Astral Plane.
- Causal Plane.
- Mental Plane.
- Etheric Plane.
- Soul Plane.

Explore this dimension at your leisure. On subsequent voyages you can select other planes to experience. Ask for the presence of one of your spirit guides to accompany you.

Play new age music for 3 minutes.

You've done very well. Now we're going to send your astral body to the upper Astral plane or beyond. If you would like to explore the Causal, Mental, Etheric or even the Soul plane, just concentrate on the name of this dimension.

As I count forward from one to 10, on the count of 10 you will arrive at your destination. One, 2, 3, moving toward this plane. Four, 5, halfway there. Six, 7, 8, almost there. Nine, 10, you are there.

Now begin exploring this dimension at your leisure. Record everything you see, hear, touch, taste, and feel in your subconscious, to be remembered later. Do this now.

Play new age music for 3 minutes.

Now begin your trip back to Earth by first entering a brilliant white light you now see before you. Descend back to your room and merge with your physical body. Note the warm feeling now spreading and permeating throughout your entire body. Stay with this feeling for a few moments.

Experience a feeling of total love and peace. Let yourself immerse your complete awareness in a sense of balance and centering of your soul's energy.

Stay with this feeling for a few more moments.

Play new age music for 2 minutes.

Alright now. Sleep now and rest. You did very, very well. Listen very carefully. I'm going to count forward now from I to 5. When I reach the count of five you will be able to remember everything you experienced. You'll feel very relaxed, refreshed, and you'll be able to do whatever you have planned for the rest of the day or evening. You'll feel very positive about what you've just experienced and very motivated about your confidence and ability to play this tape again, to voyage to other dimensions. Alright now. One, very, very deep. Two, you're getting a little bit lighter. Three, you're getting much, much lighter. Four, very, very light. Five, awaken. Wide awake and refreshed.

Here is another OBE self-hypnotic exercise to meet a spirit guide:

Now listen very carefully. I want you to imagine a bright white light coming down from above and entering the top of your head. Filling your entire body. See it, feel it, and it becomes reality. Now imagine an aura of pure white light emanating from your heart region. Again surrounding your entire body. Protecting you. See it, feel it, and it becomes reality. Now only your masters and guides and highly evolved loving entities who mean you well will be able to influence you during this or any other hypnotic session. You are totally protected by this aura of pure white light.

Now focus in on how comfortable and relaxed you are, free of distractions, free from physical and emotional obstacles that prevent you from safely leaving and returning to the physical body. You will perceive and remember all that you encounter during this experience. You will recall in detail when you are physically awake only these matters which will be beneficial to your physical and mental being and experience. Now begin to sense the vibrations around you and in your own mind begin to shape and pull them into a ring around your head. Do this for a few moments now.

Play new age music for 2 minutes.

Now as you begin to attract these vibrations into your inner awareness, they begin to sweep throughout your body making it rigid and immobile. You are always in complete control of this experience. Do this now as you perceive yourself rigid and immobile with these vibrations moving along and throughout your entire body.

Play new age music for 3 minutes.

You have done very well. Pulse these vibrations. Perceive yourself feeling the pulse of these vibrations throughout your entire awareness. In your own mind's eye, reach out one of your arms and grasp some object that you know is out of normal reach. Feel the object and let your astral hand pass through it. Your mind is using your astral arm, not your physical arm, to feel the object. As you do this you are becoming lighter and lighter and your astral body is beginning to rise up from your physical body. Do this now.

Play new age music for 3 minutes.

You've done very well. Now, using other parts of your astral body (your head, feet, chest, and back) repeat this exercise and continue to feel lighter as your astral body begins to rise up from your physical body. Do this now.

Play new age music for 3 minutes.

Now think of yourself as becoming lighter and lighter throughout your body. Perceive yourself floating up as your entire astral body lifts up and floats away from your physical body. Concentrate on blackness and remove all fears during this process. Imagine a helium filled balloon rising and pulling your astral body with it up and away from your physical body. Do this now.

Play new age music for 3 minutes.

Now orient yourself to this new experience. You are out of your body, relaxed, safe, and totally protected by the white light. Concentrate on your sanctuary on the upper Astral plane and request one of your spirit guides to meet you there.

Play new age music for 3 minutes.

You've done very well. Now I want you to travel to a destination much farther way with your guide. It can be a location across the country or anywhere around the world. Take a few moments and think of this destination and you will be there in a few minutes. Allow your mind to be receptive to any instructions from your spirit guide.

Play new age music for 3 minutes.

Alright now. Sleep now and rest. You did very well. Listen very carefully. I'm going to count forward now from 1 to 5. When I reach the count of five you will be back in the body. You will be able to remember everything you experienced and reexperienced. You'll feel very relaxed, refreshed, you'll be able to do whatever you have planned for the rest of the day or evening. You'll feel very positive about what you've just experienced and very motivated about your confidence and ability to play this tape again to experience leaving your physical body safely and contacting a spirit guide. Alright now. One, very, very deep. Two, you're getting a little bit lighter. Three, you're getting much, much lighter. Four, very, very light. Five, awaken. Wide awake and refreshed.

I have discussed the concept of the fifth dimension previously. This is a dimension that functions as an overall foundation for the Astral, Causal, Mental, Etheric, and Soul planes. It can also be a form of a way station between these lanes in which spirit guides can "hang out."

Try this exercise to take a trip to the fifth dimension to contact a spirit guide:

Now listen very carefully. I want you to imagine a bright white light coming down from above and entering the top of your head. Filling your entire body. See it, feel it, and it becomes reality. Now imagine an aura of pure white light emanating from your heart region. Again surrounding your entire body. Protecting you. See it, feel it, and it becomes reality. Now only your masters and guides and highly evolved loving entities who mean you well will be able to influence you during this or any other hypnotic session. You are totally protected by this aura of pure white light.

In a few moments I am going to count from 1 to 20. As I do so you will feel yourself rising up to the superconscious mind level where you will be able to communicate with your Higher Self. One, rising up. Two, three, four, rising higher. Five, six, seven, letting information flow. Eight, nine, 10, you are halfway there. Eleven, 12, 13, feel yourself rising even higher. Fourteen, 15, 16, almost there. Seventeen, 18, 19, number 20 you are there. Take a moment and orient yourself to the superconscious mind level.

Now I want you to merge with your Higher Self and be prepared to enter a blackhole. Take a few moments and perceive yourself actually entering and merging with the white light of your Higher Self. Do this now.

Play new age music for 2 minutes

Now that you have become one with your Higher Self, you are free to control this experience completely protected and out-of-your body. See a blackhole in front of you and enter it. This is a gateway into the fifth dimension. From here you can travel to parallel universes, the past, the future, or just remain in this fifth dimension hyperspace.

Focus on meeting spirit guides in this hyperuniverse. Take a few moments and open yourself to encountering other entities. You are perfectly safe and protected and you will only attract positive people and souls into your awareness. Do this now.

Play new age music for 3 minutes.

You have done very well. At this time I would like you to attract a particular spirit guide that has worked with you before into your particular location in the fifth dimension. You will be able to communicate with this guide by telepathy. Do this now.

Play new age music for 4 minutes.

Very good. Now I want you to explore this wormhole we call the fifth dimension and travel anywhere in time and to any other dimension with your spirit guide. You will be exiting through a whitehole when you do this. Do this now.

Play new age music for 3 minutes.

Alright, you have done very well. In just a few moments I am going to count up from 1 to 5. When I reach the count of 5 you will be back in hyperspace from where you began this voyage. One, you are returning to hyperspace, two, moving closer, three, halfway there, four, almost there and five, you are there. I'm going to count forward from 1-5. When I reach the count of 5 you will be back in your physical body in the present. You will be able to remember everything you experienced and reexperienced. You'll feel very relaxed, refreshed, and be able to do whatever you have planned for the rest of the day or evening. You'll feel very positive about what you've just experienced and very motivated about your confidence and ability to play this tape again to experience the Fifth Dimension and a spirit guide. One, very, very deep. Two, you're getting a little bit lighter. Three, you're getting much much lighter. Four, very, very light. Five, awaken. Wide awake and refreshed.

Soul Plane Ascension

The Soul plane is where our subconscious travels to be escorted by our Higher Self following death on any of the lower five planes. It is here that we are in direct communication with our Higher Self and high-level spirit guides. We now review our Akashic Records and choose our next lifetime from this dimension. Ascension is only possible from the Soul plane after perfection of the soul is achieved.

Another technique we can do on this dimension is to receive information from the higher planes. Although we cannot enter these higher dimensions, an eavesdropping capability is within universal laws.

Try this Soul plane ascension exercise, which is an advanced superconscious mind tap, to experience the most uplifting realm yourself:

Now listen very carefully. I want you to imagine a bright white light coming down from above and entering the top of your head. Filling your entire body. See it, feel it, and it becomes reality. Now imagine an aura of pure white light emanating from your heart region. Again surrounding your entire body. Protecting you. See it, feel it, and it becomes reality. Now only your Higher Self, masters and guides, and highly evolved loving entities who mean you well will be able to influence you during this or any other hypnotic session. You are totally protected by this aura of pure white light.

In a few moments I am going to count from one to 20. As I do so you will feel yourself rising up to the superconscious mind level where you will be able to receive information from your Higher Self and your masters and guides. One, rising up. Two, three, four, rising higher. Five, six, seven, letting information flow. Eight, nine, 10, you are halfway there. Eleven, 12, 13, feel yourself rising even higher. Fourteen, 15, 16, almost there. Seventeen. Eighteen, 19, and 20. You are there. Take a moment and orient yourself to the superconscious mind level.

Play ascension music for 1 minute.

Now from the superconscious mind level you are going to rise up and beyond the karmic cycle and the 5 lower planes to the Soul plane. The white light is always with you and you may be assisted by your Masters and guides as you ascend to the soul plane. One, rising up. Two, three, four, rising higher. Five, six, seven, letting information flow. Eight, nine, 10, you are halfway there. Eleven, 12, 13, feel yourself rising even higher. Fourteen, 15, 16, almost there. Seventeen, 18, 19, and 20, you are there. Take a moment and orient yourself to the Soul plane.

Play ascension music for 1 minute.

From the Soul plane you are able to perceive information from various sources and overview all of your past lives, your current lifetime, and future lives, including all of your frequencies. Take a few moments now and evaluate this data and choose your next lifetime. Get a feel for the entire process.

Play ascension music for 6 minutes.

You have done very well. Now I want you to further open up the channels of communication by removing any obstacles and allowing yourself to receive information and experiences that will directly apply to and help better your present lifetime. Allow yourself to receive more advanced and more specific information from the higher planes this time. Your Higher Self and masters and guides may assist you in receiving this all-important information that will help you raise your frequency and improve your karmic subcycle. Do this now.

Play new age music for 8 minutes.

Alright now. Sleep now and rest. You did very well. Listen very carefully. I'm going to count forward now from 1 to 5. When I reach the count of 5 you will be back in the present and on the Earth plane. You will be able to remember everything you experienced. You will feel very relaxed, refreshed, and you will be able to do whatever you have planned for the rest of the day or evening. You will feel very positive about what you've just experienced and very motivated about your confidence and ability to play this tape again to experience the Soul plane. Alright now. One, very, very deep. Two, you're getting a little bit lighter. Three, you're getting much, much lighter. Four, very, very light, Five, awaken wide awake and refreshed.

As with the other techniques I have presented, music selection is very important. I have specially prepared New Age music for different techniques. If you would like a list of those tapes, simply contact my office.

Teleportation

Unlike OBEs, which entail the astral body separating from its physical counterpart and voyaging to other dimensions, teleportation actually transports the physical body to these different planes.

When you teleport your physical body, it dematerializes (disappears) from one dimension and rematerializes (reappears) in a new plane. This experience is often characterized by a "pop" sound heard just prior to dematerialization and immediately following your rematerialization to your original location.

Some of our natural teleportation experiences take place during the dream state. The difference between this and other dreams, including lucid dreams, is that your physical body is relocated to dream world. Consciously directed teleportation is characterized by a noticeable increase in the energy of your aura vibrating at high speed, accompanied by a tingling, buzzing sensation and/or a feeling of spiraling upward, and a "pop" sound from the top of the head.

In order to facilitate your own teleportation to other dimensions, you need to focus your mind and remove any environmental or other distractions from your awareness. A well-rested body and practicing this technique at night will speed up your mastery of teleportation.

It is natural to hold your breath during this process. Make sure you breathe deeply and slowly. Do not be alarmed if you feel somewhat lightheaded, or experience a swirling and upward sensation during this exercise. A tightness across the Third Eye region of your forehead may be felt in the beginning. The view you have during a teleportation may appear as if you were looking through a keyhole at first. Each of these oddities disappears with practice.

When you teleport to a different dimension, you want to see yourself as if you were viewing this new place from inside your body (first-person perspective), not as if it were a dream or a movie. Always state clearly your intention to travel to a certain dimension. For example, state, "I intend to teleport to the Causal plane to meet with my spirit guide to review my Akashic Records." Try this exercise in teleportation and be prepared to meet a spirit guide:

Now listen very carefully. I want you to imagine a bright white light coming down from above and entering the top of your head, filling your entire body. See it, feel it, and it becomes reality. Now imagine an aura of pure white light emanating from your heart region, again surrounding your entire body, protecting you. See it, feel it, and it becomes reality. Now only your Higher Self, Masters and guides, and highly evolved loving entities who mean you well will be able to influence you during this or any other hypnotic session. You are totally protected by this aura of pure white light.

In a few moments, I am going to count from one to 20. As I do so you will feel yourself rising up to the superconscious mind level where you will be able to receive information from your Higher Self and Masters and guides. You will also be able to overview all of your past, present and future lives. One, rising up. Two, 3, 4, rising higher. Five, six, seven, letting information flow. Eight, nine, 10, you are halfway there. Eleven, 12, 13, feel yourself rising ever higher. Fourteen, 15, 16, almost there. Seventeen, 18, 19, number 20. Now you are there. Take a moment and orient yourself to the superconscious mind level.

Play new age music for 1 minute.

You are now in a deep hypnotic trance and from this superconscious mind level, you are in complete control and able to access this limitless power of your superconscious mind. I want you to be open and flow with this experience. You are always protected by the white light.

At this time I would like you to ask your Higher Self to assist you in the teleportation of your physical body to another dimension to meet a spirit guide. Trust your Higher Self and your own ability to allow any thoughts, feelings or impressions to come into your subconscious mind concerning this goal. Do this now.

Allow all outside thoughts during this relaxation phase to drift passively through your mind. Suggest to yourself that at any time you may experience a teleportation and this projection would be terminated if your physical body felt in any way uncomfortable. You may begin to detect a faint "pop" sound in one ear. This indicates you are about to teleport your physical body. Choose a dimension where you wish to visit a spirit guide and focus on this location. Use your five senses at this time; see the colors, smell the flowers, and so on. If you are having trouble with visualization, merely think about this destination or a spirit guide with which you have previously communicated.

Shortly, you will find yourself standing in the center of this scene. Wherever you place your thoughts, your physical body is bound to follow. Be wary of your thoughts, your physical body is bound to follow. Be wary of your thoughts at this time, as each cognition may direct the physical body to return to your present location instantly. To return to your original site, all you need to do is think about it and that will be accomplished instantaneously. Let yourself now experience an actual teleportation to another dimension to meet a spirit guide.

Play new age music for 6 minutes.

Alright now. Sleep now and rest. You did very, very well. Listen very carefully. I'm going to count forward now from 1 to 5. When I reach the count of five you will be back in the present, you will be able to remember everything you experienced and reexperienced. You'll feel very relaxed, refreshed and you'll be able to do whatever you have planned for the rest of the day or evening. You'll feel very positive about what you've experienced and very motivated about your confidence and ability to play this tape again, to experience teleportation and spirit guide contact. One, very, very deep. Two, you're getting a little bit lighter. Three, you're getting much, much lighter. Four, very, very light. Five, awaken. Wide awake and refreshed.

A Comprehensive Self-Hypnosis Exercise to Meet a Spirit Guide

Before I present additional exercises to meet spirit guides and establish relationships with them, some suggestions concerning how to present questions to them are in order. Consider these carefully:

1. Ask clear and specific questions. It is helpful to formulate these before your meeting.

2. Do not ridicule your spirit guide or ask silly questions. Never show disrespect for this teacher. Your spirit guide can read your mind so always have pure motives in what you ask.

3. Refrain from asking questions that require a simple yes or no response. You want to ask questions that are clear and succinct, encourage a dialogue, and will give you the opportunity to verify its accuracy.

4. In the beginning, do not ask questions that require a prediction of an extreme nature. For example, do not ask such questions as, "When will I find happiness?" or "When will I meet the right man?" Ask instead questions concerning the truth about some issue. You might ask how you can go about improving your relationship at this time, or any other aspect of your life.

5. Refrain from asking a question that is too broad in the beginning. A question such as, "When exactly will I become fulfilled in life?" is far too general and complex for your initial guide contact. Also avoid questions that are too emotional. Do not ask, "Does _____ love me for the right reasons?" A better question would be, "What is the truth about my relationship with _____?"

6. Record your session. It is important to keep records in a journal to compare contacts with your guide at a later date. After the session is over you can play back this tape and summarize this communication in your journal. It is easier to more objectively evaluate communication with your guide at a future date.

Here is an exercise that assists you in establishing a rapport with your spirit guide:

1. Request information for friends and follow up on this data for accuracy. Be patient, as some of this material may take time to materialize. When it does, you will increase your trust for this spirit guide.

2. Consciously ask your spirit guide to accompany you on a walk. Converse with this guide in a leisurely way about several topics. Occasionally ask this spirit something of importance and verify its accuracy.

3. Specifically request information for yourself from the spirit guide. Make sure this material will be applicable in a short time in your life. You can quickly and easily confirm the validity of this information and establish trust with this spirit.

4. Do not be afraid to ask for favors from your spirit guide. Make these simple requests, such as a solution to a simple problem, the location of an unimportant missing object, a parking space and so on.

5. Request a certain dream from your guide that you will remember and one that will contain valuable information for you to use.

6. Ask your guide to create opportunities for you. These spirits can help open doors to paths that might otherwise be closed to you.

7. Ask your guides to assist you in times of indecision, crisis or transition. This is a bigger test for these spiritual advisors, and should only be requested after you have developed sufficient trust in them.

After your first communication with your spirit guide, ask yourself these questions:

◎   Did I feel comfortable with this experience?

◎   Was I able to establish a rapport with my spirit guide?

◎   How did I feel emotionally as a result of this contact?

◎   What did the guide's answers to my questions mean to me?

◎   Did I learn anything significant about myself or the universe as a result of this exposure?

◎   Was this experience different from what I expected?

◎   Can I recognize this guide in the future?

◎   Did I sense anything suspicious about what my guide told me or his/her behavior in general?

Upon successful completion of this exercise go on to the next one. It may require several attempts to initiate this contact with your guide. Do not try the next procedure until the previous one is mastered.

Following your initial contact with a spirit guide the following occurrences may be observed or felt:

◎   A positive mood (tranquility, peace of mind).

◎   An experience of unity or oneness with the environment; what the ancients called the joining of microcosm (man) with macrocosm (universe).

◎   Sensations of tingling and heat will be noted. These feelings are mostly felt at the moment of your spirit guide's entry.

◎   An enhanced sense of reality and meaning.

◎   A sense of inability to describe the experience with words. An alteration in time/space relationships.

◎   You may find it necessary to speak the words you receive telepathically before the next words appear in your inner mind. Just let this information flow and it will come easier and feel more natural.

◎   Paradoxicality—that is, acceptance of things that seem paradoxical in ordinary consciousness.

◎   Your first messages may take the form of a mental picture, a sense of expanded energy or a verbal communication.

◎   Often colors and lights are seen, but not a definite form. Feelings of floating and other dissociated states are commonly experienced. With continued practice you are establishing a stronger link with your spirit guide.

◎ You will detect the vibratory presence of your guide as being different from your own. These differences can be observed in your breathing patterns, your posture, and your speech rhythm pattern and speed.

It is easiest to engage a spirit guide by meeting him/her in your sanctuary. Here is a sophisticated technique to establish a meaningful relationship with a spirit guide:

Now listen very carefully. I want you to imagine a bright white light coming down from above and entering the top of your head, filling your entire body. See it, feel it, and it becomes reality. Now imagine an aura of pure white light emanating form your heart region, again surrounding your entire body, protecting you. See it, feel it, and it becomes reality. Now only your Higher Self, Masters and guides, and highly evolved loving entities who mean you well will be able to influence you during this or any other hypnotic session. You are totally protected by this aura of pure white light.

Sit back, relax, breathe deeply, and send a warm feeling into your toes and feet. Let this feeling break up any strain or tension, and as you exhale let the tension drain away. Breathe deeply and send this warm feeling into your ankles. It will break up any strain or tension, and as you exhale let the tension drain away. Breathe deeply and send this feeling into your knees, let it break up any strain or tension there, and as you exhale let the tension drain away. Send this warm sensation into your thighs so any strain or tension is draining away. Breathe deeply and send this warm feeling into your genitals and drain away tension.

Send this warm feeling into your abdomen now; all your internal organs are soothed and relaxed and any strain or tension is draining away. Let this energy flow into your chest and breast; let it soothe you and as you exhale any tension is draining away. Send this energy into your back now. This feeling is breaking up any strain or tension and as you exhale the tension is draining away. The deep, relaxing energy is flowing through your back, into each vertebra, as each vertebra assumes its proper alignment. The healing energy is flowing into all your muscles and tendons, and you are relaxed, very fully relaxed. Send this energy into your shoulders and neck; this energy is breaking up any strain or tension and as you exhale the tension is draining away. Your shoulders and neck are fully relaxed. And the deep relaxing energy is flowing into your arms; your upper arms, your elbows, your forearms, your wrists, your hands, your fingers are fully relaxed.

Let this relaxing energy wash up over your throat; your lips, your jaw, your cheeks are fully relaxed. Send this energy into your face; the muscles around your eyes, your forehead, your scalp are relaxed. Any strain or tension is draining away. You are relaxed, most completely relaxed.

And now float to your space, leave your physical body and move between dimensions and travel to your space, a meadow, a mountain, a forest, the seashore, wherever your mind is safe and free. Go to that space now. And you are in your space, the space you have created, a space sacred and apart. Here in this space you are free from all tension and in touch with the calm, expansive power within you. Here in this space you have access to spiritual guides, their information and energy. Here is the space where you can communicate with your spirit guides. Your flow is in harmony with the flow of the universe. Because you are part of the whole creation you have access to the power of the whole of creation. Here you are pure and free. This is your personal sanctuary.

Visualize yourself in a beautiful room. This room has no real boundaries, but is surrounded by feelings of love. Note different colored lights all around you and experience the joy that accompanies this place.

Sense the presence of at least one pure being of light and love. Be open now to receive communication from this spirit guide. You see a door surrounded by a brilliant white light in front of you. Beyond this door this spirit guide is located.

Open up this door and experience this dimension of pure love and light. This region of a higher vibration is waiting for you. As you walk into this spiritual realm, feel the light surrounding and healing you. It cleanses your aura.

Take a few moments to orient yourself to this dimension. Observe the presence of your guide. This spirit may appear as a human, white light, a series of colored lights, or any way that will make you feel comfortable. It may be a sound. Do not be concerned with this representation, just open up your heart and soul to receive its communication. Refrain from preconceived images of what a guide should look like. It is not necessary to perceive an actual figure as a guide.

Ask your spirit guide to present itself and begin this contact. Note the feelings and sensations you feel as the spirit guide approaches. Memorize what images accompany this pure spirit. Observe the surroundings as your guide approaches you.

Greet your guide and ask if it has some special information that is of value to you at this time. Telepathically carry on a conversation with this guide.

Request that your spirit guide assist you in opening up and establishing this path of communication. If you are given a name, say that name out loud or to yourself this time. Greet this spirit when it appears and remove any doubts or fears concerning this encounter. Focus only on feelings of love and joy.

Visualize your spirit guide's energy entering your aura. Feel the intensity of this loving energy and note how it becomes stronger. If you sense any negativity or resistance, dismiss this spirit and ask for your higher guide now.

Play new age music for 3 minutes.

If you do not know the name of your guide, ask for that at this time. Repeat this name out loud or to yourself and, again, offer greetings to your guide. If there are several guides present, request that only one come forward to represent the others in this communication. Ask if your guide represents some particular specialty.

Begin asking your questions. Start with the simple ones first and verbally state these questions to your guide. Repeat any responses you receive out loud by saying, "My spirit guide _____ says..."

Continue with these questions for as long as you feel comfortable. Ask your guide if there are specific days or times of the day or evening that are best for future sessions.

Play new age music for 5 minutes.

When you have completed asking your questions and have verbalized the guide's responses, sit calmly and enjoy the presence of your guide's energy. Before saying goodbye to your spirit teacher, ask it to strengthen the link so it will be easier to reestablish at some future sessions.

Request that your spirit guide assist you in opening up and establishing this path of communication. After conversing with your guide for a short time, thank this spirit, say goodbye and slowly return to your conscious state. You have made an initial comprehensive contact with your spirit guide. Write down your experiences in your journal, especially the guide's answers to your questions.

Repeat this exercise as many times as it is necessary until you have established verbal communication with your spirit guide. Always request that your guide assist you in any way to initiate and maintain this contact. Be open to any advice it may offer.

Sometimes it helps if you have a partner with you who can ask your questions while you remain in trance with your eyes closed. Your partner should practice the protection, balancing, and trance exercises in this book first. He or she must be in a trance state prior to asking your questions. The rest of the instructions remain the same, and you are encouraged to verbalize all data received from your guide.

The following questions can be asked by you of your partner:

1. How do you feel at this time?

2. What do you sense, feel or see now?

3. Can you hear anything? If so, what do you hear?

4. Tell me, in your own words, what you are receiving at this time?

5. Is there anything you observe that is preventing this connection from being established?

6. What message is your guide trying to convey to you at this time?

7. Has the environment you are observing changed in any way?

You can help your partner by asking your spirit guide for assistance in strengthening this connection.

The following are sample questions of a personal nature that you may ask your spirit guide in your communications.

1. What is it that I am supposed to learn in this lifetime?

2. How can I facilitate my spiritual growth?

3. What decisions can I make at this time to place me on the path to fulfilling my karmic purpose?

4. What specific actions can I take to facilitate entering this spiritual path?

5. What can I do to create more abundance in my current life?

6. How can I best help others?

7. What is my highest spiritual goal at this time?

8. How can I become more creative?

9. What exactly is the purpose of my relationship with
    _____ at this time?

10. What can I do to improve my communication with my spirit
    guides?

Feel free to expand this list and add any questions that will assist you in your life now.

Personal Questions   Date

1. _____

2. _____

3. _____

4. _____

These next questions deal with a more universal nature. Do not ask too many of these questions at any one sitting. These questions are as follows:

1. Is there a consciousness to the Earth itself? If so, what is it like?

2. How is the Higher Self different from the soul? What can people do to access this Higher Self? What does the Higher Self feel like?

3. What can we do to help world peace? How can we add to the quality of the universe?

4. Is there free will? Can people see their own future and change it?

5. Why do we have a conscious will? How does it fit into the karmic pattern of the universe?

6. Do we all have a karmic purpose? Is anyone on the Earth just to exist for the sake of existence itself?

7. How did the universe begin?

8. Is the universe friendly?

9. Is there a purpose to every relationship we have in a lifetime?

10. What is the mechanism for ascension?

11. How can each soul positively contribute to the spiritual evolution of the universe?

12. Can we be affected by other people's negative thoughts and emotions? If so, how can we protect ourselves from this exposure?

13. Can you describe the upcoming consciousness shift in detail?

14. Please describe the God energy complex.

Again, you may add to this list with your own questions of a universal nature.

Universal Questions   Date

1. _____

2. _____

3. _____

4. _____

5. _____

6. _____

Always record your responses in your journal. Every month or so I suggest you review this log and observe patterns in the answers you receive. This also gives you the opportunity to verify the accuracy of the information given to you by your spirit guide.

After you have established this initial contact, there are several positive patterns that will become evident in your life. Among these are:

1. Your wishes of growth and desires will be fulfilled more rapidly than in the past.

2. Healing affects will be observed physically, mentally, emotionally and spiritually. You will experience a more positive and optimistic attitude and a new lease on life.

3. Every area of your life will be improved, some dramatically.

4. You will find yourself becoming more loving and open to communication. This will improve your relationship with others.

5. People will be attracted to your new energy, and you will be able to help them on several levels.

6. The ability to see the future will be developed.

7. Others who are also interested in spiritual growth and metaphysics will enter your life.

8. Your "luck" will improve and good fortune will surround you.

These are only a sample of the positive things you will encounter.

Contacting Unborn Children

Spirit guides have informed my patients that it is quite possible for parents to contact the souls of their unborn children. There is reportedly a two-way communication established during the gestational period.

My work with past life regression hypnotherapy has demonstrated that we select our own names on the Soul plane prior to incarnating and telepathically communicate this name to our parents, who then name us according to what they assume is their choice.

In this exercise to contact the souls of your unborn children I first present affirmations to facilitate this mechanism. We will also use the sanctuary method to meet with and communicate with the soul of your unborn child.

If you already have a name for this child, use it during this exercise. If not, simply use the term unborn child as I have. Try this technique with an open mind:

Now listen very carefully. I want you to imagine a bright white light coming down from above and entering the top of your head, filling your entire body. See it, feel it, and it becomes reality. Now imagine an aura of pure white light emanating from your heart region, again surrounding your entire body, protecting you. See it, feel it, and it becomes reality. Now only your Higher Self, Masters and guides, and highly evolved loving entities who mean you well will be able to influence you during this or any other hypnotic session. You are totally protected by this aura of pure white light.

In a few moments, I am going to count from one to 20. As I do so you will feel yourself rising up to the superconscious mind level where you will be able to receive information from your Higher Self and Masters and guides. One, rising up. Two, 3, 4, rising higher. Five, 6, 7, letting information flow. Eight, nine, 10, you are halfway there. Eleven, 12, 13, feel yourself rising even higher. Fourteen, 15, 16, almost there. Seventeen, 18, 19, and 20. Now you are there. Take a moment and orient yourself to the superconscious mind level.

Play new age music for 1 minute.

You are now in a deep hypnotic trance and from this superconscious mind level I would like you to focus and incorporate the following affirmations:

I am of pure light and pure energy.

I am connected to my Higher Self and can communicate with my unborn child.

I am a free and powerful being.

I now open up my mind to establish communication with my unborn child.

I send out and receive only unconditional love.

I have no fear.

And now float to your space, leave your physical body and move between dimensions and travel to your space, a meadow, forest, the seashore, wherever your mind is safe and free. Go to that space now. And you are in your space, the space you have created, a space sacred and apart. Here in this space you are free from all tension and in touch with the calm, expansive power within you. Here in this space you have access to spiritual information and energy. Here is the space where you can communicate with your spirit guides and your unborn child.

Your flow is in harmony with the flow of the universe. Because you are part of the whole creation you have access to the power of the whole of creation. Here you are pure and free. This is your personal sanctuary.

Now open up your mind to telepathically communicate with the soul of your unborn child. Your Higher Self and spirit guide will assist you with this process. Begin with these simple questions:

What is your name?

Have we been together in past lives?

Do you have a special purpose in my life at this time that I should be aware of?

What can you tell me about my karmic purpose?

Continue asking any other questions that will assist you in your own spiritual growth.

Play new age music for 4 minutes.

Alright now. Sleep now and rest. You did very, very well. Listen very carefully. I'm going to count forward now from 1 to 5. When I reach the count of five you will be back in the present, you will be able to remember everything you experienced and reexperienced. You'll feel very relaxed, refreshed and you'll be able to do whatever you have planned for the rest of the day or evening. You'll feel very positive about what you've experienced and very motivated about your confidence and ability to play this tape again and to communicate with your unborn child. Alright now. One, very, very deep. Two, you're getting a little bit lighter, Three, you're getting much, much lighter. Four, very, very light. Five, awaken. Wide awake and refreshed.

Accessing Your Akashic Records With Your Spirit Guide

Although all of our Akashic Records are kept on the Causal plane, spirit guides and we ourselves may access them on any of the lower five planes, in addition to the Soul plane. There are learning temples on the Astral, Mental, Etheric, and Soul Plane where this procedure is made user friendly.[1]

We will use the sanctuary technique to obtain the assistance of a spirit guide to enable you to view your Akashic Records with this exercise:

Sit back, relax, breathe deeply, and send a warm feeling into your toes and feet. Let this feeling break up any strain or tension, and as you exhale let the tension drain away. Breathe deeply and send this warm feeling into your ankles. It will break up any strain or tension, and as you exhale let the tension drain away. Breathe deeply and send this feeling into your knees, let it break up any strain or tension there, and as you exhale let the tension drain away. Send this warm sensation into your thighs so any strain or tension is draining away. Breathe deeply and send this warm feeling into your genitals and drain away any tension.

Send this warm feeling into your abdomen now; all your internal organs are soothed and relaxed and any strain or tension is draining away. Let this energy flow into your chest and breast; let it soothe you and as you exhale any tension is draining away. Send this energy into your back now. This feeling is breaking up any strain or tension and as you exhale the tension is draining away. The deep, relaxing energy is flowing through your back, into each vertebra, as each vertebra assumes its proper alignment. The healing energy is flowing into all your muscles and tendons, and you are relaxed, very fully relaxed. Send this energy into your shoulders and neck; this energy is breaking up any strain or tension and as you exhale the tension is draining away. Your shoulders and neck are fully relaxed. And the deep relaxing energy is flowing into your arms; your upper arms, your elbows, your forearms, your wrists, your hands, your fingers are fully relaxed.

Let this relaxing energy wash up over your throat, and your lips, your jaw, your cheeks are fully relaxed. Send this energy into your face, the muscles around your eyes, your forehead, your scalp are relaxed. Any strain or tension is draining away. You are relaxed, more completely relaxed.

Now listen very carefully. I want you to imagine a bright white light coming down from above and entering the top of your head, filling your entire body. See it, feel it, and it becomes reality. Now imagine an aura of pure white light emanating from your heart region, again surrounding your entire body, protecting you. See it, feel it, and it becomes reality. Now only your Higher Self, masters and guides, and highly evolved loving entities who mean you well will be able to influence you during this or any other hypnotic session. You are totally protected by this aura of pure white light.

In a few moments, I am going to count from one to 20. As I do so you will feel yourself rising up to the superconscious mind level where you will be able to receive information from your Higher Self and masters and guides. You will also be able to overview all of your past, present and future lives. One, rising up. Two, three, four, rising higher. Five, six, seven, letting information flow. Eight, nine, 10, you are halfway there. Eleven, 12, 13, feel yourself rising even higher. Fourteen, 15, 16, almost there. Seventeen, 18, 19, and 20. Now you are there. Take a moment and orient yourself to the superconscious mind level.

Play new age music for 1 minute.

And now float to your space, leave your physical body and move between dimensions and travel to your space, a meadow, a mountain, a forest, the seashore, wherever your mind is safe and free. Go to that space now. And you are in your space, the space you have created, a space sacred and apart. Here in this space you are free from all tension and in touch with the calm, expansive power within you. Here in this space you have access to spiritual information and energy. Here is the space where you can communicate with your spirit guides. Your flow is in harmony with the flow of the universe. Because you are part of the whole creation you have access to the power of the whole of creation. Here you are pure and free. This is your personal sanctuary.

Turn your attention inward and center it on the area of the Third Eye. See it glow with a golden white radiance and feel it pulsate with energy. As you do this, your realization of the sounds, colors, and temperature in the room around you should gradually fade and as they do so the subtle psychic stirrings will become more noticeable.

At first, this may be only an impression of inner light, or of brilliantly illuminated geometrical figures, or of stars shooting by in ordered procession, or some other visual appearance that will probably be meaningless. Or your first impression may be of sound.

Now request your spirit guide to appear and state your interest in reviewing your Akashic Records. Your guide may show you a hologram, accompany you to a learning temple, or simply describe them to you. Do not be surprised if you find yourself drifting into a scenario-like dream.

In the earlier stages of your development you may not get clearly defined data that you can recognize as such, so don't expect them. Accept the dreamlike sequence that passes before your consciousness as you sit in reverie. Remember what you observe and write it down as soon as possible thereafter.

Using the instructions on questioning your spirit guide I previously presented, ask specific questions concerning your Akashic Records. For example, you might want to trace past life ties with a loved one, or inquire as to your karmic purpose. Think carefully about your questions and make the most out of this experience.

Play new age music for 3 minutes.

Now begin obtaining data about your future. Begin with a short range, say one week to a month. Remember what you observe and write it down as soon as possible upon awakening from this trance. Log all of your observations into a journal and occasionally verify the accuracy of this information.

Continue inquiring about events farther into the future, say five, ten, fifty years and beyond. Ask about your own future lives and relate these to your karmic purpose.

Last, tap into the general Akasha of the Universe and allow your consciousness to tune into future world events, inventions, lifestyle changes and so on.

Play new age music for 6 minutes.

Alright now. Sleep now and rest. You did very, very well.

Listen very carefully. I'm going to count forward now from 1 to 5. When I reach the count of five you will be back in the present, you will be able to remember everything you experienced and reexperienced. You'll feel very relaxed, refreshed, and you'll be able to do whatever you have planned for the rest of the day or evening. You'll feel very positive about what you've experienced and very motivated about your confidence and ability to play this tape again, to experience your Akashic Records and spirit guides. Alright now. One, very, very deep. Two, you're getting a little bit lighter. Three, you're getting much, much lighter. Four, very, very light. Five, awaken. Wide awake and refreshed.

During these practice sessions you should "feel" this connection between your consciousness and the Akasha, with your spirit guide assisting you at every step. Your Higher Self is also involved in this and every one of these exercises.

When this has been accomplished and you can recall an incident from the past as simply as you can look up an account in the encyclopedia, once you have developed a working connection between your subconscious and spirit guide, it is not too difficult to contact the Akasha. But because these embrace in detail every event since this world began and many events still to come, your first attempts may appear confusing. Be patient with this rather advanced exercise.

CHAPTER 7

What We Can Learn From Spirit Guides

In this chapter I will relate information given by spirit guides that have contacted my patients over more than two decades. A variety of topics ranging from the nature of reality to ascension will be discussed. Remember the expression, "There are no absolute truths, including what I just said." Read this chapter with an open mind and accept or reject what you like. Your own spirit guide contacts will undoubtedly add to these paradigms.

The Nature of Reality

We live in a multidimensional universe, which is characterized by an interrelationship between the various planes and parallel universes. Modern physics tells us we can enter the fifth dimension through a blackhole, travel through a wormhole and eventually exit through a whitehole into the past, future, or another parallel universe.

Certain contact points (blackholes, stargates, and so on) exist that permit entering and leaving these dimensions. Spirit guides use these contact points as a form of travel, as do other less-evolved entities.

You literally create our own reality through the use of your subconscious. This inner reality was far better developed in primitive man and most of us have lost contact with this natural ability.

The only way for you to change the state of the world in which you live is to change yourself by altering your consciousness. You are responsible for your life and you must never blame circumstances on any outside force. You form your own dreams and you form your own physical reality. The world is what you are. It is the physical materialization of the inner energy you have created.

What goes around comes around. The energy you send out (love, hate, compassion, greed, and so on) will come back in kind to affect your life. This all takes place in a multidimensional universe that is impossible to accurately describe in human terms. Beyond your physical body is an Astral, Causal, Mental, Etheric, and Soul plane body.

Each of the bodies we possess, or selves, has its own identity. The personality we exhibit is chosen to be compatible within the reality (universe or dimension) in which we are functioning. All of our being is composed of energy patterns. What we assume is reality is merely an illusion. The illusory world of our dreams is far more real than the physical plane we have come to know and accept.

It is natural and common for us to reach out and inquire about each of these systems. You can look to your consciousness as the force behind the creation of matter. It forms all of the other dimensions besides the Physical plane. It is incorrect to assume that physical reality is the true mode of existence.

The source and power of your present consciousness has never been physical. Our human race is merely a testing ground for consciousness growth. As thought and emotion manifest themselves on the Physical and Astral planes, respectively, you must learn to control both in order to grow spiritually. When you master the positive desire for creativity and love over destruction and hatred and eliminate fear from your being, the karmic cycle ends and you may ascend to rejoin with the God energy.

Many of the spirit guides that assist us have perfected their souls, while others are in their last Earthly cycle. Some spirit guides were never in physical form or human at all.

Because we create our reality, we function both as producers and actors in the play of life. There is a play within a play, as represented by other dimensions. The actions within the play, not the results, are what count the most in regard to our spiritual evolution. All the world is truly a stage.

Learning occurs by continually transforming mental energy (thought or psychic energy) into physical reality and responding to our creations with deeds and actions. We participate in physical reality so that we can operate and experience within this dimension. Here, you can develop your abilities, learn, create, solve problems, and help others. Matter is the shape that basic experience takes when it comes into our three-dimensional system. Our dreams, thoughts, expectations, beliefs, and emotions are literally transformed into physical matter.

In order for us to comprehend the world in which we live, these materializations of our emotions, energy, and mental environment are created. They function as focal points where highly charged psychic impulses are transformed into something that can be physically perceived. Nerve impulses now travel outward from the body along invisible pathways and carry telepathic thoughts, impulses, and desires, containing all the codified data necessary for translating any thought or image into physical actuality, altering seemingly objective events. Without this telepathic mechanism the physical universe would collapse in chaos. Each of us must maintain a certain framework for our world, and this can only be stabilized by a conglomerate form of telepathy with our fellow planetary inhabitants.

It is this inner self, out of massive knowledge and the unlimited scope of its consciousness, that forms the physical world and provides the stimuli to keep the outer ego at the job of awareness. The inner self organizes, initiates, projects, and controls the transformation of psychic energy into matter and objects. The more intense the thought, the greater the likelihood that it will materialize in our realm.

The physical reality we are aware of is the result of a cooperation among many fellow citizens of the Earth. We have a vast storage of knowledge within our subconscious to select from. The ego is not privy to this data. It only receives what the subconscious allows it to and this data mostly comes from the five senses.

We will function better if we learn to listen to the voice of the inner self and work with it. Some of these voices reflect spirit guide contacts. You create your reality according to your beliefs and expectations, therefore you should examine these carefully. If you do not like some aspect of your world, then examine your own expectations. You must learn to erase a negative thought or picture by replacing it with its opposite. A negative thought, if not erased, will almost certainly result in a negative condition. Do not repress these negative thoughts, but rather recognize, confront, and replace them.

You create your own problems. You cannot escape your own attitudes, for they will form the material world you see. If changes are to
occur, they must be mental and psychic changes. These will be reflected
in your environment. You are not your emotions. They flow through you,
you feel them and then they disappear. When you try to hold back they
build up. You are independent of your thoughts and emotions. You have
emotions. You use your thoughts and emotions in your mental composition. You must learn to trust your own spontaneous nature.

This spontaneity to which I am referring is that of nature. Our bodies
will be healthy automatically if we do not project false ideas upon them.
Physical symptoms are communications from the inner self, indications
that we are making mental errors of one kind or another. You are a part
of the inner self. It is *not* manipulating your actions.

Consciousness is a dimension of action which allows the inner structure of the universe to both experience and express itself. We can look
upon identity as an action that is conscious of itself. An identity is also a
dimension of existence, actions within action, an unfolding of action upon
itself. Through this interweaving of action with itself, through this reaction, an identity is formed. Identity and action cannot be separated, and
both contribute to our spiritual development.

Without identity, action would be meaningless, for there would be
nothing upon which action could act. Action then must, by its very nature, create identities. Identity, because of its characteristics, will continually seek stability, while stability is impossible. Action would seem to
destroy identity, because action must involve change, and any change
seems to threaten identity, however, identities are never constant, for
consciousness without action would cease to be conscious. Identity must
seek stability while action must seek change; yet identity could not exist
without change, for it is the result of action and a part of it. Identity is
not the same as individual personality. Personality represents only those
aspects of identity which are able to be actualized within three-dimensional existence.

The self with which we identify is but a small component of our entire
multidimensional identity. This self is our ego and is quite distinct from
our subconscious, which has lived before in thousands of past lives. Personality and identity are not dependent upon physical form.

As our consciousness grows out of its experience, it forms other "personalities" or fragments of itself. These fragments are entirely independent

as to action and decision, while constantly in communication with the whole self of which they are a part. These "fragments" themselves grow, develop, and may form their own personalities. You have constant contact with the other parts of your whole self, but your ego is so focused upon physical reality and survival within it that you do not hear the inner voices, some of which reflect your Higher Self and spirit guides.

The Nature of Time

There is no past, present and future per se as isolate fragments of time, the fourth dimension. All events occur simultaneously in the space-time continuum. The past, present, and future only appear to those who exist within three-dimensional reality. Because the Higher Self and spirit guides exist in other dimensions, they are able to see your past, present, and future all at once. Quantum physicists use terms such as parallel universes and the fifth dimension to describe the multidimensional reality that exists.

The ego chooses a single event from all the probable ones. Until the ego observes the event, it is only one of all the other probable ones. It becomes actual in your reality only when it is experienced by the physical self. These other probable events become just as "real" within other dimensions. We use the term antimatter to describe the physical constitution of parallel universes. There are an infinite number of systems or universes between matter and antimatter. We can detect these other dimensions in our dream state or through the use of alpha techniques, such as hypnosis. They are as real as our physical world. We just do not focus on them normally.

Each of these dimensional bodies experiences time in its own manner according to the nature of its perceptions. Their various realities merge in the overall perceptions of the whole self, supervised by the Higher Self and spirit guides. There is a constant subconscious interchange of information between all these layers of the whole consciousness.

God

God is an energy gestalt, the sum of all consciousness. In this case, the whole is far greater than the sum of its parts. This God energy is an ever-expanding consciousness that simultaneously and instantly creates each one of the infinite dimensions and universes that exist today. Its energy is within and behind all universes. We experience the God energy as our Higher Self and spirit guides.

What this means quite simply is that there is always a connection between our subconscious and the God energy. We naturally constantly seek the knowledge of God and don't have far to look. God is within each of us as represented by the Higher Self. Our very existence is dependent on the God energy. By addressing your Higher Self and spirit guides, you are communicating with God, by way of its Oversouls that created us.

In a certain way we are all creators. We create our physical reality, as God created the universe. Thought is energy and is the mechanism of our creative potential. Our expectations, fears, and other emotions create telepathic signals which help in the final version of the reality we experience.

Ascension

The true purpose of each soul on this planet is to reunite with the God energy, a process called Ascension. This natural, ongoing evolutionary mechanism is an alteration in our levels of conscious that requires perfection of the soul.

Reincarnation is the process of providing our souls the learning opportunity to accomplish this spiritual unfoldment by inhabiting physical bodies, as well as other dimensional incarnations. Spirit guides assist us in this endeavor and provide many helpful hints as to how we may accomplish this end to the karmic cycle of birth and death.

When we get overly concerned with the physical plane and forget our true karmic purpose, ascension becomes elusive. All life is ascending, the plants, the rocks, the animals, each in its own time in its own individual way. The Earth, as a living being, is also ascending. It is happening according to the Divine Plan and all will take place when a consciousness shift occurs.

Spirit guides will never force us to do anything. They merely advise. It is our awareness and free will choices that determine whether we accept inner peace, joy, compassion, love, and other higher qualities that lead to ascension.

Some guides relate that it is possible to ascend in a resurrected body as Jesus is reported to have done. To do this all cells in the physical body are expanded to a higher fvr and now a radiant glow of a brilliant white light (Higher Self) can be seen. This radiating body vibrating at a higher fvr is teleported to the Soul plane where ascension actually takes place. When ascension is completed, there will no longer be a body of any type on the higher planes. A resurrected body merely facilitates the ascension process on the Soul plane.

In order to speed up this all-important mechanism, it is necessary that you begin now to take care of each of your physical, mental, emotional, and spiritual needs. Self-discipline and contact with your Higher Self and spirit guides are required to accomplish this.

An incentive to improve your attitude and degree of compassion, love, and so on is that these alterations result in your sending out a higher vibrational energy signal that attracts higher quality people and experiences into your life. Eating right, exercise, proper rest, and maintaining a balanced lifestyle provides a solid physical and emotional foundation for your consciousness-raising techniques through self-hypnosis.

Self-hypnosis is a very simple and effective tool for improving the physical body, as so often stated by spirit guides. By calming the mind and body much stress is relieved. It is up to you to honor your physical body by establishing this balance and expressing this focus of your soul's expression.

The first step in this process is to overcome fear and feelings of guilt and inadequacy. If you don't feel worthy of spiritual growth and ascension, the process so necessary for external bliss is curtailed.

Becoming aware of the different bodies and dimensions that exist is the next step in this ascension mechanism. Physical matters, emotions, and spirit energy all vibrate at different rates. Unless you access your Higher Self and increase your psychic ability to tune into these different frequencies, your focus will be entirely on the physical level and unaware of the others.

Self-hypnosis is the most efficient mechanism to increase your awareness. Spirit guides recommend any alpha technique you feel comfortable with to achieve this goal. You must allow both your Higher Self and spirit guides to flow freely throughout your very being. This has the immediate advantage of allowing you to experience yourself as primarily spiritual energy capable of love and inspirational thoughts and actions.

Self-forgiveness is another quality that spirit guides emphasize as a necessary step to ascension. A simple technique to accomplish this is to stand in front of a mirror, view yourself with love and compassion and say, "I forgive you for any thought, deed, emotion, or inaction throughout this or any past, parallel, or future lifetime. I unconditionally love and appreciate you for your very being."

This exercise can be repeated in reference to forgiving others (parents, spouses, children, coworkers, siblings, neighbors, or friends) and the universe in general. You must say, "I forgive anyone from this or any other lifetime or dimension that may have harmed me or expressed a negative thought in relationship to my being. I hereby forgive actions, regardless of motive, erase all karma, let go any vengeance or any other form of negativity and surround myself and the rest of the universe in a brilliant white light."

Another step in the ascension process requires a shift from conscious functioning, represented by a fear-based rigidity, separateness, and limited growth capacity to a subconscious-superconscious mind level of awareness based on love, togetherness, and openness with unlimited potential for growth.

Moving from a judgmental to a nonjudgmental mentality in which all souls are worthy of respect and energy is not wasted on lower-level emotions. When you function from the spiritual level (assisted by spirit guides) loving and peaceful thoughts and feelings easily flow through your stream of consciousness.

We need also to recognize that we are not alone in this process. In addition to having the continual presence of our Higher Self within our consciousness, at the crown chakra and Soul plane, we have the audience of spirit guides. Some of these advisors come to our assistance in times of great need—angels for example. We must learn to accept these spirits and work with them.

Throughout our history we have tended to worship these guides as gods. This process entails giving up our power to them. These entities do not want our power and ascension is impossible unless we empower and repower ourselves by developing self-love, trust, forgiveness, compassion, and many other desirable traits.

Spirit guides have their own hierarchy and function both in groups and individually to train us in the ascension process. It is up to us to listen to these highly evolved advisors. The Physical plane is far too limiting to attain this growth. That is why most of our spirit guide contact takes place during our dreams and other OBEs.

When certain guides speak of Ascended Masters, they discuss beings of light who descended from higher orders of entities to teach us how to ascend. There are 144,000 of these Ascended Masters and the precise mechanism in which the physical bodies are chosen to house them depends upon their previous work in earlier lives on Earth.

Certain "Councils of Light" oversee the functions of these masters. These councils are spiritual universes continually being evolved and reevolved beyond the visible spectrum. They transmit knowledge to us in a Light Force and a Love Force.

When our physical bodies are close to ascension, they create an eighth and ninth chakra. A series of biomagnetic energy resonances are balanced with the eighth and ninth chakra levels so as to open the human vibratory field through a complete energy conversion. Now the soul and Higher Self can merge forming one energy complex that is perfect and able to travel to the higher planes.

We live in an open-ended local universe which is part of other universes and spiritual realms which constitute the Universal Mind. The spirit guides use light and love to facilitate our final ascensions when we are ready. The Third Eye is the receptor of these two forces.

A special light grid entering the inner eye transforms the soul's energy so that it can evolve faster. You will notice that throughout history the term light has consistently been used to describe higher states of consciousness.

With the assistance of our Third Eyes, our souls are prepared to receive and respond to a higher language of light and love. This functions to accelerate the entire ascension process and allows you to enter a point of no return, at which you finally become one with your Higher Self.

None of us are truly isolated or alone. Cosmic understanding is always available to us. Spirit guides function within each of us, if we allow them to, and from a higher dimensional perspective. These spirit guides, along with our souls, are integral components to the universe in general and the divine plan of the God energy.

What is the Core Essence?

The true nature of your soul's essence is made available to you only when your purity of mind and spirit increases to the extent that it raises your level of awareness high enough to receive and comprehend this vast amount of data.

As you open the pathways to higher and higher dimensions, you will receive clearer messages, more profound information, more information that is entirely new to you. Much more about your role in the grand design of the future will become manifest as gateways become open and expanded at an accelerated rate, due to the upcoming consciousness shift. This will result in a far more rapid rate of awakening and spiritual unfoldment.

The true essence of your being has been hidden due to fears, subjective beliefs, judgment, falsehoods, propaganda, and other limitations. One result of this is hopelessness and helplessness reflected in codependency behavior.

The shift in consciousness that is about to occur is a true window of opportunity to both acknowledge and empower your core essence, which is your true spiritual identity. You are far more than a physical body with a subconscious. You are even more than an extension of your Higher Self. It is your destiny to return to the God energy from whence you came.

The other dimensions, including the physical plane, represent an experiment in the cosmos. It is time to end this experiment and learn the secrets of universal knowledge and experience that will reveal our core essences and facilitate the ascension mechanism we discussed previously.

Buried deep within your brain cells and subconscious are memories of this core essence. Many of us are now beginning to recall our true origin as spiritual beings who came to this planet to both watch over and participate in its development. Some of us were responsible for the installation of this planet with electromagnetic energy in the form of *ley lines* (energy grids that joint hilltops, churches, and prehistoric monuments that are theorized as functioning as condensers of electrical forces and uniters of spiritual energy) and other magnetic grids that have created energy gateways.

This history involved extraterrestrials and time travelers who were able to travel interdimensionally, as well as through space, to help seed this planet. Some brought fantastic psychic powers, others scientific wonders, and still others genetic material to assist in the establishment of the five major races and advanced ancient civilizations such as Atlantis and Lemuria (Mu).

After our core essences became trapped in the karmic cycle, many of us felt abandoned and betrayed by our advisors. This was not the case, as it was our responsibility to integrate the spirit with the physical body and perfect Earth plane existence by way of mental, emotional, and psychic gifts, along with free will.

The misuse of the physical body, and subsequent ethical and moral degeneration of our core essences, was our choice. We cannot blame the spirit guides or the system for this occurrence. Consider the disappointment of moving from a highly evolved spiritual being, who had some say in the design of the universe, to a subservient and dysfunctional animal unable to resist the temptations of the material world. No wonder there is so much anger in the world. Much of it is directed against ourselves for messing up a beautiful system.

All is not lost, as we can change at any time and depart from this stress cycle of birth and death by listening to and following the wisdom of spirit guides. You have the right of free will to misuse the great knowledge of the universe to amass wealth and control humankind. Have not governments, religion, and the corporate world demonstrated this tendency, some even in the name of God?

For those souls who came to Earth with overwhelming love for this planet and the recognition of its status as a living entity, much pain has been felt as the result of this cosmic experiment. You know who you are. You feel most fulfilled when in natural surroundings (the mountains, seashore, woods and so on) and when experiencing a great affinity for the majestic grandeur of nature. This feeling is often nullified by the neglect, destruction, and misuse that has characterized the human race down through the ages.

Some of you came to this planet to transmit universal wisdom, teach, and guide others to awaken them to their ultimate truths. The integrity, love, joy, peace, honor, and unity you have tried to impart has often been ignored and replaced by limitation, isolation, guilt, hate, and fear.

Others have had a difficult time adjusting to the confines of the physical body and responded by rejecting all forms of material comforts and desire under the assumption that any association with the Physical plane would interfere with their spiritual progress. Others have starved their bodies, numbed their brains with drugs, or abused themselves through various forms of self-mutilation.

None of the above-mentioned responses were the correct paths to ascension. Our task originally was to function as a cocreator with the God energy and to experience all of the beauty and wonder our spiritual nature has in a physical vehicle we call the body. In that vein most of us have failed so far. But there is still time to live in the splendor, harmony, beauty, and perfection of the universe. That is why we create our physical reality with our mind, so state the spirit guides.

Death

Death is a process of the Physical plane, as well as other dimensions, that frightens people more than anything else I know. The spirit guides teach us and demonstrate the fact that death is nothing but a change of dimensions. Think of it as a peaceful transition from the physical body (assuming you haven't mastered the art of resurrecting the physical body) to an astral body and eventually to a Soul plane form. Eventually, a new astral body and then a physical one is occupied.

Most of us fail to demonstrate the confidence to reject the idea that death is a finality and that the rest of eternity is a black void of nothingness. The evidence that there are other dimensions can be found in near-death experiences (NDEs).

My patients have received spirit guide data pointing out that all clinical (physical) death, or crossing into spirit examples, are NDEs, with the single exception that the silver cord connecting the physical to the astral body is severed. This severed cord prevents the soul from being able to return to its former physical form.

We can summarize what precisely takes place at the moment of death as follows:

- There is a brilliance emanating from a white light.
- There is no pain.
- Peace and love are noted immediately.
- The soul emerges and is transformed to be with its Higher and perfect Self.

- ☉ The silver cord is severed.
- ☉ Telepathy and other ESP are exhibited.
- ☉ Unusual sounds are heard.
- ☉ The tunnel experience begins.
- ☉ The presence of other loving entities is felt.
- ☉ There is total awareness of the physical world left behind and the nonphysical one just entered.

The white light so commonly reported is actually the Higher Self. I have made this point several times already, but it bears repeating. The only way the departed soul can travel to the Soul plane to select its future life is to enter this white light. Descriptions of a blinding, yet peaceful aura of pure white light are not surprising, since it represents the perfect energy of the Higher Self.

Death also requires telepathy as the mode of communication. The Astral plane uses telepathy as we depend upon speech. It is impossible to distort the truth when any entity can instantly read your thoughts.

Always remember the spirit guide's chief message: There is no death, merely a shift of awareness (fvr), and a change of dimensions. Hypnotic techniques, along with other alpha disciplines, allow us to merge with our Higher Self at the moment of death and leave the karmic cycle behind once and for all. I refer to this as *conscious dying*.

Consider this letter from one of my readers who spends a bit of time in hypnosis and has developed her psychic abilities, as well as presenting a story illustrating the permanence of the soul:

> My brother, who lived in Georgia, had been seen at the emergency room that night. He had been diagnosed as having pneumonia earlier in the week and despite the antibiotics he was taking, a repeat chest X-ray showed no improvement in his condition.
>
> At the emergency room that night he was medicated for pain and a lung biopsy was scheduled for the following day. The night before the biopsy results were known to us, my father came to me. He had passed away almost five years before that night and although I have communicated with others of the spiritual realm this was the first and only time that dad has come.

As dad stood at the foot of my bed, impressions were shared between us, making spoken words unnecessary, "Jack will soon be here with me" dad told me "when his time there is finished I will come for him." Before dad left my presence I understood that he had wanted to tell me how seriously ill my brother was before the doctors did and he wanted to assure me as well, that he would be there for Jack when the time came for him to cross over.

Jack was diagnosed with squamous cell carcinoma, the most virulent of lung cancer. Because of the advanced nature of the disease, all we could hope for was that the tumors would shrink enough to allow the pain medication to keep Jack comfortable until the end came.

About a month into the therapy, X-rays revealed that the cancer was rapidly spreading in spite of the radiation and that his immune system and heart were severely damaged. The treatments ended ominously.

Jack was 44 years old when he discovered that he had inoperable cancer. The disease relentlessly took away his strength, his livelihood, and eventually his earthly life but it never took his joy. The beginning of the end began with a visitation from God.

In December, during one of our many visits to Jack, some family members were praying for Jack. With great difficulty Jack rose from the couch and joined hands with us as we prayed. Soon afterwards I sensed a holy presence in the room and simultaneously Jack began to exclaim that God was in the room standing next to him. He started to cry as God's love and mercy ministered to him. From that night onward Jack was serene in his acceptance of God's will for him.

Jack's condition remained critical but stable until one Sunday morning in February when he awoke in severe respiratory distress. The oxygen brought no relief and he was taken by ambulance to the hospital where he was admitted for terminal care.

Jack possessed revelation knowledge during this time. Our grandmother passed away on the very night that Jack entered the hospital and because of his condition we decided not to tell Jack about it; but even I was not prepared for what happened next.

Jack awakened from a short nap and expressed surprise that he had just seen grandmother with our grandfather in the spirit world. When I tried to explain to him why we had not told him about her passing away he said, "You might as well have told me, I would have found out about it anyway."

An Angel flew into the room through the door leading into the hallway and stopped directly over the bed where Jack lay. He reached down and took Jack in his arms and they flew away through the window. At that exact instant I looked over at where Jack's body lay and could see that he was no longer breathing.

The angel was magnificent. He wore a long, white, flowing robe, gathered at the waist by a gold braided cord. His appearance was majestic. His skin was rosy and flawless, his face framed by curly hair, the color of wheat. He wore no shoes, his feet were perfect in form. It was as if I were a spectator that night, he did not acknowledge my presence but with joy and purpose he did as he was bid.

For some time after seeing the Angel of God, my sense of spirituality was heightened. During this time I kept a pad and pen by my bed at night, so frequent were the messages I received from the Holy Beings of the spiritual realm. My gifts of prophesy and discernment were never as acute as they were during that time.

It was during this time that I experienced a spontaneous past-life recall in which I saw my true self in the body of a woman of a different race. I was totally consumed with love for others; anger and discontentment were not part of my spirit.

There is no fear in my life now, fear of death has been replaced by assuredness that my state here is temporary and that a loving God awaits me at the end of each trial. There we will all be reunited with our loved ones.

The transition from the physical body allows us to identify with our spirit guides by placing us in their universe of simultaneous time, telepathy, traveling at the speed of light and easier access to our Akashic Records. Once the departed soul enters the white light, all bereavement on the Earth plane ends, because the magnetic pull from the astral body to the physical body's aura is impossible from the perspective of the Soul plane.

Crossing into spirit finally proves to us that death is simply a transition into a life that is larger, fuller, and more meaningful than the one we left behind. Still, the ever-present emotion of fear is evident. We must eliminate fear from our awareness to grow spiritually, especially the fear of death.

For those of you who have successfully mastered OBEs, this will come as no surprise. The astral body feels no pain from its physical predecessor. You are completely free of all discomforts and your senses are particularly well developed, especially the sense of hearing.

Even though you have crossed into spirit and have been instructed by both your Higher Self and spirit guides to enter the white light, your free will is active. You can reject that advice and remain on the lower Astral plane as a ghost in the form of a troubled spirit. This explains haunted houses and the like. You have the choice to remain in this condition indefinitely.

Seeking the Truth

I am a retired priest of the Episcopal Church and have been interested in the paranormal for most of my life. I have had vivid out-of-body experiences as well as several mystical experiences.

In the past few years, largely through meditation, I have begun hearing voices purportedly of "Guardian spirits." These voices are addressed to the inner mind and always speak about issues which are important to me. In several instances they have foretold events which seemed very unlikely to transpire, but which, nonetheless, materialized against all logic.

The voice is never judgmental but merely indicates that something is about to transpire within a given time frame.

I cannot, however, determine whether this is all coincidence, contact with the astral, or simply my own inner voice (or wishful thinking). I do not expect you to determine which of the above this may be, but I only report this as an interesting phenomenon. The voice has been correct on any number of issues even in things trivial. I have been retired for some years mostly of boredom when the routine was deadly dull but the voice has made things interesting and, since it began, life has become much more pleasant.

I do firmly believe in an afterlife and also that death does not sever a loving relationship. The voice I hear is that of a woman who genuinely loved me platonically. I like to think that her love continues to guide me.

The above letter was sent to me by a man whom I never worked with clinically but who is a devoted reader of my books. This example demonstrates both the accuracy and true spiritual motive of a guide. We can all benefit from this form of contact from a guide's inner voice, or any other manifestation of high level energy. In seeking his truth this man has found a greater purpose in his golden years.

In seeking the truth, spirit guides emphasize the development of telepathy as a necessary prerequisite. Telepathy is a natural and continual process that is experienced by all of us. This psychic gift has the capability of producing positive changes in our moods and mental functioning.

We can enhance our relationships and interactions with others through telepathy. This method can empower us by way of channeling positive thoughts inwardly, resulting in peace of mind, increased creativity, raised self-image, and myriad other benefits.

An interesting protective mechanism is provided by telepathy. Although a psychic attack may be initiated through telepathy, an individual protected by white light techniques, or similar methods, is able to transmit this negative energy back to the sender. A "boomerang effect" results in the perpetrator receiving the malice he or she tried to direct at you.

We can use telepathy on a global basis to raise planetary consciousness and bring about an end to world hunger, injustice, disease and even world peace. It is always important to consider the fact that our futures are determined by our free will choices, rather than predestination or chance. Spirit guides assist us in making the right choices.

When we have OBEs, we experience the very core of our beings. This liberation from our physical bodies allow us the opportunity to have direct contact with spirit guides and receive their illumination that facilitates the search for the truth. We expand our consciousness, become aware of other realities and see evidence of life following death of the physical body, an all-important truth.

When out-of-the body, our perceptions become more detailed, vivid, and meaningful. We can now visit learning temples and significantly expand our creative and problem-solving skills. Freed from the confines of the physical body and the ego, you can tune into a more real universe and become enlightened.

All of our psychic talents come into play while astral voyaging. We can view the past (*retrognition*), the present (clairvoyance, *clairaudience, clairsentience*), the future (*precognition*), and several other gifts to make inroads to the truth.

One of the concepts that spirit guides try to explain to us is that the other dimensions exist alongside the Physical plane, just at different fvrs. Each dimension has a different density, determined by how fast it vibrates, and they all coexist in the same space as does time, temperature, and barometric pressure. The reality we perceive is based upon our points of view. In our physical bodies we sense the physical world. The mental plane is observed when our souls inhabit our mental bodies and so on. The exception is seen by those who have well-developed psychic powers while in their physical bodies.

Spirit guides do monitor our thoughts, but are careful not to infringe upon our thoughts or actions. This free will principle is etched in stone in spirit world. Because the God energy is all things, is in all places, and represents all of consciousness, all of our thoughts are generated by God.

We humans have become isolated in our thinking we have separated from God, not the other way around. Spirit guides only attempt to bring these divine ideas and concepts to us for consideration.

The Physical plane is an illusion created by our minds. As long as we continue to give this illusion power, we will be subject to its laws. We can return to the true reality of a spiritual universe through self-hypnosis. These guides are quite adamant about our using mindfulness techniques. Some guides stress meditation, while others emphasize self-hypnosis.

Self-hypnosis gives us the power to quiet the distracting conscious mind (ego), which continually seeks immediate gratification within the illusory material world. We can easily reduce the illusion most of us experience on the Physical plane through self-hypnosis. Even these illusions function to teach us to recognize them for what they really are. Let us listen to these guides and use these illusions to grow spiritually.

After you have mastered recognizing and learning about the illusions of the Earth plane, your next step in finding the truth is to accept and express your love of God. Using hypnosis speeds up this process due to its natural mindfulness effect.

Hypnosis teaches us that we obtain what we expect. Whatever you desire with intense concentration, repetition, and proper mindset will become your reality. This is part of God's plan. You must put aside intellectual analysis and other cognitive abilities to appreciate and experience this principle. Cognition only creates more illusions and inhibits spiritual unfoldment.

Cause and effect paradigms, for example, are a component of these physical plane illusions. The multidimensional universe and parallel universe theory illustrating that all time is simultaneous nullifies any form of cause and effect as being a truth. It is God's love that created us and the universe in general. We can identify with this in hypnosis.

No amount of cognition or evaluation of any book, scripture, or other data will lead you to this truth. The universe is based on free will, not by what you think is fair or an injustice. We are all part of God's energy and we were conceived not only as part of this gestalt, but as a unique component of that macrocosm.

Spirit guides are not the ultimate representative of God's truth. They are a heterogeneous group of souls in various levels of growth themselves. All they do is provide guidance in such a manner that the ultimate decisions are left up to free will.

An important truth is that love is the most important quality in the universe. This truth must be realized from within our very being, not by the way of the external, Physical, and illusory plane. Spirit guides emphasize that they can only teach those of us who seek the truth. Their simple message is that all that there is can be expressed by one word: love.

What we send out to others and the universe comes back to us in kind. Service to others is service to one's self. We can look upon others and ourselves and find no similarity, but there is identity, completion, and unity. Each of us is a completed and free being whose identity is unique within the multidimensional universe.

We can more easily receive communication from guides through self-hypnosis. This natural state will foster our ability to reach out to our fellow citizens of the universe and assist in both their enlightenment and our own.

Spirit guide activity is greater now than it has been in the history of our species. This is not merely due to the increased population of this planet, but more so explained by the increased desire of us to make this spiritual breakthrough when the consciousness shift takes place. Deep within our subconscious we know that this major change in consciousness is on the horizon.

Part of the confusion we feel comes from the inability to consciously remember our karmic purpose. When we reincarnate into a new physical body, all memories of past lives and karmic purpose are eliminated from our physical brain. But our subconscious retains these memories and self-hypnosis can restore them to our conscious awareness. That is why I presented the Access your Akashic Records exercise in the previous chapter.

Our conscious mind loves to avoid change and it procrastinates learning these required karmic lessons as evidence of its unwillingness to grow. By using hypnosis we are removing this formidable obstacle to spiritual development, so we are better prepared to remember these tests and complete them. It is important to use self-hypnosis techniques to reinforce the concept of complete unity of self, especially in times of stress or doubt.

Spirit guides do not like to simply tell us what is going to happen in the future. For one thing, there are many probable paths which are influenced by our motives. Second, the farther ahead in time they view, the more difficult it is for them to pinpoint precisely what we will experience, as I have previously discussed.

These beings of light warn us not to fear predictions of Armageddon and geological disasters on a massive scale as prophesized by the *Book of Revelations* and psychics. Only those individuals who program themselves to experience a pole shift, or Armageddon-like scenario, will have that as their reality. For us spiritually evolved souls a major consciousness shift will bring with it a new vibration of space and time that represents a path so positive it is impossible to describe.

You will not be allowed to enter this new age unless you have mastered the lessons of love and of the God-created universe of which we are a part. Shortly, we will all be given a choice to make and there will be no middle ground. Either you raise your soul's energy and select the path of love and light, or choose the Armageddon-like fate of the ancient continent of Lemuria (Mu) and Atlantis. Never forget the concept of forgiveness. Forgiveness erases karma.

It is our fvr of the component of consciousness that we term soul that will determine which path we select. There will be no God apart from us who supervises a Judgment Day. Rather, a God within us that assists our ability to learn light and love and ascend to this New Age. For others who fail this test a series of additional lessons will be required. It will not be Hell or Armageddon, merely summer school.

Healing

The guides discuss rather complicated paradigms involving vibratory sound complexes that are involved in the healing of our body. The subconscious is by far the most important component of our natural defense against disease and recovery from any form of trauma. Consciousness represents a microcosm of the God energy complex. This gives us many creative and curative powers.

A balance established between that all-important love and wisdom in the manner in which we use our bodies are another healing force at our disposal. The third factor represents our connection with the Higher Self. Self-hypnosis is the most efficient method to maintain this link.

Vibrational sound complexes involve the electromagnetic forces in the universe and the fabric of space-time. They limit our natural healing capabilities and can be bypassed by eliminating the polarities that comprise the illusions of the Physical plane. If we can use self-hypnosis to assist us in believing that all things are one and that disharmony doesn't exist except in our minds, we are well on our way to be healed.

When we come to understand and accept that all is one and that this one is love and light as represented by God, we will be healed. The elimination of imperfection and disharmony of energy forces that cause disease and chronic pain can be brought about when our mind-body complex accepts the love of God. Balancing our chakras is part of this mechanism.

Illusions of the physical plane disappear when we identify with the God energy complex completely. Healing then functions as a catalyst for this individual mechanism and a reward for our faith. All healing takes place within our consciousness first. The mind must be opened spiritually for this to occur. We are all complete healers, as our mind contains all things, things that we obtain from God.

Proper healing is assured when we place our mind-body complex in a place of love and light. Attuning to our Higher Self is a way of letting the perfect God energy into our very essence. This pure energy can heal anything and open our minds up to receive spirit guide wisdom. We can even see healing brought about through an increase in creativity, as the next two examples will demonstrate.

The Spirit Guides of William Blake

One of my favorite artists and writers is William Blake. This creative genius was born in England in 1757 and crossed into spirit in 1827. In addition to functioning both as an artist and poet, he illustrated and printed his books as well. He even saw an image of his dead younger brother, Robert, who instructed William on a process of copper engraving that proved both valid and practical in the production of Blake's books.

Blake saw spirit guides in his visions. These light beings gave him creative inspirations. He referred to these guides as the "Immortals." Blake's *Songs of Innocence* and *Songs of Experience* dealt with his spiritual advisors. These divinely inspired creative insights helped him deal with bouts of depression.

We can look to Blake's art as expressions of universal knowledge. He spoke of the Hall of Los, in which the figures of this dimension appeared as statues until one observed them. They then became animated and represented one's past lives. This Hall of Los was in actually the Causal plane, where our Akashic Records are housed.

Robert Louis Stevenson's "Brownies"

The famous writer Robert Louis Stevenson would create elaborate stories to tell himself prior to falling asleep in order to eliminate his childhood nightmares. He stated that certain "little people" he called "Brownies" provided him with the inspiration for his tales.

We can see how spirit guides could take the form of Brownies to assist Stevenson in honing his skills as a writer. Stevenson explained the role of these guides in inspiring one of his best-known works, *The Strange Case of Dr. Jeckyll and Mr. Hyde*, as follows:

> "I had long been trying to write a story on this subject, to find a body, a vehicle for that strong sense of man's double being, which must at times come in upon and overwhelm the mind of every thinking creature."

And

> "For two days I went about racking my brains for a plot of any sort; and on the second night I dreamed the scene at the window, and a scene afterwards split in two, in which Hyde, pursued for some crime, took the powder and underwent the change in the presence of his pursuers. All the rest was made awake, and consciously, although I think I can trace in much of it the manner of my Brownies."[1]

Extraterrestrials

Spirit guides mention thousands of groups of extraterrestrials (ETs) from a multitude of galaxies that have come to Earth and experimented with our species genetically. These guides speak of 25,000-year planetary cycles during which much evolutionary progress is made.

Often ETs from Mars are described as coming to Earth, due to inhospitable conditions existing on their planet. Some guides speak of nuclear war on that red planet long ago. In order to inhabit Earth these ETs had to undergo a type of genetic alteration conducted by guardians of interplanetary colonization.

The details of these guardians are somewhat sketchy. Some describe them as dimensional guardians that transferred the Martians from their planet to Earth after that race exterminated themselves by various methods. A form of melding took place between the social memories of the ETs and our physical bodies. This also resulted in a genetic alteration of our chromosomal makeup.

In addition to our evolution being sped up, various wars among other competing ETs took place that were contrary to our spiritual growth. Some guides describe time travelers from our very own future as interceding and protecting us from these highly advanced ETs. My book, *Time Travelers from Our Future* explains this in greater detail.

This seeding of our species has taken place during a period of about five million years. Some of the negative consequences from these ETs have involved making use of energy forces or black magic. Telepathic techniques were used by rather disturbed individuals to access negative forces from the lower Astral plane and manipulate or attack others on the physical plane. The very same methods that can heal and assist our spiritual growth can be used for evil purposes. Fortunately, our Higher Self is always with us and this explains the effectiveness of white light spiritual protection techniques through hypnosis. We can always call on our spirit guides with this natural alpha state.

We can look to the Old Testament for an example of ET spirit guides. The Jewish prophet Ezekiel lived in exile by the Chebar Canal in Babylon. He wrote, "I looked, and behold, a whirlwind came out of the north, a great cloud, and a fire infolding itself, and a brightness was about it." He went on to describe four strange other worldly creatures that had the physique of man but with a few unusual differences: The heads of these creatures each had four faces (one human, and one each of a lion, an ox, and an eagle) and two pairs of wings. Some kind of "terrible crystal" extended from the top of the creatures' heads, and "their appearance was like burning coals of fire."[2]

Ezekiel went on to describe how each of these beings were connected to a fiery wheel intersecting with another wheel. The wheels could change direction without turning around, and their rims were covered with eyes. The sound made by the creatures' wings was "like the noise of great waters, as the voice of the Almighty."[3]

Later a vision was seen by the prophet of a fiery human stationed on a throne composed of sapphire. The result of this entity's message to Ezekiel assisted the latter in guiding the Jewish people back to God by convincing them to abandon their evil behaviors.

Scholars have long debated whether Ezekiel's vision was one of angels or an encounter with ETs in their flying saucers. Either way these beings functioned as spirit guides.

A Christmas Angel in Uniform

We have discussed angels and described them as nonhuman messengers of God whose only purpose is to teach love. At times these spirit guides manifest themselves as human in order to assist us in times of dire need. Marissa's case that I am about to present is one such example. This example defies all logical explanation except one divine intervention by a spirit guide.

The case of Marissa was reported in my book *Soul Healing* in the chapter titled "Angelic Healing." This patient described an angelic encounter that occurred on Christmas day in 1988.

Marissa was an eighteen-year-old devout Christian and a virgin. She had few friends, as her communication skills were not very good and most of her classmates considered her a prude and not fun to be around. Her best friend was Carla, who was quite the opposite in personality and morals, as compared to Marissa. Carla was a party girl with no respect for Christian values, and repeatedly tempted Marissa in "broadening her horizons" with sex and drugs. It was not uncommon for Carla to smoke pot, use cocaine, and have sex with boys.

Marissa had no other friends who regularly paid as much attention to her as did Carla. What Marissa didn't realize at that time was that Carla's motives were strictly to corrupt and humiliate Marissa. For example, Marissa had never tried drugs and wouldn't even drink alcohol. Carla was well aware of this and the fact that Marissa was a virgin, but still persisted in tempting her.

Christmas day in 1988 fell on a Sunday. Carla's parents had gone to Palm Springs for the weekend, but Carla chose to remain at home in Los Angeles. This provided Carla the opportunity to throw an unsupervised party at her parents' home.

Marissa was invited to this party on Sunday (Christmas day) and was told that only a dozen people would be there. She readily accepted the invitation and looked forward to this event with excited anticipation.

When Marissa arrived she was shocked. In addition to the presence of over 150 people at the party, there were drugs all over the place. People were smoking pot, popping pills, and even syringes were in use.

Because meeting new people was difficult for Marissa on her best day, the shock of this degenerate scene literally immobilized her. Two of

Carla's friends named Todd and James approached Marissa and told her to go into the den because Carla had a special Christmas present for her. As Carla painted for a hobby, this was not a suspicious request.

While in the den, Todd and James tore Marissa's blouse and announced they were going to rape her. Marissa froze and prayed for a moment. A loud knock at the front door changed everything. A man announced, "This is the police—open this door!" Marissa noted his name, badge number, and patrol car number, and then left the party. She did not file any charges against Todd or James.

The officer escorted Marissa to her car and told her that she was fortunate not to have been molested by Todd and James. When she said to the policeman, "Are you sure God didn't send you here today?" he just smiled and returned to his patrol car.

A few days later Marissa called the precinct to express her gratitude to the officer. She was amazed to learn that the police had no record of an officer with his name. The patrol car number and badge number were not on their records either. Last, no official call was made or reported to Carla's house that night.

When Marissa told me of this incident four years later in my Los Angeles office, she asked me who this man could possibly be. I informed her that it was probably her "guardian angel."

Marissa came to see me to deal with insomnia, depression, low-self image, poor communication skills, and loneliness. The main technique in my office is the superconscious mind tap. This method consists of introducing the patient's subconscious mind to his or her Higher Self (superconscious mind) through hypnosis, as I have discussed previously. One result of this "cleansing" mechanism is to raise the quality of the subconscious mind's energy level to rise above an issue. You may think of this approach as an energy immune system.

Whereas a patient may previously have been vulnerable to issues such as depression, overeating, procrastination, and other "self defeating sequences" they now rise above this susceptibility and can permanently effect a new positive behavior pattern and lifestyle. This technique also trains the patient to communicate with their guardian angels and other spirit guides.

Marissa was able to utilize this cleansing mechanism to overcome her low self-image, improve her communication problems, eliminate depression, and remove the insomnia that plagued her for over five years.

Another side effect of this approach is a change in the energy she sent out to others. Marissa almost immediately began attracting new and positive friendships in her life. During one of her superconscious mind tap sessions she saw the image of her policeman angel in uniform who saved her honor in 1988.

By the late spring of 1993 Marissa met Warren. They immediately fell in love. On Christmas day 1993, Warren proposed to her and she accepted. They were married the following spring.

Marissa called me in June of 1995 to inform me that she was in marital bliss. She did remain a virgin until her wedding night as was her goal. Warren is a man of like qualities, a devout Christian and a loving husband.

One final thing Marissa shared with me was that she is the proud mother of a baby boy. This entire experience has only further strengthened Marissa's belief in God and in the power of faith and spirit guides.

An Uninvited Spirit and an Angelic Encounter

In 1995 a woman named Elaine came to my Los Angeles office from out of state. Part of her problems revolved around her bereavement over the death of her father five years prior. Because he left her mother shortly after her birth, she always blamed herself for his abandonment of the family.

Elaine was depressed throughout most of her life. The passing of her father now made it impossible for Elaine to confirm or reject her worst fear—that she was the cause of her parents' breakup. Elaine's spirit guides had other plans.

She was able to channel the soul of her late father in my office. His spirit cleared up her abandonment issue once and for all by letting her know that he left because he felt he could not provide for the family, being disabled and unable to work.

As this eliminated Elaine's longstanding guilt for thinking her birth was responsible for her father's departure, her spirit guide contact proved most beneficial and therapeutic. Another turn of events took place in my office as she channeled the spirit of her late husband's late sister without attempting to do so. This uninvited soul told that she had died as a young child in order for her parents to be able to have two additional children, one of which is Elaine's husband.

This case took another surprising spiritual turn on the morning of her final session. On her way to my office she nearly missed her turn. She avoided the incident by swerving her car to refrain from colliding with two vehicles coming from different directions. Elaine then stopped her car and tried to locate these two cars, but they were nowhere to be seen.

Because there were no driveways or intersections for these cars to enter, it was literally impossible for them to have turned off the road. Did they simply vanish into thin air, or were they holograms created by spirit guides? Elaine and I will never know for sure, but she arrived at my office on time and safe and sound.

An Actor's Angel

The late actor Gordon MacRae, who starred in such films as *Carousel* and *Oklahoma*, had a life-saving encounter with an angel. In 1946 Gordon was in the Air Training Army Air Corps Pilots when, at about 11 a.m., the copilot panicked and froze at the controls.

Advice came from the ground for them to jump. Gordon instead unlocked the copilot's hands and eventually landed the plane. It was fortunate that he didn't jump because one of his crew did and was killed due to the low altitude of the plane.

Gordon MacRae was assisted again some time later. He was stationed at Pope Field in North Carolina and routinely flew to New York to spend the weekend with his wife and children, who lived on Long Island.

His wife, Sheila, "sensed" that he shouldn't fly to New York one particular Friday and instead made arrangements to take a train with their daughter to visit him. Later that evening she and Gordon attended a party at the home of one of the colonels. They were informed that the very flight Gordon would have taken to New York crashed as it was about to land at Roosevelt Field, killing everyone aboard.

In 1982 I had the pleasure of being interviewed by their daughter, Meredith MacRae, when she hosted a local Los Angeles television talk show. She most definitely appeared open to my work, as my first book, *Past Lives—Future Lives*, was just released. Perhaps the angel's influence on her parents kept spiritual growth "all in the family."

A Television Host's Spirit Guide Contact

Marilyn Kenz (one of the "Mommies" of television fame) had a rather dramatic spirit guide contact that was televised.

On November 22, 1961, when she was 14, Marilyn Kenz—one of the hosts of *Caryl and Marilyn's Real Friends*—had an argument with her father on the way to school. He wanted her to cut her hair and wear it more conservatively. Marilyn slammed the car door as her father drove off—her way of having the last word.

He died of a heart attack later that day. Guilt-stricken, Marilyn wrote a note to him, crumpled it up, and tossed it into the fireplace. For the next 35 years, she struggled to remember what her note had said, but the memory remained buried in her subconscious. She tried various types of therapy, including conventional hypnotherapy, to obtain this memory. Nothing worked.

On February 10, 1997, I went to Marilyn's home, where a crew was set up to tape a hypnosis session with Marilyn. We were going to try to retrieve her repressed memory. I helped her regress to the day of her father's death.

On the day of the fight, while she was in gym class, Marilyn felt dizzy and fainted at the precise moment her father died of a heart attack. She was taken to the nurse's office and told to lie down on a cot. Another student was on the cot next to her. A few minutes later, the nurse informed both girls that there had been a death in one of their families—but she didn't know which one at that time. Marilyn turned to the other student and said, "I hope it's my father." Then they both laughed.

Before long, Marilyn's neighbor Vivian arrived with bad news. Vivian drove Marilyn home. When she arrived there, she didn't want to acknowledge her father's death. "I just walked through them [other people in her home] and past them," she said. "I didn't want to be there. I didn't know where anybody was." She was crying during this part of the session.

Marilyn said she didn't want to see her mother because it would give too much reality to the fact that her father had died. She went to her room and tried to deal with the tragedy.

Dr. G.:   Do you feel anything in particular?

Marilyn: A hole, a hole. I've got a hole inside of me…It's in my chest. It's a huge hole. (I asked Marilyn about the note she wrote to her father.)

Marilyn: I am writing, "I'm so sorry."

Dr. G.:   What else?

Marilyn: "I love you."

That was the answer that had eluded Marilyn for more than 35 years. The note she wrote simply said, "I'm so sorry. I love you."

After the session, Marilyn said, "That was the hardest thing I've done."

The experience was important for many reasons. At the time of her father's death, Marilyn could not express her emotions. She didn't cry or express any feelings concerning this incident for more than 15 years. Conventional psychotherapy (including hypnosis) had been unable to retrieve her repressed memory. But in only 20 minutes, I was able to elicit the details of this all-important note.

Following this revelation, I guided Marilyn into a communication with the spirit of her late father. She described a surrealistic scene: She saw herself as a child—prior to her father's death—and as a mother repressing his death. Suddenly, another image of the adult Marilyn sprang from this mother image. The vision represented an empowered Marilyn undergoing soul healing. She watched as the image of her father appeared in a swirling light. Marilyn rose up above the Earth and joined him. They embraced and laughed.

I asked Marilyn why she was laughing. She told me that both she and her father found it hilarious that Marilyn at age 49 was communicating with her father, who was only age 42 when he died.

I concluded the session with a technique in which Marilyn guided her father's spirit into the white light. I trained her to access her Higher Self to heal her grief and raise her soul's energy.

The show aired on April 7, 1997.

As a side note, before the show, Marilyn said she did not believe in life after death, and to this day she does not believe in reincarnation. Her session was an out-of-body experience.

"I really feel grateful," she said later. "It was really good for me. I, at last, got to the point where I could look at the most scary portion of it." Belief is not necessary for soul healing to work. No matter how long a memory has been buried, when you contact your Higher Self, you can obtain any information you desire.

A Policewoman's Angel

This case of spirit guide intervention comes from my good friend and colleague Brad Steiger and was reported in his book *Guardian Angels and Spirit Guides*. A southern U.S. city policewoman named Christa Evans rescued a female motorist trapped in a submerged car in a local river. An ambulance took this woman to a local hospital for treatment.

Later a witness stated that another passenger was in that same car. Although no prior reports of another individual appeared, Officer Evans stated, "I had better check it out. We can't risk leaving someone who might still be alive down there to drown. And in any event, it's my job to bring the victim to the surface."

It was unfortunate that the woman Christa rescued was not available to confirm the presence of this other passenger, as she was dazed and her statements could not be relied on as being completely accurate. Christa returned to the submerged car and found no other person alive or dead.

However, a sudden lift shift in water pressure closed the car door shut on Christa's left pinky finger. As she could not open the door and the oxygen supply in her tank was low, her only choice was to cut off her finger or drown.

Christa prayed for help and was rewarded, and summarized what happened next as follows:

"A bright light approached me. It came within arm's length...and then it disappeared. But my finger was free! I rose to the surface and was pulled into a boat by two other members of the rescue squad. Neither of them had entered the water...I am convinced that it was my guardian angel that saved me from drowning."[4]

An Angel Cliffhanger

Chantal Lakey of Murrieta, California, had an encounter with several angels that saved her life. She and her fiancé, Dale, were hiking at a place called Lookout Point near Ophir, Oregon. Dale was "showing off" his athletic skills to Chantal. Suddenly, the trail ended at a rocky cliff. As it began raining, the rock became slippery.

As they descended this rock it became steeper and more treacherous. Dale reached out to help guide Chantal's foot toward the ledge and fell to his death! Chantal was in shock and had no idea how to descend the cliff. She screamed, "Please, God, I don't want to die!"

She soon saw angels surrounding her and preventing her from Dale's fate. They held her up, but she still felt great fear and slowly continued with her descent. When she was about 75 feet above the beach, she lost her footing and began to slide down the face of the cliff out of control.

Then she felt a "hand" supporting her from behind that stopped her from falling further. She then completed her descent without incident. Later on she was able to flag down a passing motorist who drove her to the sheriff's office. Chantal felt the many spirit guides with her the rest of the day.

Dale did die on that day, but Chantal was spared. The rescue team could not figure out how she possibly could have descended that cliff relatively unharmed. This incident left Chantal not with anger over the loss of her fiancé, but with an unshakable realization that God exists and is a loving being.[5]

One must ask why Chantal was saved and not Dale? Dale did act somewhat immature by showing off and most certainly did not call upon his spirit guides. Chantal, on the other hand, did specifically request God's assistance in her time of need.

There is more to this scenario than that. In the scheme of the universe and both Dale's and Chantal's karmic purpose, one was supposed to survive, but not the other. Let us not forget the old adage: "God works in mysterious ways." One last point is that later Chantal met her soulmate, Andy Lakey, and married him. Their first child was born in 1993. His angelic encounters were also described in Freeman's book *Touched by Angels*.

Spirit guides have assisted us in all types of times of need by the process of entering our consciousness as an inner life. Consider the case of one of my patients named Ava.

Ava had a lifelong history of being victimized by men. As a nine-year-old child she was molested by an older cousin.

Ava's boss, "Frank," made more than a few suggestive remarks to her. One day Frank called Ava into his office and grabbed her around the waist. Her initial response was just to let it happen. Suddenly, her inner voice prompted her to tell Frank that if he didn't let go of her immediately, she would scream at the top of her lungs and file suit against him for sexual harassment. Frank let go. This was the first time Ava had ever stood up to a man.

Oscar's case illustrates a different type of scarring aided by his guide. He had undergone an existential crisis several years ago and lost his faith in relationships of any kind. After being used and scarred by several women, Oscar decided never to date again. At his corporate job Oscar was being blocked from a well-deserved promotion by a jealous female colleague. This only fueled his disgust with women.

One day Oscar's inner voice directed him to go to lunch at a restaurant serving a kind of food he disliked. While there, he encountered one of his female supervisors, dining alone. She invited Oscar to join her. He related his problem to her and was surprised when she listened intently and promised to assist him. Three weeks later he received the promotion and found out it was this same female supervisor who had made it possible. Because his faith in women has been restored, and he is dating once again.

Being Part of God's Energy Complex

If there is one common message conveyed by spirit guides, it is that we represent a microcosm of the God energy complex. Our subconscious is far from perfect, but we do have the Higher Self. This superconscious mind is the perfect energy component of your essence and represents your link to God and spirit guides.

The path to perfection of our soul requires us to eventually merge with our Higher Self and become one with it. First, we must become aware of this part of our souls' energy, and next we have to eliminate all fear. Determining the truth has always been difficult for us, because we are given so many contradictory messages from religion and other organizations.

We all aspire to attain love. When we can recognize false paradigms, it is easier to perceive and understand the opposite, the truth. When we adopt an attitude reflecting love, the truth becomes more readily available, often with the assistance of spirit guides.

Spirit guides foster our understanding of the truths of the universe. The OBE exercises presented in the previous chapter are an important preparation to receive one of the most important truths: the soul is eternal and death is merely a change in dimensions.

When contemplating the origin of our universe, we have deduced that energy preceded matter. Spirit guides reinforce this paradigm and emphasize that your Higher Self is a remnant of the perfect God energy complex and that you should communicate with your Higher Self as often as possible, preferably through self-hypnosis.

In between lives your soul journeys to the Soul plane to evaluate your most recent lifetime and compare it with past lives and future incarnation options. At this time our spirit guides, along with your Higher Self, assist you in making choices.

We may spend the equivalent of centuries before deciding on reincarnating. For those who believe in a Heaven and Hell or Bardo paradigm, the stay on the lower Astral plane is lengthened. Now we truly become a creator of our reality, as our thoughts manifest themselves faster and more directly on other dimensions. There is no possibility of growth on the lower Astral plane, so it is wisest to listen to our guides and learn how to select the upper Astral dimension following the transition from the Physical plane. A more detailed discussion of this is presented in my book *Peaceful Transition*.

When on the Soul plane we overview precisely where our subconscious is on the karmic evolutionary ladder. From the most basic levels of perception and function we see where our assets and liabilities in reference to our own growth lie. We must consider all components of physical, emotional, mental, and spiritual growth and exactly how to achieve it. Spirit guides provide valuable assistance in integrating these goals and making a proper choice for a new life. However, your free will can reject their recommendation at any time. Even if we make an intelligent choice for a future life, our free will actions and thoughts determine the ultimate quality of that life. Nothing is predestined.

The eternal now is how many guides refer to the higher planes. This eternity lacks any form of cause and effect and polarity. We can begin to relate to this concept as we become more aware of consciously directed OBEs. Now the idea of space and time can be seen to be confined to the three-dimensional physical plane. I have previously discussed the nowness, isness, and hereness of these dimensions.

Infinity and eternity signify a limitless expansion of the universe. We place various limitations upon ourselves in understanding and accepting this truth. By assimilating and adopting the truth as presented by high-level guides, we can make great inroads to incorporating these truths in our own energy complex. A review of history illustrates that our race has gone through many 2,000-year cycles of development as part of the overall 25,000-year cycle of planetary evolution. It is time to end these cycles and ascend.

Fear is the only real obstacle to our spiritual growth. This concept of fear is based upon a separation of our soul from that of God. We now create polarities of good and evil, right and wrong, acceptable and unacceptable, and so on. This creates prejudice, and violence is almost always the result. How many wars, religious and otherwise, have been caused in order to protect a certain population from the presence of those who were different in physical appearance, or ideology?

The actual basis of fear is this concept of "other" because the other is always in opposition to the self. Dualism is now propagated and now becomes the phenomenal manifestation of the universe. First we develop a "me" perspective and then an "other" polarity is used to balance out the first premise. What we have now is a subject (me) which perceives and cognitizes, and an object (other) which is perceived and cognitized.

A result of this duality is the creating of the separate entities of self (ego) and the other. This is a major component of the illusion of the physical plane because it is the mind that creates these polarities. The God energy complex has nothing to do with this division. We create our own reality.

The simplest manner in which to rid ourselves of fear, as repeatedly stated by the guides, is to understand who and what we (microcosm) are in relation to the universe as a whole (macrocosm). We see a universe on the Physical plane that is created by our consciousness. All of our analyses and intellectualizations fail to comprehend and accept the big picture: All of what we perceive and experience is nothing but a manifestation within our consciousness. There is nothing other than consciousness and herein lies the basis of the illusions of the Physical plane.

As a dreamer dreams a dream, the characters portrayed in the dream have no part in the creation of this dream. All that exists is that dream and that dream represents our consciousness on another dimension. Our species and everything we observe in the physical world function like characters in a dream. They are not truly living their lives, but being lived as part of our consciousness in action.

To further emphasize the illusory nature of the physical plane, the guides point out that because we create this dream, the characters portrayed (the material world in general) have no independence, choice, or free will from our perspective. They must respond to our thoughts and emotions. In this analogy, the dreamer is real but all characters and environments are only an illusion created by the dreamer.

This is further complicated by the fact that every other consciousness on our dimension is manifested as other human beings, and each one of them creates his or her own dreams. We now become mere actors in their play and our role is one of no violation. This further reinforces a separation of beings (me versus other) and gives way to fear that can only be resolved through a complete understanding of universal truths and an acceptance of love.

This polarity of me and other only adds fuel to the illusions of the physical plane with an added disadvantage of expressing an aggressive attitude (based on fear) to many of our fellow beings. Our ego can only restrict us and prevent expansion of our awareness.

When we set the ego aside, as in hypnosis, the soul is open and receptive to the concept of nonbeing. Now we can experience a nowness so characteristic of the higher planes and receive pure knowledge from our spirit guides and Higher Self. This principle explains the spontaneous and intuitional inspiration that acted as the driving force behind all great artistic and scientific achievements.

It is important to consider the aspect of time in this paradigm. The physical brain significantly restricts our consciousness from its timeless universality and limits our functioning to that of an individual consciousness. The ego now is caught in the crossfire between desire and fear operating in conceptual time. Our perspective is trapped between desire and fear in the context of time, desire, fear, and time merging as one aspect of consciousness.

Identification with separate and discriminated phenomena creates the illusory ego-self and our subsequent bondage to the karmic cycle. It is this illusory ego-self that considers itself subject to causality at the cycle of birth and death. Identification with these illusions creates the limitations in our soul's growth. Liberation from the karmic cycle is brought about by disidentification. Spirit guides assist us in this disidentification.

Here is a letter from one of my readers with whom I have not had the pleasure of working. This communication illustrates some of the many things we can learn from spirit guides:

I am a 65-year-old recently retired, typical workaholic. I was the goody-goody kid who did exactly what he thought his parents would expect for the never-coming or never-expected "approval." I was the "white sheep" of the family and was supposed to make their lives worthwhile. I made good grades, became a Christian at the acceptable age of 12, became a fundamentalist preacher for about two years, and then became a physician. I literally "denied myself" what happiness was there for me. At about age 56, totally unhappy with my life, which consisted of a successful radiology practice, patients who loved me as well as a wife and two boys who also loved me, vice chairman of the deacons at one of America's largest churches, and so on, I seriously considered suicide.

I was surprised when my spirit began to rise from me as a bluish white mist. I interjected, "Wait, we are supposed to be going inside!" My spirit replied, "Don't worry, I will be back with love." I obeyed. Soon, the spirit turned into a seagull and flew around the cliffs, ocean and giant trees. He landed on a large pine tree branch. A female seagull joined him and they built a nest. An egg soon appeared and became ready for hatching. The egg broke open and I looked out and saw my parents for the first time. They were beautiful and I was beautiful. I grew swiftly and my parents taught me to fly, soar, feed, and sing. After awhile, they said, "It is time to go back."

They flew back to me and turned into the mist. My spirit entered my body.... I heard beautiful music and I was love.... The story goes on from here to witness my immediate loss of my fear situations, especially of death. I am, in fact, excited about my passage into my next existence. I recreated myself. I gained peace of mind and contentment and at that point realized what the scriptures really meant about being content where one is. My life has been fantastic for the past two years as I have learned to receive and to be open to what is there for me. I have beautiful positive energy which is obvious to energy people. I quit my practice and now communicate with letters, on Prodigy, and play African drums.

My goal for the few short years that I remain on this Earth is to develop a more open communication with my subconscious and my Masters and guides. I thought this before I read that section in your book. We shall see. I know that my cup runneth over and I don't know where I would put more happiness than I have.

The following is another correspondence from someone I haven't met who reported spirit guide benefits through his dreams:

...In this dream with my deceased father in a setting that can only be described as heavenly.

My father died of cancer of the stomach in 1972. He had lived a life of hard work and poverty in the Arkansas Ozarks. He had experienced mental illness in his adult years, becoming increasingly mentally ill during my teenage years.

Over the years, as my father's illness became increasingly worse, he became more and more paranoid and hallucinatory, which caused a great deal of difficulty for other family members. I worked closely with him during this period of time, on our hill country farm, when I wasn't in high school.

At the age of 19, during the Korean war, I enlisted in the Navy for four years. During this four years my father's illness continued to worsen. Shortly after I was discharged from the Navy, I had to help get him committed to the state mental hospital, where he received electro-shock therapy. He made fair recovery from this and was able to come home. He was able to live a reasonably happy life, without too much difficulty, for the remainder of his life, even though his mental functioning was somewhat impaired.

I have digressed to give this background information because I felt that it was necessary to give a proper perspective to this portion of the dream. I have necessarily left out most of the details of a very difficult period of time in my life, and in the lives of other members of my family.

I had been fairly depressed for a period of time after the death of my father, probably to a great extent because I had developed a pattern of holding in my feelings as a teenager, because this had been necessary in dealing with my father. I also had the feeling after his death that he had lived a very difficult life, experiencing poverty all of his life, experiencing mental illness, and then suffering terribly with cancer for three months before his death. I am sure that his death also aroused buried psychological conflicts remaining from our relationship during those difficult years.

The dream seemed to have a purpose of communicating to me that all was well with him, and there really wasn't anything for me to be depressed about. In the dream it seemed that I went to the edge of this beautiful setting of vivid color. It was as if I was looking across a beautiful landscape of the most vivid colors that can be imagined. The color was more vivid, and more beautiful than any landscape I have ever seen. There were no buildings, roads, power lines, or other imperfections to clutter up the landscape. I seemed to go to the edge of this landscape, and my father seemed to float toward me across the landscape.

My father appeared younger looking than I ever remembered him having looked. (He was 30 years of age when I was born.) There was no verbal communication, but it seemed to be communicated to me that all was well with him. There was no problem of cancer, or of mental illness. It was as if he was in the prime of life, with no problems of any kind.

This experience was a totally positive, warm experience, which seemed to be for my personal benefit. There was no involvement at all of any conflicts that I may have still had unresolved from the difficulties in our relationship during the years of his mental illness. This experience seemed to be for my reassurance that I didn't need to feel depressed over the difficulties he had experienced in life; that life did have meaning, and also to possibly strengthen the thinking I already had about the nature of the hereafter.

Conclusion

In my practice, I train my patients to empower themselves, and among the many clinical issues I train my patients to overcome, the following have been most easily resolved with the assistance of spirit guide contact through hypnosis:

- Weight loss.
- Anxiety.
- Depression and suicidal tendencies.
- Alcohol and other drug addictions.
- Sexual dysfunction.
- Fear of death and other phobias.
- Chronic pain.
- Grief over the death of loved ones.
- Concentration problems and poor memory.
- Extreme negativity.
- Antisocial behavior.
- Psychic attack.
- Insomnia.
- Existential conflicts.

Your spirit guides are within the realm of other dimensions and are connected to your reality by way of your Higher Self. They assist us in our spiritual growth by advising us on how to overcome the only real block to our psychic empowerment:

Belief in spirit contact is universal. It has and is a part of all countries throughout the world through the history of civilization. All of the major world religions have taught about the existence of a spiritual world. It is referenced in all holy scriptures. Jesus Christ himself believed in the reality of the spiritual dimensions.

As far as channeling is concerned, many examples exist of people accurately detailing future events and describing activities taking place in another room or thousands of miles away. Those who channel, or contact spirit guides in other ways, tend to exhibit psychic abilities and possess knowledge that they do not have when not in a hypnotic trance state.

Other evidence of channeling can be seen in changes observed in breathing rate, voice changes (a woman's voice becomes deep), and alterations in facial features and expressions. The late Jane Roberts, for example, exhibited all three of these characteristics.

We have several spiritual bodies, namely the Astral, Causal, Mental, Etheric, and Soul plane bodies. Each of these spiritual bodies access our Akashic Records and may also tap into the divine plan of the universe by way of spirit guide contact. Because this divine plan contains all possible outcomes, it therefore encompasses all of the potential you are not yet able to use. Spirit guide contact can assist us in utilizing our other bodies to ascend the ladder of awareness, the unlimited potential of the divine plan.

As you practice self-hypnosis and access both your Higher Self and spirit guides, you improve your ability to love in a wise and compassionate way. Now you find that there is nothing that cannot be solved, influenced, or brought to a greater order and increased by love. With love we heal our hurts, our feelings of inadequacy, our issues, our problems. We become less fearful and feel less negativity. This form of psychic empowerment is the ultimate key to our becoming conscious of ourselves as spirit.

Your Higher Self is pure love and, as you become one with love, you become one with your Higher Self. In time, wisdom is added to this love. Your thoughts become more positive and you begin to make great strides in your ultimate ascension. All you need do is practice the self-hypnosis exercises presented in this book and request your spirit guides to send the frequencies from the higher dimensions through you to Earth and its inhabitants.

Love nourishes our hearts and souls—then the body. It gives us the strength and the courage we need to effectively address difficult issues in a caring way. Love is a healing force for our physical, mental, emotional, and spiritual aspects. Love allows us to live a day that is filled with peace, contentment, joy, and delight. We may look upon the God energy complex as a concentration of love. Love allows the realization of who and what we truly are.

As a spirit, you are pure light and pure love. You are constantly changing, growing, and learning. Each of your lifetimes holds the potential for awakening to your true nature. To accomplish this you must eliminate the only real obstacle you face: fear. The message from spirit guides is clear: Stop living in fear and start living in love and joy.

Dreams help us see ourselves as we really are. We don't lie to ourselves in our dreams. Dreams serve as an unrivaled connection to our Higher Self and spirit guides. These nighttime movies give us insight about life lessons, and you can take those insights into waking reality and use them to your advantage by allowing us to achieve the highest levels of wellness and creativity. By working with dreams you will move naturally into higher levels of consciousness and understanding, which have the power to transform yourself and your life.

Spirituality has been in man's quest since the beginning of time. Most people think that they are separate from the spirit—that God is outside of them or "somewhere else," or that you have to die in order to be with God. You cannot separate yourself from God. There is a part of us that has complete understanding of everything—our universe, our world, our physical existence, our life goals, our karmic purpose. This is that part of us we call our Higher Self. We are not our bodies. It is our soul that represents our true essence and this soul originated from God.

The evolving body of evidence for psychic phenomena demands a careful reexamination of the thinking and a restructuring of our traditional views about human life and experience. The fact that mind seems capable of experiencing realities beyond the known limits of sensory perception challenges our conventional systems and raises new questions about the nature of reality and human existence itself.

Are we not all searching for more meaning in our lives? This karmic purpose gives us a deeper understanding of our place in the universe and our ultimate destiny. The answers lie within our consciousness and spirit guides assist us in obtaining these insights. Hypnosis is, in my experience, the most efficient and self-empowering mechanism to obtain these goals.

Too often we turn outward for the very answers that lie within our consciousness by way of our Higher Self and spirit guides. Every day the universe provides us with opportunities to advance our level of spiritual unfoldment. All we have to do is practice mindfulness techniques and be aware of these karmic lessons that we are given. If we don't learn these lessons now, they will return to haunt us with interest and penalties until they are mastered.

Because our guides are not continually with us and usually refrain from making their presence obvious so as not to interfere with our lives, it is easy to assume that any such contact is imagination or delusional behavior. Never forget that the sole purpose of these beings of light is to en-Lighten us. Your consciousness will gradually expand as your awareness of other realities and possibilities becomes evident.

The new awareness and knowledge that has been brought forth in this last 35 years is only the beginning of what is to come. There is a global consciousness shift on the horizon, and old beliefs, those so firmly entrenched in the mass consciousness, the old ways of functioning, are no longer acceptable. This harmonic convergence of energies will result in the realization that we are the creator of both our internal and external world.

It is time for our species to accept the responsibility for the condition of the world we perceive. Originally we were all given the tools to create paradise. We failed, but it is not too late to rectify these errors. Our spirit guides will show us the way, if only we will listen to them.

Spirit guides emphasize both *psychic empowerment* and a *repowering* of our being. This requires us to take back the power we were originally given (repowerment) and live a life reflecting our own ultimate truth with integrity, valor, and authenticity (empowerment).

We must shed all fears of allowing ourselves to experience this Power, and being completely responsible for our actions, always using our influence for the highest good. One of the main fears to eliminate is that of the need to dominate and control others.

Being prepared to accept the responsibility for this spiritually propagated knowledge and power allows us to move well beyond the limitations of the Physical plane and transcend old controlling beliefs to advance to a level on par with that of our Higher Self and spirit guides.

Historically we have seen Western civilization move from blindly accepting the Truths of the Bible and the writings of the classical Greeks, most notably Aristotle, to modern scientific inquiry.

It took courage for Renaissance man to challenge Aristotle's concept that a heavy stone dropped from a certain height will hit the ground before a lighter stone. Galileo showed the folly of this paradigm by conducting such an experiment and discovering that both stones landed at exactly the same time.

Another observation arrived at by Galileo that the Earth revolved around the sun, not the other way around, came about with his telescope. Spirit guides had a lot to do with these and most of our scientific discoveries. These beings of light have assisted us in expanding our psychic gifts so that some of us could detect the thoughts of others, leave our bodies, perceive future events, exhibit levitation, teleportation, and so on.

Aristotle reported that the *spirit body*, or *eidolon*, exhibited all of the senses we know of on the Physical plane. Buddhist and yogic texts mimic this view about the astral body. The *ka* of the ancient Egyptians and the *energy body* of the Tibetans also represented the *eidolon*. Analogous examples are the *doppelganger* of the Germans, the *astral* or *desire body* of the Theosophists, and the *vardger* of the Norwegians. Spirit guides have been responsible throughout history for disseminating these concepts.

Reincarnation is the main mechanism of the karmic cycle of birth and death. Communication from spirit guides have tried to teach us that there is no such thing as death, just a shift from one dimension to another, and that we need not fear death. There is a thread of reincarnation found in most of the major religions in the world today for this very reason.

It is only by opening ourselves up to the wisdom of the spirit guides that we will come to the realization that there most definitely is a soul, an afterlife, and other dimensions. Although the physical body may die, your subconscious is eternal and will eventually merge with your Higher Self as we ascend.

We find extraordinary similarities between the independently produced *Egyptian Book of the Dead* (*Chapters for Coming Forth by Day*) and the *Tibetan Book of the Dead* (*Bardo Thödol*). In both books nearly identical depictions are presented of how the astral body is elevated from the physical body at the moment of death. In addition, the judgment scenes in both scriptures discuss a weighing of the soul following death to determine the fate of the transitee.

The Egyptian version weighs the heart of the deceased against truth, as represented by a feather. An ape-headed god Thoth functions as the judge. A weighing of black versus white pebbles presided over by a monkey-headed god Sinje characterizes the Tibetan text. We even find Tibetan lamas embalmed and mummified in a manner quite similar to that exhibited in ancient Egypt. This most definitely suggests a common origin; spirit guides are a distinct possibility.

Spirit guides try very hard to educate us as to the laws of the universe and its truths. For instance, the reincarnation process is viewed by many as being one of two mechanisms. One such school states that our current karma is the direct result of previous lives and we are helpless to change it. Another school avers that we can improve our future lives and the present incarnation by following intricate religious rituals.

Both views are incorrect. In the first case a life of apathy and depression would result. Why worry about spiritual growth if you are doomed from the moment of birth to a life of pain and frustration? The second school gives all of the power to others. It is our natural gift to seek our own spiritual growth from within. Psychic empowerment can never be achieved by relying on others or their rituals.

Hypnosis is my recommendation for achieving spirit guide contact because this natural state detaches you from your conscious mind and allows you to access your subconscious, Higher Self and spiritual advisors. It introduces you to the concept of tuning in to the vibratory force or energy surrounding other advanced beings. The white light presents you with the protection technique that will assist you in avoiding any negative consequences from this communication.

You must always acknowledge universal laws as you expand your psychic skills. As you develop these abilities they will increase in power. However, with such power comes responsibility. The energy you send out always comes back to you. When you send out love, you get love in return. If you attempt to hurt or manipulate others, you may succeed initially but you will have to pay back this energy misuse down the road. You may be tempted to use your newly developed psychic powers to seek vengeance on someone who has wronged you. Do not give into this temptation. Your spirit guides only preach love and spiritual growth and will never compromise your free will.

The only obstacles in the world are the ones we create. Contacting spirit guides can facilitate your spiritual growth enormously. If you allow potential obstacles to interfere with this communication, you will miss these opportunities. You have free will. Free will allows you to grow spiritually, stay the same, or regress negatively and dysfunctionally. You can adapt any way you choose to the continual flow of information to which you are exposed daily.

You can choose to remember what you learn and observe, or you can discard any data you receive. Your subconscious permanently stores everything your five senses and your psychic abilities teach you. Using the exercises and techniques in this book with discipline, proper motivation, and confidence can give you a properly trained mind that can work with these guides to psychically empower yourself and enhance your spiritual development.

The universe is filled with obstacles. The strongest is your own ego. The reason for this is simple. Your ego is part of you. It lives with you and contributes to your thoughts. It censors what you do and say. Your ego has only been with you in this lifetime. It will die when your physical body crosses into spirit. Your soul or subconscious is eternal. As pure energy it cannot be destroyed—not even when you die.

The subconscious is a computer that is programmed daily. The world in which we live has more negative than positive energy. You must control this programming or you will lose your greatest asset in overcoming these obstacles. Without the proper use of your subconscious you cannot access your Higher Self. This book trains you to program your subconscious positively and establish a regular communication with your Higher Self and spirit guides. By using this book, you can understand your karmic purpose and recognize the connection you have with other souls. This will allow you to rise above these self-made obstacles.

The universe has plenty of knowledge to share. In order for you to acquire it, you must be open to receive it. Society does not promote this openness. Many Americans, for example, do not believe in reincarnation and American society looks askance at this truth. As a soul you desire spiritual growth. Part of that growth requires a certain knowledge. Much of what you were taught as truth is incorrect. You cannot grow unless you obtain this knowledge. One of your obstacles is society and your greatest assets lie in your Higher Self and spirit guides.

You are limited only to your beliefs. This obstacle can easily be removed by psychic development. Society cannot prevent you from communicating with your Higher Self. Only you can do that. Even if you were put to death for your beliefs, you would reincarnate and continue your quest for knowledge and truth in a future life.

Using self-hypnosis facilitates this openness and establishes the all-important connection with your Higher Self and spirit guides. Many spiritual growth opportunities are available to the psychically developed soul, but you must look for them. When you accept the concept of a soul and a Higher Self, you enter a different universe where anything is possible and spiritual guide contact is the norm.

Used with perception and common sense, self-hypnosis can help you, more than any other ability, to succeed in your most sincere endeavors. The only real limits to spirit guide contact are those you create.

In order to facilitate your spirit guide contact I recommend the following:

◎ Accept yourself for who you are and take an inventory of your own needs.

◎ Do not allow negative influences to affect you.

◎ Trust in yourself and keep your motives pure.

◎ Recognize that certain things and situations are outside your control and that you cannot change them.

◎ Initiate changes that you can control and that result in your spiritual growth.

◎ Take care of your body.

◎ Do not allow any person or institution to victimize you.

◎ Establish balance in every aspect of your life.

My final recommendation is to conscientiously practice self-hypnosis. Make tapes of the scripts presented in this book, or contact my office for a list of professionally recorded cassettes and CDs.

Continue to contact your spirit guides and psychically empower yourself. Let your Higher Self assist you in this endeavor and may the Force be with you. Feel free to contact me and share your experiences. Perhaps we will meet on one of the many dimensions that compose the real universe. As we say in Los Angeles, "Have your spirit guide contact my spirit guide."

Chapter Notes

Chapter 1

[1] Corinthians 15:39, 42-44.

[2] B. Goldberg, *Peaceful Transition: The Art of Conscious Dying and The Liberation of the Soul* (St. Paul: Llewellyn, 1997).

[3] Daniel 4:20.

[4] Hebrews 1:14.

Chapter 2

[1] B. Goldberg, *Peaceful Transition*, op cit.

[2] B. Goldberg, *Time Travelers from Our Future: A Fifth Dimension Odyssey* (Sun Lakes, AZ: Book World, Inc., 1999).

[3] R. Moody, *Life After Life* (New York, Bantam, 1975).

[4] B. Goldberg, *Peaceful Transition*, op cit. p.14.

[5] B. Goldberg, *Time Travelers from Our Future*, op cit.

Chapter 3

[1] B. Goldberg, *Protected by the Light: The Complete Book of Psychic Self-Defense* (Tucson, AZ: Hats Off Books, 1999).

[2] 2 Samuel 19:35.

[3] 1 Kings 3:9.

[4] Ezekiel 44:23.

[5] Jonah 4;11.

[6] Malachai 3:18.

7 Hebrews 5:14.

8 B. Goldberg, *Protected by the Light*, op cit.

Chapter 4

1 B. Goldberg, *Soul Healing* (St. Paul: Llewellyn, 1996).

2 B. Goldberg, *Astral Voyages: Mastering the Art of Interdimensional Travel* (St. Paul: Llewellyn, 1999),

Chapter 6

1 B. Goldberg, *Astral Voyages*, op cit.

Chapter 7

1 R. L. Stevenson, *Memories and Portraits, Random Memories, Memories of Himself* (New York: Scribner, 1925) p. 172.

2 Ezekiel 1:4.

3 Ibid.

4 B. Steiger, *Guardian Angels and Spirit Guides: True Accounts of Benevolent Beings from the Other Side?* (New York: Penguin, 1995) pp. ix-xi.

5 Eileen Freeman, *Touched by Angels* (New York: Warner Books, Inc., 1993).

Bibliography

Abbott, David P. *Behind the Scenes with the Medium*. Chicago: Open Court, 1907.

Atkinson, W. *Mind-Power*. Chicago: Progress, 1908.

Bach, Marcus. *Miracles Do Happen*. New York: Waymark Books, 1968.

Bagnall, O. *The Origin and Properties Of the Human Aura*. London Routledge and Kegan Paul, 1957.

Barbanell, Maurice. *This Is Spiritualism*. London: Jenkins, 1959.

Bardens, D. *Ghosts and Hauntings*. New York: Taplinger, 1968.

Baxter, Richard. *Certainty of the World of Spirits*. London: Joseph Smith, 1834.

Bayless, Raymond. *The Other Side of Death*. New Hyde Park, New York: University Books, 1971.

Bennett, Hal, Z. *Spirit Guides: What They Are, How to Meet Them, and How to Make Use of Them in Every Area of Your life*. Ukiah, CA: Tenacity Press, 1997.

Bentine, Michael. *Doors of the Mind*. London: Granada, 1984.

Besterman, T. *Crystal-Gazing*. London: Rider, 1924.

Blundson, Norman. *A Popular Dictionary of Spiritualism*. London: Arco, 1961.

Bozzano, Ernesto. *Discarnate Influence in Human Life*. London: John N. Watkins, 1938.

Bradley, D.B. and R.A. *Psychic Phenomena*. New York: Parker, 1967.

Brown, Slater. *The Heyday of Spiritualism*. New York: Hawthorn, 1970.

Buckland, Raymond, and Carrington, Hereward. *Amazing Secrets of the Psychic World*. New York: Parker, 1975.

Buckland, Raymond. *A Pocket Guide to the Supernatural.* New York: Ace Books, 1969.

Budge, W.E.A. *The Egyptian Book of the Dead.* New York: Dover, 1967.

Burr, Harold. *Blueprint for Immortality.* London: Neville Spearman, 1972.

Butler, William E. *How to Develop Clairvoyance.* York Beach, Maine: Weiser, 1971.

Carrington, Hereward. *The Invisible World.* New York: Beechhurst Press, 1946.

————. *Modern Psychical Phenomena.* New York: American Universities Publishing Co., 1920.

Chaney, Earlyne and Messick, William L. *Kundalini and the Third Eye.* Upland, Calif.: Astara, Inc., 1980.

Chaney, Earlyne C. and Chaney, Robert G. *Astara's Book of Life: The Holy Breath in Man.* Second Degree, Lesson 4. Upland, CA: Astara, Inc., 1966.

————. *Astara's Book of Life: The Science of Rebirth.* First Degree, Lesson 21. Upland, CA: Astara, Inc., 1966.

Chevreuil, L. *Proofs of the Spirit World.* New York: E. P. Dutton and Co., 1920.

Christopher, Milburne. *Mediums, Mystics and the Occult.* New York: Crewell, 1975.

Crookall, Robert. *Casebook of Astral Projection.* New Hyde Park, N.Y.: University Books, 1972.

————. *During Sleep.* London: Theosophical Publishing House, 1964.

————. *The Interpretation of Cosmic and Mystical Experiences.* London: James Clark and Co., 1969.

————. *Intimations of Immortality.* London: James Clark and Co., 1965.

————. *The Mechanisms of Astral Projection.* Moradabad, India: Darshana International, 1968.

————. *More Astral Projections.* London: Aquarian Press, 1964.

————. *The Next World—and the Next.* London: Theosophical Publishing House, 1966.

————. *Out-of-the-Body Experiences: A Fourth Analysis.* New Hyde Park, N.Y.: University Books, 1970.

————. *The Study and Practice of Astral Projection.* London: Aquarian Press, 1961.

————. *The Supreme Adventure.* London: James Clarke and Co., 1961.

————. *The Techniques of Astral Projection.* London: Aquarian Press, 1964.

David-Neel, Alexandra and Yongden, Lama. *The Secret Oral Teachings in Tibetan Buddhists Sects*. San Francisco: City Lights, 1968.

Eben, Martin. *Reincarnation in the Twentieth Century*. New York: Signet, 1970.

————. *True Experiences in Communicating with the Dead*. New York: New American Library, 1968.

Daniel, Alma, Wylie, Timothy, and Ramer, Andrew. *Ask Your Angels*. New York: Ballantine Books, 1992.

Edwards, Harry. *The Healing Intelligence*. New York: Taplinger, 1971.

Eliade, Mircea. *Shamanism, Archaic Techniques of Ecstasy*. New York: Pantheon Books, 1963.

Evans-Wentz, W. Y. *The Tibetan Book of the Dead*. New York: Causeway Books, 1973.

Fahler, Jarl. "Does Hypnosis Increase Psychic Powers?" *Tomorrow, 6:96*, autumn 1958.

Fodor, Nandor. *Between Two Worlds*. Englewood Cliffs, N.J.: Parker Publishing Co., 1964.

————. *Encyclopedia of Psychic Science*. New Hyde Park, N.Y.: University Books, 1966.

Fox, Oliver. *Astral Projection*. London: Rider and Co., 1993.

————. "The Pineal Doorway—A Record of Research," *Occult Review, 31:4*, April 1920.

Freeman, Eileen. *Touched by Angels*. New York: Warner Books, Inc., 1993.

Garfield, Laeh M., and Grant, Jack. *Companions in Spirit*. Berkeley: Celestial Arts, 1984.

Garrett, Eileen. *Adventures in the Supernormal*. New York: Creative Age Press, 1949.

————. *Beyond the Five Senses*. Philadelphia: J.B. Lippencott Co., 1957.

————. *Many Voices*. New York: Putnam's, 1968.

Goldberg, Bruce. *New Age Hypnosis*. St. Paul: Llewellyn Pub., 1997.

————. *Dream Your Problems Away: Heal Yourself While You Sleep*, Franklin Lakes, N.J.: New Page Books, 2003.

————. *Past Lives—Future Lives Revealed*, Franklin Lakes, N.J.: New Page Books, 2004.

————. *Peaceful Transitions: The Art of Conscious Dying and the Liberation of the Soul*. St. Paul: Llewellyn Pub., 1997.

————. *Soul Healing*. St. Paul: Llewellyn Pub., 1996.

————. *The Search for Grace: The True Story of Murder and Reincarnation*. St. Paul: Llewellyn Pub., 1997.

————. *Protected by the Light: The Complete Book of Psychic Self-Defense*. Tucson, AZ: Hats Off Books, 1999,.

————. *Time Travelers from Our Future: A Fifth Dimension*. Sun Lakes, Ariz.: Book World, Inc. 1999.

————. *Astral Voyages: Mastering the Art of Interdimensional Travel*. St. Paul: Llewellyn Pub., 1999.

————. "Quantum Physics and its application to past life regression and future life progression hypnotherapy." *Journal of Regression Therapy*. 1993, 7(1), 89-93.

————. "The treatment of cancer through hypnosis." *Psychology—A Journal of Human Behavior*. 1985, *3*(4), 36–39.

————. "The clinical use of hypnotic regression and progression in hypnotherapy." *Psychology— A Journal of Human Behavior* 1990, *27*(1), 43–48.

————. "Your problem may come from your future: a case study." *Journal of Regression Therapy*. 1990, *4*(2), 21–29.

Green, Celia. *Out-of-the-Body Experiences*. Oxford, Eng.: Institute of Psychophysical Research, 1968.

Greenhouse, Herbert B., *The Book of Psychic Knowledge*. New York: Taplinger Publishing Co., 1973.

————. *In Defense of Ghosts*. New York: Simon and Schuster, 1970.

Holy Bible. King James Version.

Howe, Quincy, Jr. *Reincarnation for the Christian*. Wheaton, Ill.: Theosophical Publishing House, 1987.

Kalima, Norma. *Angels in the Army of God*. New York: Signet, 1997.

Kardec, Allan. *The Book of Mediums*. York Beach, Maine: Weiser, 1970.

Kilmo, Jon. *Channeling*. Los Angeles: J. P. Tarcher, 1987.

Kilner, Walter J. *The Human Aura*. New York: University Books, 1965.

Knight, Marcus. *Spiritualism, Reincarnation and Immortality*. London: Duckworth, 1950.

Krippner, Stanley and Vaughan, Allan. *Dream Telepathy*. New York: MacMillan, 1973.

Lee, Jung Young. *Death and Beyond the Eastern Perspective: A Study Based on the Bardo Thödol and the I Ching*. New York: Gordon and Breach, 1974.

LeShan, Lawrence. *The Medium, the Mystic and the Physicist*. New York: Viking Press, 1974.

Levine, S. *A Gradual Awakening*. New York, NY: Anchor books, 1989.

Martin, Joel, and Romanowski, Patricia. *We Don't Die*. New York: Putnam's, 1988.

Mead, G.R.S. *The Doctrine of the Subtle Body*. Wheaton, Il: Theosophical Publishing House, 1967.

Moody, Raymond Jr. *Life After Life*. New York: Bantam, 1975.

Moss, Thelma. *The Body Electric*. Los Angeles: J. P. Tarcher, 1979.

Northgate, Ivy. *Mediumship Made Easy*. London: Psychic Press, 1986.

Perkins, James. *Through Death to Rebirth*. Wheaton, IL: Theosophical Publishing House, 1974.

Pike, James A. *The Other Side*. Doubleday, 1968.

Pratt, J.G. *Parapsychology: An Insider's View of ESP*. New York: Doubleday, 1964.

Premananda, Swami. *Katha Upanishad: Dialogue of Death and Vision of Immortality*. Washington, DC: Self-Realization Fellowship, 1943.

Proes, Serena. *Eden Isles: A Journey Through Time and Space with Spirit Teachers and Guides*. Phoenix: Crystal Star Pub., 1986.

Puri, R.P. *Mysticism: The Spiritual Path*. Punjab, India: Radha Soami Satsang Beas, 1988.

Roberts, Jane. *Seth Speaks*. Englewood Cliffs, N.J.: Prentice Hall, 1972.

————. *The Seth Material*. Englewood Cliffs, N.J.: Prentice Hall, 1970.

————. *The Nature of the Psyche: Its Human Expression*. New York: Bantam Books, 1979.

————. *The Nature of Personal Reality*. Englewood Cliffs, N.J.: Prentice Hall, 1974.

Rolt, C. E. *Dionysius the Areopagite—The Divine Names and the Mystical Theology*. Kila, Mont.: Kessinger Publishing Co., 1997.

Rossi, E. L. *Dreams and the Growth of Personality*. New York: Pergamon, 1972.

Scholastico, Ron. *The Earth Adventure: Your Soul's Journey Through Physical Reality: The Wisdom of the Guides/133*. Carson, Calif.: Hay House, 1991.

Sculthorp, Frederick. *Excursions to the Spirit World*. London: Cambridge University Press, 1940.

Sherman, Harold. *You Can Communicate with the Unseen World*. New York: Fawcett, 1974.

Smith, Susy. *The Enigma of Out-of-Body Travel*. New York: Garrett-Helix, 1965.

Stearn, Jess. *Edgar Cayce—The Sleeping Prophet*. New York: Bantam, 1967.

Steiger, Brad. *Guardian Angels and Spirit Guides: True Accounts of Benevolent Beings from the Other Side*. New York: Penguin, 1995.

Stevenson, R. L. *Memories and Portraits, Random Memories, Memories of Himself*. New York: Scribner, 1925.

Vasiliev, L. L. *Experiments in Mental Suggestion*. Hampshire, England: Institute for the Study of Mental Images, 1963.

————. *Mysterious Phenomena of the Human Psyche*. New York: University Books, 1965.

Whiteman, J.H.M. *The Mystical Life*. London: Faber and Faber, 1961.

Wolinshky, S. and Ryan, M.O. *Trances People Live: Healing Approaches in Quantum Psychology*. Falls Village, Conn.: The Bramble Company, 1991.

Xavier, F., and Vieira, W. *The World of Spirit*. New York: Philosophical Library, 1966.

Yarbo, Chelsea Quinn. *Messages from Michael*. New York: Playboy Paperbacks, 1979.

Zolar. *Zolar's Book of the Spirits*. Englewood Cliffs, N.J.: Prentice Hall, 1987.

Index

About the Author

DR. BRUCE GOLDBERG holds a B.A. degree in Biology and Chemistry, is a Doctor of Dental Surgery, and has an M.S. degree in Counseling Psychology. He retired from dentistry in 1989, and has concentrated on his hypnotherapy practice in Los Angeles. Dr. Goldberg was trained by the American Society of Clinical Hypnosis in the techniques and clinical applications of hypnosis in 1975.

Dr. Goldberg has been interviewed on the Donahue, Oprah, Leeza, Joan Rivers, Regis, ABC Radio, Art Bell, Tom Snyder, Jerry Springer, Jenny Jones, and Montel Williams shows; by CNN, CBS News, NBC, and many others.

Through lectures, television and radio appearances, and newspaper articles, including interviews in *TIME,* the *Los Angeles Times, USA Today*, and the *Washington Post,* he has conducted more than 35,000 past-life regressions and future-life progressions since 1974, helping thousands of patients empower themselves through these techniques. His CDs and tapes teach people self-hypnosis, and guide them into past and future lives and time travel. He gives lectures and seminars on hypnosis, regression and progression therapy, time travel, and conscious dying; he is also a consultant to corporations, attorneys, and the local and network media. His first edition of *The Search for Grace*, was made into a television movie by CBS. His third book, the award winning *Soul Healing*, is a classic on alternative medicine and psychic empowerment. *Past Lives— Future Lives* is Dr. Goldberg's international bestseller and is the first book written on future lives (progression hypnotherapy).

Dr. Goldberg distributes cassette tapes to teach people self-hypnosis and to guide them into past and future lives and time travel. For information on self-hypnosis tapes, speaking engagements, or private sessions, Dr. Goldberg can be contacted directly by writing to:

Bruce Goldberg, D.D.S., M.S.
4300 Natoma Avenue, Woodland Hills, CA 91364
Telephone: (800) Karma-4-U or (800) 527-6248
Fax: (818) 704-9189
email: karma4u@webtv.net
Website: www.drbrucegoldberg.com

Please include a self-addressed, stamped envelope with your letter.

Other Books by Dr. Bruce Goldberg

Past Lives—Future Lives

Soul Healing

The Search for Grace: The True Story of Murder and Reincarnation

Peaceful Transition: The Art of Conscious Dying and the Liberation of the Soul

New Age Hypnosis

Secrets of Self-Hypnosis

Unleash Your Psychic Powers

Look Younger and Live Longer: Add 25 to 50 Quality Years to Your Life Naturally

Protected by the Light: The Complete Book of Psychic Self-Defense

Time Travelers from Our Future; A Fifth Dimension Odyssey

Astral Voyages: Mastering the Art of Interdimensional Travel

Custom Design Your Own Destiny

Self-Hypnosis: Easy Ways to Hypnotize Your Problems Away

Dream Your Problems Away: Heal Yourself While You Sleep

Past Lives, Future Lives Revealed

Ascension: The Art of Soul Perfection and the Attainment of Grace